Iggy & The Stooges

On Stage 1967-1974

Per Nilsen

SONIC**BOND**

sonicbondpublishing.com

Sonicbond Publishing Limited
www.sonicbondpublishing.co.uk
Email: info@sonicbondpublishing.co.uk

First Published in the United Kingdom 2021
First Published in the United States 2021

British Library Cataloguing in Publication Data:
A Catalogue record for this book is available from the British Library

Copyright Per Nilsen 2021

ISBN 978-1-78952-101-6

Typeset in ITC Garamond & ITC Avant Garde
Printed and bound in England

Graphic design and typesetting: Full Moon Media

Iggy &
The Stooges
On Stage 1967-1974

Per Nilsen

sonicbondpublishing.com

on stage ...
Iggy & The Stooges

Contents

Acknowledgments

This book is the product of many years of research. The work started in the late 1980s after I published a book on Iggy Pop with Dorothy Sherman, *The Wild One*, which is long out of print. I am indebted to a number of people who have assisted me, in one way or another, in the process of gathering information for the book: Tim Middleton, Jim Lahde, Natalie Schlossman, Michael S. Begnar, Brian Zabawski and Paul Trynka. Particular thanks to Tim for fact-checking and research and to Natalie for fantastic reporting in the *Popped* newsletter devoted to The Stooges.

A great deal of information and many quotes were derived from interviews conducted by Dorothy Sherman for *The Wild One* book: Ron Asheton, Leee Black Childers, Michael Davis, Danny Fields, Wayne Kramer, Ron Richardson, John Sinclair, Jimmy Silver and Tony Zanetta. Information is also based on interviews by Paul Trynka for *Open Up And Bleed* (the most definitive Iggy Pop biography): Bob Baker, Leo Beattie, Bill Cheatham, Doug Currie, Bob Czaykowski (Nitebob), Dave Dunlap, Ben Edmonds, Danny Fields, Skip Gildersleeve, Bob Sheff, Michael Tipton and Don Waller. Additional interviews for the book were conducted with Chris Ehring, Jimmy Silver and James Williamson. Thanks also to Carlton P. Sandercock for protecting the Stooges' legacy. Further thanks to Steve Babor, Heather Harris, Kurt Ingham and John Catto for fantastic photos, to Richard Adams and Madeline Bocchiaro for kind assistance, and to the *Independent Voices* website for information.

Reports from people who witnessed Stooges gigs are credited throughout the text. I am grateful for the accounts from Chazz Avery, Mike Barich, Wayne Bruce, Jeffrey Burdin, Randy Foley, Harvey Gold, Tommy Keene, Chaz Miller, Jim Nash, Phil Natta, Raul Pineda, Ron (Ann Arbor music fan), Natalie Schlossman, Richard Taylor, Bill W. Ten Eyck, Chris Yarmock and Brian Zabawski. Peter Cavanaugh's blog also provided interesting recollections.

Many publications and press reports were consulted for reviews of various Stooges performances; these are acknowledged throughout the text. Several interviews with Iggy and/or band members provided particularly valuable insights: *Goldmine* (Ralph Heibutzki); *Ballroom Blitz* (Mike McDowell, Jim Heddle); *The Wire* (Edwin Pouncey); *Guitar Player* (Cliff Jones); *Black to Comm, I-94 Bar* (Kim Shimamoto); *Furious* (Jason Gross); *Raw* (Phil Alexander); *New Musical Express* (Nick Kent, Edwin Pouncey, David Donohue); *The Aquarian Weekly* (Keith Lyle); *Mojo* (Cliff Jones, Paul Trynka); *Mean* (Gregg Lagambina); and *RCD* (Neil Cooper). Interviews with Stooges members and associates were also helpful: *Metro Times* (interview with Ben Edmonds); *You Want My Action* CD release by Easy Action (interview with Jimmy Recca by Kim Shimamoto); and the 'PKM Interview' (interview with James Williamson by James Marshall).

Some CD liner notes were important sources of information: *1970: The Complete Fun House Sessions* (Ben Edmonds); *The Stooges* 2005 re-issue (Ben Edmonds); *Fun House* 2005 re-issue (Paul Trynka); *Raw Power* 2010 re-issue (Kris Needs, Brian J. Bowe); *Live at Goose Lake, August 8th, 1970* (Jaan Uhelszki); Easy Action's *You Want My Action* (Lisa Gottlieb, Craig Petty); and Easy Action's *Heavy Liquid* (Brian J. Bowe, Bob Matheu).

A number of books also provided essential information and background: *Total Chaos* (Jeff Gold; astonishing book); *Open Up And Bleed* (Paul Trynka); *I Need More* (Iggy Pop with Anne Wehrer); *The Complete Iggy Pop* (Richard Adams); *The Stooges – A Journey Through The Michigan Underworld* (Brett Callwood); *The Stooges – The Authorized And Illustrated Story* (Robert Matheu); *Raw Power* (and various iterations of the book by Mick Rock); *Ron Asheton: The Stooges, Destroy All Monsters & Beyond* (John Wombat, Ruth Moreira); *Your Pretty Face Is Going To Hell* (Dave Thompson); *Gimme Danger* (Joe Ambrose); *Detroit Rock City* (Steve Miller); *Apathy For The Devil – A 1970s Memoir* (Nick Kent); *Any Day Now: The London Years 1947–1974* (Kevin Cann); *The Complete David Bowie* (Nicholas Pegg); *Please Kill Me – The Uncensored History Of Punk* (Legs McNeil, Gillian McCain). *There Goes Gravity* (Lisa Robinson); and *Hunky Dory (Who Knew?)* (Laurence Myers).

Every effort has been made to acknowledge and contact copyright owners. If any have been inadvertently omitted, the publisher will be pleased to make the proper acknowledgment at the earliest opportunity.

The Stooges may have played some concerts that are not listed here, but not too many, because their concerts from 1971 to 1974 are quite well documented. Missing concerts are more likely to be from the 1968–1970 period. Some of the gigs that have been mentioned or hinted at in various sources include Lima, Ohio, 1970 (according to Iggy, he confronted Scott Asheton in this city about a change in pace in playing and the lack of tom-tom playing) and Star Theatre, Flint, Michigan, late 1970 (Bill Cheatham mentioned this as a concert where the band members were paid in heroin instead of money). Various lists of Stooges concerts on the internet also include numerous erroneous and unverified dates and/or concerts that were never actually played.

Prologue

The story of The Stooges began in 1967 in Ann Arbor, outside Detroit. The group was formed by Jim Osterberg with friends from Ann Arbor and brothers Ron and Scott Asheton. Jim had learned his trade as a drummer with the band, Iguanas, thus his nickname Iggy. The Iguanas had assembled at the local high school in 1962 and, after going professional in 1965, occasionally backed up bands such as The Shangri-Las and Four Tops. Jim was the featured vocalist on a few songs in the Iguanas' set. He left The Iguanas in August 1966 for The Prime Movers, an older, more bohemian band that played blues. With The Prime Movers, Iggy developed quite a local reputation as an accomplished drummer.

Iggy met Ron, Scott, and their friend Dave Alexander on the Ann Arbor music scene. Ron and Dave had dropped out of high school in 1966 to travel to London to check out the English music scene. Once home, they hung around outside the local hotspot, Discount Records, where Iggy was working. Iggy managed to get Ron the bass player's position in The Prime Movers, but he lasted only a short time, failing to meet the band's exacting musical standards. Instead, Iggy found him a job with a fellow Discount Records employee, Scott Richardson, in The Chosen Few. At one point, that group also included future Stooges guitarist James Williamson. Meanwhile, Iggy left The Prime Movers in late 1966 to go to Chicago on a personal quest to discover the source of the blues. He played South Side bars as a pick-up drummer with local blues stars.

The more Iggy hung around the Chicago bluesmen, however, the more contempt he felt for the white guys trying to play the blues. He reached the conclusion that only Afro-American musicians could really play the blues. Iggy returned home to Ann Arbor in March 1967 with the intention of forming a band that would be as intuitive in its approach to music as the bluesmen who plied their trade in the Chicago bars. What Iggy had in mind was an avant-garde group that would play music that was based on his enthusiasm for musicians such as Harry Partch, Cab Calloway and Screaming Jay Hawkins. More up-to-date, Iggy was impressed by *The Velvet Underground & Nico*, especially the possibilities of pure noise showcased on the album and by the unconventional mix of instrumentation. Iggy was also influenced by the factories and construction sites that characterized the industrial sprawl that he called home. Having grown up with a soundtrack of interstates being built and sheets of metal being fashioned into automobiles, he wanted to 'make a big noise: monolithic, metallic, like a big machine – like the drill presses at the Ford plant, stamping out fenders.'

Ignoring the large pool of competent, locally established musicians, Iggy chose Dave Alexander and brothers Ron and Scott Asheton to be members of his group. Although Ron previously had played guitar and bass, the members were basically unskilled musicians. Iggy helped Scott improve his skills as a drummer. 'Iggy might have taught him some tricks or refined his drumming, but Scotty played before that,' said Bill Cheatham, a friend of the Asheton

9

brothers who would go on to work for The Stooges as a roadie and guitarist. Rehearsals were held in the Asheton basement. Iggy lived with his parents in a trailer park on Carpenter Road, on the fringe of Ann Arbor. He would take the bus into Ann Arbor, where the Asheton brothers lived in a house with their mother and younger sister, Kathy.

Slowly but surely, Iggy's group began discovering their musical identity. They wanted to be different from everybody else, experimenting with unusual instruments and sounds. Iggy would alternate between an electric organ and a Hawaiian guitar, which he played seated with all strings tuned to E. Scott played a self-made drum set that had a pair of oil drums instead of bass drums, with the words 'tits' and 'pussy' painted with day-glo psychedelic colors so they would light up in the dark. He played with marching drum mallets to achieve a thunderous sound. Meanwhile, Ron dealt with a huge, droning bass sound.

In the summer of 1967, they christened themselves The Psychedelic Stooges, drawing inspiration from reruns of *The Three Stooges* television series. Iggy said, 'We were sitting in Ron's bedroom on the University of Michigan (in Ann Arbor) campus, stoned on acid, looking for our sound and identity, realizing the fierceness of the competition – we weren't dumb guys. We thought about "psychedelic" because that was happening then, and "stooges" because we loved the one-for-all/all-for-one of The Three Stooges, and the violence in their image. We loved violence as comedy. Besides sounding right, "stooge" also had different levels of meaning: is calling yourself a stooge a self-insult?' Jimmy Silver, who would go on to manage the band, commented on the band name, 'In the beginning, the name was a joke. It was a put-on: The Psychedelic Stooges. But they loved The Three Stooges, and they loved the way they felt about The Three Stooges. They didn't want people to take them too seriously.'

The band set up headquarters with a friend, Ron Richardson, nicknamed 'The Professor' for his appearance and academic background. Richardson knew Ron from his Chosen Few days, having booked them and other local acts into the local frat house circuit. Ron Asheton remembered, 'We tripped all that summer (1967) and Ig was doing acid every day for six months. We talked about music all the time. We just liked that free form, making those noises, being fans of Jimi Hendrix. We found great release in it. We'd say, "Just let one go, whatever happens, physically, musically, just do whatever you feel like doing. Let the music take over."'

The band's early music was dirge-like and monotonous. It would often feature a motif as a basis for various excursions as the music seemingly plotted its own route. One of their first identifiable numbers was called 'The Razor's Edge,' for which The Who's 'A Quick One, While He's Away' (from *A Quick One*, 1966) provided inspiration. Iggy described it as '...totally far-out music. It had no time structure at all or anything like that. It was influenced a lot by Indian music and a lot by some of the opera I used to listen to, but mainly by these poems of motion. The format grew, and Scotty was there, the drummer, and we had a kind of motion. We proceeded to play just this thunderous, racy music, which would drone on and on, varying the themes. It was entirely instrumental at this time, like jazz gone wild. It was very North African, a very tribal sound: very electronic.'

Iggy's future performance style was influenced by seeing Jim Morrison perform with the Doors at the University of Michigan in Ann Arbor, 20 October 1967. Iggy watched in astonishment as Morrison berated the crowd and stumbled around the stage, making strange noises, swearing and generally antagonizing the audience: 'The Doors were a tremendous influence on me. Seeing them was what made me decide to become a singer. I was very excited. I loved the antagonism; I loved that he was pissing them off. Yes, yes, yes. They were all frat people, football killers, the future leaders of America – the people who today are the rock stars of America – and not only was Morrison pissing them off, but he was mesmerizing them at the same time. The gig lasted only 15 or 20 minutes because they had to pull Morrison offstage and get him out of there fast because the people were gonna attack him. It made a big impression on me.'

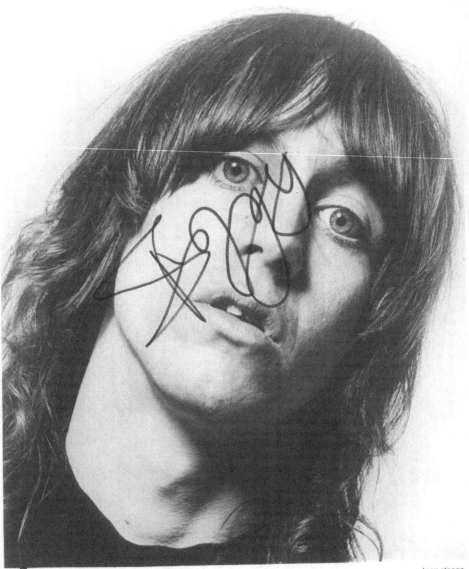

iggy stooge

the stooges

EXCLUSIVELY ON ELEKTRA RECORDS

elektra

Signed promo shot for first album. (*Elektra/Joel Brodsky*)

1967–1968

The Psychedelic Stooges revealed their mind-blowing version of contemporary music on Halloween 1967 in the house of their manager Ron Richardson. Shortly after this, the band moved from Richardson's house, where they had rehearsed. They continued temporarily in the Asheton basement before a friend of Richardson, Jimmy Silver, took over the managerial reins. 'They had energy that they needed to get off in some way,' said Richardson. 'It was hard being around that energy. It's like a marriage in some ways. It's hard enough for two to live together. It's even harder for five people living together. We parted ways. It was time for me to do something different. They were heading in one direction and I was heading in some other direction. I wanted to get away from it all. It was just like being in debt and deeper in debt. It was not happening as fast as you should think it should happen. Then we went our separate ways.' Silver found them a farmhouse where they could live and practice together in the communal spirit of the day. Life at the Fun House centered around smoking pot, watching television and rehearsing. There were also healthy periods when Iggy and the guys were served macrobiotic food by Jimmy Silver and his wife, who moved into the band house.

The Psychedelic Stooges public debut was on 20 January 1968, although it was an unannounced performance because they filled in on a bill at the Grande Ballroom in Detroit. The band played over 20 shows at the Grande Ballroom throughout 1968, typically on Saturdays and Sundays, to the extent that they more or less became the house band. Ron Asheton was grateful for the opportunity to play there: 'We were lucky to have the Grande in full swing; that was a good venue for us. There'd be sympathetic people there. The people that came there were supposedly, most of them, hip, so that's where the old Psychedelic Stooges really learned how to play. Thank God for the Grande Ballroom, or we wouldn't have worked.'

Inspired by the emergence of concert venues like The Avalon and The Fillmore in San Francisco, the 2,000-seat Grande Ballroom was the brainchild of 'Uncle' Russ Gibb, a high school teacher and local DJ, who acquired the building in 1966. Catering to what Gibb hoped would be hipper and more musically mature crowds, the Grande proved to be the perfect classroom for young Michigan bands learning their craft. Gibb worked closely with John Sinclair, MC5's manager and key Detroit counterculture figure, and Hugh 'Jeep' Holland, an agent, producer and manager of many local bands. According to Silver, 'Previously there was a club scene, but the clubs weren't big enough to have enormous amounts of kids attend them. There were a whole bunch of clubs in Ann Arbor, Birmingham, Leonard, etc. But it really wasn't until Grande Ballroom opened and the ballroom scene got big, that you could have a couple of thousand kids in one place in one night.'

Gibb and Holland brought in national artists and presented local bands as opening acts. The Psychedelic Stooges and all the Detroit and Michigan bands, MC5, The Rationals, SRC, Jagged Edge, The Woolies, Thyme, The Frost,

13

The Amboy Dukes, Third Power, Up and Savage Grace, played the Grande Ballroom regularly, either as headliners or opening for the national acts. Supported by the enthusiastic and loyal Detroit audiences, the locally bred groups often received wilder audience response than the top acts on the bill. 'There were a lot of great bands there all at once, fighting for the same few gigs, all fighting for national attention,' Iggy commented. 'When you're young and fighting to make it, you're concerned with every other band on the block.'

While every major US city had some sort of a local music scene, few reached the proportion of Detroit during the 1967-1970 period. The Detroit/Michigan scene was dominated by bands playing hard, energetic rock music, performed with intensity and total belief, which seemed to reflect the industrial factory climate of Detroit. The scene was distant enough geographically and culturally from New York and California to shield it from the pretentiousness that had come to characterize the music of both scenes. Detroit music often had a raw, down-to-earth quality, which contrasted with the more intellectual approach to music typical of many bands from cities like San Francisco and New York.

The early performances by The Psychedelic Stooges were quite experimental, with the band members playing home-made instruments and the music being largely improvised. Silver would occasionally perform with the band: 'They had a very bizarre collection of instruments. When they first started performing, they had me play this bizarre instrument that they had designed. We took an oil tank that people put outside their houses – not an oil drum – an oil tank that people use to store oil in. It's got pipes coming out of it everywhere. We took this thing and spray painted it white, took it to Grande Ballroom, and as the finale to the act, we took the PA microphone and dropped it down inside this thing and they had me beat on it with a rubber mallet that is used for body repair on an automobile.' Iggy described his instruments: 'I had a Waring blender with about two inches of water in and if you miced that up, you got a great sound like a waterfall, very beautiful, very spacey. I played vacuum cleaner at the first few gigs and then I got an air compressor that was more powerful. If you put your thumb over the end of a vacuum nozzle, you get this real weird wailing sound. I used to wear golf shoes and dance on this piece of galvanized sheet metal too. It was different, you know?'

Iggy performed in whiteface make-up, usually without a shirt: 'The first few times we literally played just two or three ultra-simplistic pieces, just a couple of chords, a simple riff, and I didn't use the English language at the time. I'd just say "wooooh...," anything that came out that I liked, which was pretty to me, beautiful, but only with the understanding that it was the best I could do, and still understanding that it's the best I can do, and that's all that it is.' Ron remembered, 'Usually we basically just got up there and jammed one riff and built into an energy freak-out until finally we'd broken a guitar or one of my hands would be twice as big as the other and my guitar would be covered in blood. I wouldn't even realize it at the time I was doing it. A lot of our shows were like that until we started finding little bits that were starting to get more musical.'

Around this time, Iggy became Iggy Pop, as he adopted and adapted the surname of a friend called Jim Popp. Scott Asheton said, 'Iggy had shaved off his eyebrows. We had a friend named Jim Popp, who had a nervous condition and had lost all his hair, including his eyebrows. So when Iggy shaved his eyebrows, we started calling him Pop.' Iggy explained, 'Iggy was a nickname that stuck. And Pop I took from one of my boyhood heroes, Jim Pop, who sniffed so much glue that he lost all his hair. And he would lay around the student union, just laying there, like, with these big frog eyes and looked more like a frog as he lost his eyebrows too. Every time the hair on the top of his head would start to grow back, Scott would go up to him and give him a good hard flick on the top of his head, pup! Like that, and it would fly off again. He fascinated me, fascinating creature.'

At some point in spring 1968, Iggy made the transition to becoming the band's singer and frontman. At the same time, the band's experimental format evolved into a more traditional rock band setting, with Ron Asheton playing guitar, Dave Alexander on bass, and Scott Asheton behind a regular drum set. According to Ron, 'It just all sort of evolved. I said to Iggy one day, "You should just concentrate on singing. Let Dave play the bass, I wanna play guitar". I originally wanted to play guitar. I had taken guitar lessons for years; three, four years. That's what I wanted to do anyway. We stopped using the home-made instruments when we realized we wanted to get better and make records.'

While they began employing a more conventional line-up, The Psychedelic Stooges' music was anything but orthodox or predictable. The songs were usually spontaneous, based around monotonously-repeated riffs and rhythms. Even more remarkable than the music was the live performing style of Iggy. He improvised with vocal sounds and acted out the imagery embodied in songs like 'I'm Sick' and 'Asthma Attack,' both of which had their roots in Iggy's breathing problems. The band's concerts were short and intense, typically lasting between 15 and 25 minutes. From the outset, their set featured few recognizable songs, focusing instead of jams that grew out of guitar or bass riffs. Aside from 'I'm Sick' and 'Asthma Attack,' two of their earliest songs were 'Goodbye Bozos' and 'The Dance Of Romance.'

The Psychedelic Stooges played many concerts with MC5, and the members of the two bands became close friends, although MC5 considered themselves to be superior musically. MC5's Dennis Thompson said, 'At the beginning, I thought they were God-awful musicians. I thought they sucked and they should all get a different job. But they were determined to come up with their own sound and, as we know, Iggy and the boys developed performance art.' MC5's Michael Davis said, 'All they knew what to do was get on stage and be very interesting. When we listened to them playing, we were like, "What are these guys doing? They really don't have the songs, and the music they're playing is so ridiculously simple". But there was something really charming and straight to the point about it. It was so rudimentary that it was great.'

Iggy and the band's stage act developed throughout 1968. They astounded audiences that came to see a traditional 'rock and roll' band but ended up witnessing an indelibly unique experience. Twisting and hurling himself around the stage, Iggy generated the threatening aura of a wild animal suddenly uncaged. Denying the audience its safety as passive voyeurs, Iggy would involve the spectators in the performance, often diving into the audience and walking amongst the crowd. Never before had a rock audience been so vividly confronted by such an intense performer. Bob Czaykowski – who would later work with the Stooges as a soundman – saw the band many times. 'Nobody else was going out into the audience. That was a different thing. When you were the audience, you were the audience and the band was onstage. Iggy was the first one to really push that thing where he came out into the audience.' MC5's manager John Sinclair used to watch in awe: 'We were always excited that they got over with it. You didn't know how people would respond to this. He was doing something different. He wasn't just another rock star. Iggy would go out into the audience until he made eye contact with a girl. Lock eyes with someone, zero in on them, pick them right out and go over and throw them over his shoulder or get down on the floor and kiss them. I'd go, "Wow, I wonder if this guy is going to make it back alive?" Then you'd find out that he didn't really care. He was in a different place. It really didn't matter to him if he came back alive or not. Seriously, that's the feeling I got. From a spectator's point of view, it was really exciting. He was so unpredictable. You just never knew what he would do.'

'They were never like a normal rock band,' commented Silver. 'They were always pretty far out and that was their premise. It was pretty clear to me that Iggy was trying to do something different. The music that came out of them was definitely a reaction of who they were. That is why all those kids that grew up in suburban Detroit could really relate to them, why other people would hear them and say, "Well, is this music?" It always polarized the audience. It was always a very real, very intense experience. There were people that actually hated it and there were people that loved it. There were a lot of just gonzo people that really loved it because these guys were transmitting that experience, that arrogance.'

The Psychedelic Stooges' big break came on 23 September 1968, when they played a concert in Ann Arbor with local bands MC5 and Up, attended by Danny Fields – a publicity assistant for Elektra Records. Fields had been invited by John Sinclair, who had fervently promoted the Ann Arbor/Detroit music scene to friends and associates in the media. After attending a few MC5 shows, Fields was convinced of the band's qualities and talked Elektra's Vice President Jac Holzman into signing the band. Witnessing The Psychedelic Stooges perform with MC5, Fields phoned Holzman to tell him that he had discovered *two* new groups that he wanted to sign: 'I couldn't believe what I was seeing and hearing. I had never seen a performer as incredible as Iggy, and about the music, I could only say, "At last!" I thought, "How could anybody be so good and not be signed?"' A few weeks later, Fields and Holzman returned to Ann Arbor, record contracts in hand. Thus, the band was on its way, ready to be launched beyond the Ann Arbor/Detroit music scene. 'It was a meteoric rise,' John Sinclair noted. 'They did their first gig on Halloween '67 and a year later, they were signed to Elektra, so that was incredibly fast.'

Tuesday, 31 October 1967: Ron Richardson's house, Ann Arbor, MI

The Psychedelic Stooges' first performance took place in front of an invited group of friends, including future manager Jimmy Silver and some members of local band MC5 and their manager John Sinclair. Iggy sat on the floor playing Hawaiian guitar, Ron played bass through wah-wah and fuzz boxes, and his brother Scott played his home-made drum set. Dave Alexander also helped out, rattling a Kustom bass amp in its cabinet to produce electronic crashing noises, and assisting Iggy with a battery of other instruments, including the Jim-A-Phone: a meter-high cone into which Iggy dropped a microphone to make feedback. It was an unusual experience for the audience, and some did not know if it was meant to be taken seriously or as a joke.

'It was just the most bizarre music you'd ever heard, and I thought it was terrific,' Jimmy Silver recalled. 'Scott was the drummer and Ron was playing the guitar. Jim was playing a little modified Hawaiian guitar. It made this incredible sound. Somebody was serving brownies with marijuana in them. It was a bizarre party!'

John Sinclair was present: 'I remember how loud it was, just incredibly loud in this little house. I went with a guy who had rolled up about 50 joints before going there. When he got there, he was passing out all these joints. I'll always remember it because they were inhaling freon. They were taking whipped cream and getting the freon out of it and putting it in bags. I just got really blasted. Oh God, the police! They could hear it all the way downtown and I split. That was the Psychedelic Stooges!'

Wayne Kramer of MC5 was also at the party: 'All I remember was stopping in at this party where their band was finally going to play. Iggy was sitting on the floor and he had a steel guitar with some kind of modal tuning, and he was bashing away on it. He had this vacuum cleaner too. He held it in front of the mic and made different noises with it. The whole thing was tremendously abstract and avant-garde. It was more like a preview. It wasn't songs with melodies, lead vocals, or even what ultimately turned out to be Stooges songs or Iggy songs.'

Saturday, 20 January 1968: Grande Ballroom, Detroit, MI

The Psychedelic Stooges' first public performance was unannounced, as they filled in on a bill that featured the headline act Scott Richard Case (which later became SRC) and Apple Pie Motherhood, a band from New York. The Stooges' set was a spectacular and ear-shattering event with various home-made instruments, including Scott Asheton playing two oil drums. Iggy wore white silk pajamas, his face painted white and clean-shaven, and he wore a two-foot-high wig of curled aluminum foil. Wearing golf shoes, he did some dance steps on a washboard equipped with a contact microphone. The shock of seeing something so unusual reduced most of the audience to a stunned silence; there was not much applause after the brief 15-minute set.

Ron Asheton described the performance: 'Iggy wore a nightshirt from the turn of the century. He took a piece of cardboard and corkscrewed strips of aluminum foil into it so that he had an aluminum foil afro, then he shaved his eyebrows and painted his face white. We drove to the gig, looking like that in Dave Alexander's Corvair. This is really the truth; cars tried to run us off the road. A whole bunch of guys pulled up next to us, yelling, "What the fuck is that?" and they wanted to kill us! When we got to the Grande, the neighbors were saying things like, "Motherfucker, what is that? Some kind of a mechanical man!". It was funny and we were into it, but we were embarrassed and kind of scared at the same time.'

The concert was reviewed by Steve Silverman of *Michigan Daily*, who praised The Psychedelic Stooges' music as 'easily the most imaginative' music of the evening. 'They played electronic music which utilized controlled feedback, wah-wah, pedal, slide guitar, and droned bass as well as scat-like singing and neo-primitive howling, all backed up by a strong, simple beat.'

At this point, Iggy was not sure what stage name he would use: 'I was still deciding whether my stage name would be "Jimmy James," "Junior John" or "Lance Rokkit" when the next day this college paper called *Michigan Daily* came out with a huge review of the show. In it, they kept mentioning Iggy Osterberg (the review actually referred to Iggy Osterberger), so I was stuck with it because, at the time, competition was so fierce that if you got any attention at all, you went along with it. I took great note of that piece at the time, because in the Ann Arbor area alone, there were at least twenty full-time, more-than-competent bands all busting their balls for the same few gigs in the area, all working their asses off to make it in the record business. I saw an opportunity there and never looked back. This name's catchy. People now knew me by this name, so I stuck with it.'

Sunday, 18 February 1968: Grande Ballroom, Detroit, MI

This was The Psychedelic Stooges' first officially-announced public performance. They appeared on a bill with headlining act The Byrds, The Rationals and Wilson Mower Pursuit. The concert attracted an audience of around 1,800 people, but The Byrds' performance was reported as 'hopelessly disappointing' and 'lackluster' in the Detroit newspaper *Sun*, although there was no mention of the Stooges in the review.

Sunday, 3 March 1968: Grande Ballroom, Detroit, MI

The Psychedelic Stooges were back at the Grande, this time with Blood, Sweat & Tears as the headline act. Carousel was also on the bill. An unnamed reviewer – possibly John Sinclair – in the *Sun* was enthusiastic about the

Stooges: 'The Stooges are a new Ann Arbor-based band made up of Iggy Osterberg (lead vocal, osterizer, pressure pump, meat chants, and assorted sound assaults), Ron Asheton (guitar), Dave Alexander (bass), and Scott Asheton (drums, oil drums, and other percussion blasts). Their second gig, with the BS&T at the Grande, was such an impressive triumph of modern music that people were sitting there digging them stoned out of their skulls, their mouths open, unbelieving. The Stooges combine the most beautiful stage act I've ever seen with some really incredible electronic rock & roll meat thump music – their total impact is astounding. I won't try to describe them since you can hear them at the Grande Saturday night (30 March 1968) with The Fugs.'

The Psychedelic Stooges appeared in a listing as supporting The Who along with The Soap at a concert on 9 March at the Grande Ballroom, Detroit, Michigan. However, the Stooges did not appear on the concert poster.

Sunday, 24 March 1968: Grande Ballroom, Detroit, MI
This was the first gig The Stooges played with MC5. The bill also featured Pink Peech Mob, Odds & Ends and Gold. 'I met Jim the first time that their band played with us,' said Michael Davis of MC5. 'I didn't know anything. I was a Detroiter, those guys were from Ann Arbor. Iggy had a white face on the first time they ever played. His face was completely white. He looked ghost-like. He gyrated around the stage and made a crazy fool out of himself to everyone's pleasure. Everyone liked it. They thought, "Wow, this is a wild guy." We were really the heavy critics. Nobody was as good as we were. And we thought they were alright. That meant they could come over to our house and get high with us.'

Scott Asheton commented, 'People didn't know what to think. John Sinclair, the MC5's manager, was just standing there with his mouth wide open. That was the master plan: knock down the walls and blow people's shit away. All we wanted to do was make it different.'

Saturday, 30 March 1968: Grande Ballroom, Detroit, MI
The Psychedelic Stooges appeared with The Fugs (headliner), MC5 and Sly and the Family Stone.

Sunday, 7 April 1968: Grande Ballroom, Detroit, MI
The Psychedelic Stooges played on a bill with the Chicago blues vocalist, Junior Wells, and Up: another band from the area and part of John Sinclair's Trans-Love Express collective.

Thursday, 11 April 1968: Union Ballroom, University of Michigan, Ann Arbor, MI
The Psychedelic Stooges' third gig with headlining MC5. After six concerts at the Grande Ballroom, this was the band's first professional concert in their hometown of Ann Arbor. Up was also on the bill.

Ann Arbor music fan, Ron (not Asheton), attended this concert: 'I had only heard a little about Stooges from some Ann Arbor friends. Iggy wasn't as animated as later appearances at the Grande and Eastown Theater gigs would be. I remember them mostly for how loud it was and without the expected song structures, more like "free jazz" (or "free rock" maybe). Some people I was with got up and left, which was odd back then. The Stooges were certainly different than any band I'd seen. Never saw the "white face" Iggy again. Only at that Union gig.'

Friday, 12 April 1968: Mart Room, McKenzie Hall, Wayne State University, Wayne, MI

Advertised as 'Stomp the Creeps! A Tribal Stomp,' The Psychedelic Stooges played on the bill before headliners MC5. Also on the bill, The Pigfuckers, who the *Sun* newspaper described as '...one of the first of an inevitable new wave of bands with roots in the rock scene but their ears and nerves tuned to the music of Sun Ra, Albert Ayler, Archie Shepp, Pharoah Sanders et al.' Wayne is a suburb west of Detroit.

April 1968: The Armory, Ann Arbor, MI

The Armory was constructed in 1911 to house a military unit. In addition to being an armory, the building had a large hall, which is where The Psychedelic Stooges played. According to photographer, Steve Bober, the concert was sparsely attended, with not more than 30 people in the audience. Two photos from this gig by Bober of Iggy with white face were published in *Total Chaos* by Jeff Gold: one onstage photo and one taken backstage of Iggy and a very psychedelic-looking Ron, Dave and Scott. *Total Chaos* also featured three close-ups of Iggy in whiteface, which appear to be from the same concert, attributed to the Jeff Gold and Johan Kugelberg collection (two of which first appeared in the coffee table book, *Punk – The Definitive Record Of A Revolution* by Stephen Colgrave and Chris Sullivan, and the third being previously featured in Bob Matheu's Stooges biography). These photos were not taken by Steve Bober, so they might be from another concert from around the same time.

Wednesday, 17 April 1968: Grande Ballroom, Detroit, MI

The Psychedelic Stooges performed with MC5 (headlining act) and Jagged Edge, who started life covering early Stones songs.

Sunday, 21 April 1968: Grande Ballroom, Detroit, MI

The Psychedelic Stooges played on the same bill as James Gang and Cream. However, the latter canceled their appearance, and James Gang headlined instead. It was Iggy's 21st birthday: 'I had spent the day transporting a 200-gallon oil drum from Ann Arbor to Detroit so that we could put a contact mic on it and Jimmy Silver would hit it on the one-beat of our best song. I got it up three flights of stairs into the Grande Ballroom, by myself, and then we discovered that our amps didn't work. And when we went out onstage, everybody yelled, "We want Cream! We want Cream! Get off, we want Cream!". I was on Orange sunshine acid and everyone was shouting, "We want Cream, we want Cream" all through our set. It's funny now, but at the time, phew, I was suicidal. It was one of our worst gigs ever. I went back to Dave Alexander's house with him. I was heartbroken. I thought, "My God, this is 21. This is it. Things are just not going well.". Dave's mom served me a cheeseburger with a candle in the middle of it. The idea was to keep going and things would get better. Don't give up.'

Thursday, 25 April 1968: Upper DeRoy Auditorium, Wayne State University, Wayne, MI

Billed as a 'Freek Show,' The Psychedelic Stooges appeared with MC5, Up and Pigfuckers. The bill, therefore, included Fred 'Sonic' Smith (MC5), Gary Rassmussen (Up), and Scott Asheton, all of whom would later go on to form Sonic Rendezvous, which in turn would support Iggy on tour in 1978.

Sunday, 28 April 1968: Grande Ballroom, Detroit, MI

The Stooges were advertised to support Frank Zappa and The Mothers of Invention, along with Charging Rhinoceros of Soul, who featured future Stooges members Steve MacKay and Bob Sheff, for The Mothers' first show (3 pm) – with MC5 and Carousel support for the evening show.

Iggy has said that he did his first stage dive at this concert: 'I knew The Mothers were on after us and I didn't want people to forget about us.' Russ Gibb commented, 'Iggy did invent the stage dive. The Grande was the only venue in the world where the audience could go right up to the stage. On each side were the dressing rooms, and the girls were crawling all over the place to get with the musicians. And Iggy would do that thing where he would bend over almost all the way backward. And he fell over backward, and people thought it was an accident. I don't think so. He would be in the crowd, and next thing you knew, he was floating on the audience.'

Sunday, 26 May 1968: Grande Ballroom, Detroit, MI

The Psychedelic Stooges along with MC5, provided support to Butterfield Blues Band on the last night of their run of three at the Grande. The Frost and Jagged Edge had provided support on the previous days.

Saturday, 1 June 1968: Grande Ballroom, Detroit, MI

The bill also featured Love and The Crazy World of Arthur Brown. This gig completed a run of five nights at the Grande for Arthur Brown, with Love joining (and headlining) the final two Saturday and Sunday gigs.

Sunday, 23 June 1968: Grande Ballroom, Detroit, MI

The Psychedelic Stooges played with MC5 and Blue Cheer, the latter being a West Coast trio in the Hendrix and Cream mold. According to John Sinclair writing in the *Fifth Estate*, the concert was attended by around 1,500 people and the Stooges played first at around 8 pm while '…the ballroom was still filling up with easily-recognized MC5 fans who began to wonder what the fuck was going on when the Stooges finished and the record player went back on.'

Years later, Steve Begnoche, a journalist with the *Ludington Daily News*, recalled the concert as the first he attended. It was billed as a battle of the bands between MC5 and Blue Cheer, for the mantle of the loudest band in the nation, which 'Blue Cheer won hands down.' Of the Stooges' performance, he enjoyed the show, even if not fully understanding what he had just seen. In fact, he considered it the most puzzling concert he has ever seen.

Saturday, 13 July 1968: Grande Ballroom, Detroit, MI

The Who were the headlining act, the Stooges were the support act to the second show (at 10 pm), with The Frost opening the first show (6 pm). Eyewitness reports claim that Pink Floyd also played this night, although they were scheduled the previous day.

Sunday, 28 July 1968: Oakland University, Rochester, MI

This was a benefit for ALSAC (Aid to Leukemia-Stricken American Children). Rochester is north of Detroit. MC5 were also due to play, but they canceled at the last minute for reasons given below as reported in *The Sun:* 'Apparently the legendary Oakland pigs had warrants for Rob Tyner, Mike Davis and Wayne Kramer dating back to 7/25/66 and were determined to cash them in at Oakland U when the band arrived.' MC5 turned around and went home.

Sunday, 11 August 1968: Mother's, Romeo, MI

Billed as 'a show you will not forget,' The Psychedelic Stooges played with Jagged Edge. Iggy and the band arrived late and showed up with only a guitar, bass and drumsticks, but they were able to borrow Jagged Edge's equipment. After the concert, Iggy was arrested and charged with being 'disorderly' because the crotch of his trousers split, halfway through the performance. He covered the rip with a towel and carried on, but it fell off. A girl in the audience was upset and left the show to get her father, a policeman, who was working nearby.

Ron Asheton recalled, 'He had gotten a pair of brown vinyl pants and he wore them so much; the way he twists around and does his acrobatics, the crotch just split. So he probably was just hangin' out. And then he went backstage and came back with a towel wrapped around him or something. To tell you the truth, I don't know if it was an accident or not. It was sort of like that Jim Morrison in that Miami thing. There was a girl in the audience whose father was a state policeman, and it just happened the post was right around the corner or something. And she went running on down there and said, "There's a naked man at the show." And so the old dude who was the security guard must have been in his 60s or whatever, was saying, "I'm telling you, fellas, right now, the state police are on their way." And we're going, "Huh?". So we're just sitting in the dressing room and Iggy gets the word, and he's trying to split; he's getting the hell out of there. We thought, "Well, fuck, we didn't do anything wrong. So what's the big deal?".'

Ron continued: 'So we're sitting in the dressing room, and the next thing I know the troopers start busting in, big scary dudes, crew cuts, and a couple of guns were out. They weren't pointed or nothing, but hands were on guns. And they're going, "Where's that Iggy?". We said, "He's gone, sir, and we don't know." They looked all around, and I know the Jagged Edge guy was so freaked out because those guys were speed freaks. He was just cowering in the dressing room. Hey, we were all scared. The guy goes, "You're all under arrest until we get that Iggy guy." "Oh no!". Luckily a few moments later, somebody comes up and says, "Yeah, Sarge, we got him." And what happened was Iggy had been in the trunk of a car hiding, and he was making his way to another car that was going to drive him to Ann Arbor. And that's when the police got him. So he spent the night in the clink, and then the next day his parents got him out early the next morning. For us, it was like, "Thank God we didn't have to sit in jail." That was the one and only time, at that show, that he actually got arrested. I mean, there were some close calls, but they got him crawling out of the trunk of a car.'

Romeo Observer reported on the incident: 'James Newell Osterberg, 21, of Ann Arbor, pled guilty before Justice James Schocke Monday morning and was fined $41 and costs of $9 on a charge of being a disorderly person, which had been reduced from indecent exposure. Osterberg's arrest at 10:45 pm Sunday at Mother's followed complaints both to the village and State Police. He had been performing at the local music hall as a dancer.' Iggy's arrest in Romeo would become a staple of press reporting on The Stooges in the years ahead.

Saturday, 17 August 1968: Grande Ballroom, Detroit, MI

The Psychedelic Stooges were back at the Grande Ballroom for this concert, which was listed in *Detroit Free Press*, 'The Grande Ballroom features Country Joe and the Fish, a rock group that serves up a little social commentary with their music, on Friday, Saturday and Sunday evenings. Groups playing along with Country Joe are The Frost on Friday, The Pack and The Psychedelic Stooges on Saturday, and H. P. and the Grass Root Movement plus the Stuart Avery Assemblage on Sunday.'

Friday, 23 August 1968: Grande Ballroom, Detroit, MI

The Psychedelic Stooges performed on a bill with Albert King (headliner) on the first of his three nights at the Grande. Jagged Edge were the other support band that night.

The Youth International Party Festival of Life was scheduled for 25 August 1968 at Lincoln Park, Chicago, Illinois, coinciding with the Democratic Convention being held there. Country Joe and the Fish were to headline, and a number of Detroit bands were planning to play, including MC5, the Stooges and Up. However, the city of Chicago refused to issue any permits for the festival, and most musicians withdrew from the project, including the Stooges. Of the rock bands that had agreed to perform, only the MC5 came to Chicago to play, and their set was cut short by a clash between the audience of a couple of thousand and police.

Late August 1968: Delta Community College, University Center, MI

The Stooges appeared with MC5. University Center is close to Bay City, Michigan. Peter Cavanaugh – DJ and later co-owner of the Sherwood Forest – recalled the event on his blog: 'I had seen the group perform at Delta College with the MC5 and, as I introduced them, Iggy had goosed me. I jumped about two feet in the air. It was nothing sexual, just pretextual. Iggy was quite well-behaved offstage and we had entered into an engaging conversation. He was equal parts of bafflingly brilliant and truly fucked up. He had been busted a few nights before in Romeo, Michigan, for "exposing himself," which he honestly didn't remember doing. "Bummer," summarized Iggy.'

Sunday, 1 September 1968: Baldwin Pavilion, Oakland University, Rochester, MI – Oakland Pop Festival

The bill featured Procol Harum, The Rationals, SRC, The Thyme, MC5, The Jagged Edge, The Frost and Children. Three acts were scheduled but did not play: Pink Floyd, Howlin' Wolf and Chrysalis. The festival attracted a crowd of 15,000 people, despite driving rain and intermittent lightning. The Frost's guitarist Dick Wagner remembered, 'The venue was overflowing with hippies, college kids and hardcore downtown Motor City rockers.'

MC5 played as usual with an American flag on the speakers. When the Stooges went on after MC5, they left the American flag but placed two banners over it, one that advertised Sears, and the other a Nazi banner from Ron's collection of Nazi memorabilia. Steve Mackay – who later played saxophone with The Stooges – remembered the event: 'They wanted to make a wonderful political statement: "This is the real America." Nobody came up and said, "I hate you" or anything.'

Iggy continued to draw most of the attention of the media. On the Stooges' performance, Martha Kinsella reported in *Detroit Free Press:* 'The sounds of The Psychedelic Stooges are hard to remember because listeners become so intent on watching contortionist lead singer Iggy Pop – whose actions are reminiscent of The Doors' Jim Morrison – strut around stage and dive into the front rows of the audience.'

Friday and Saturday, 6 and 7 September 1968: First Unitarian Church, Detroit, MI – Dialogue '68

The gig was presented by Unitarian Social Singles with the cooperation of Trans-Love Energies Unlimited. On the concert poster, the Stooges were billed as 'Psychedelic Stooges' (6 September) and, for the first time, as only 'The Stooges' (7 September). Detroit's *Sun* newspaper announced the event: 'Watch for news of a huge three-day Rock and Roll Frock Show at the First Unitarian Church of Detroit September 6, 7 & 8th. The church, located in the heart of Detroit's Warren-Forest community at Cass and Forest, will fill their altar and pews with rock and roll fiends for three nights and days. The concerts have been scheduled as follows: Friday, Sept. 6th: Psychedelic Stooges, Up, and Billy C. and the Sunshine; Saturday, Sept. 7th: MC5, Stooges, and the Popcorn Blizzard; Sunday, Sept. 8th: MC5, Weird Dude Employment Agency, and the Wilson Mower Pursuit. Lights by TransLove/Magic Veil all three nights. Mark those days off--more news later.' Popcorn Blizzard's frontman would later find fame as Meat Loaf.

In his review of MC5's Saturday performance in *The Village Voice*, Robert Christgau did not seem to be all that impressed by the Stooges: 'Popcorn Blizzard (good), the Psychedelic Stooges (awful) and some blather about a religion called Zenta (weird). I escaped to the weekend coffee house in the church annex during the Stooges, but even at that distance, they still managed to give me a psychedelic headache.' Christgau was indifferent about MC5's performance.

Sunday, 8 September 1968: Grande Ballroom, Detroit, MI

B. B. King headlined at the Grande Ballroom over three nights, starting on Friday 6 September. The Psychedelic Stooges were support for his last night, with other local bands Jagged Edge and The Frost providing support on the previous nights.

Sunday, 22 September 1968: Grande Ballroom, Detroit, MI

This concert was headlined by Amboy Dukes, with guitarist Ted Nugent, who had just released their second album *Journey To The Center Of The Mind*. Soul singer Rodney Knight and His Soul Sextet were also on the bill. The Stooges were billed as 'Psy. Stooges' (abbreviated) on the concert poster.

Monday, 23 September 1968: Union Ballroom, University of Michigan, Ann Arbor, MI

Billed as 'In memory of John Coltrane,' the Stooges (billed as just The Stooges) performed with MC5 (headliner) and Up. The concert was a benefit for MC5 and Children's Community School.

The concert was attended by Danny Fields, who had flown out from New York on John Sinclair's prompting. Sinclair had managed to rouse the interest of two

25

New York journalists, Dennis Frawley and Bob Rudnick, who had a radio show called *Kokaine Karma* on WFMU, a progressive New Jersey station. At the radio station, Sinclair met Fields, who had a show just before Frawley and Rudenick. Sinclair found out that Fields was also working as a publicity assistant for Elektra Records in New York and cajoled him into going to Ann Arbor to experience MC5. After attending a few MC5 shows, Fields was convinced of the band's qualities and talked Elektra's Vice President Jac Holzman into signing the band. During one of his visits to Ann Arbor, band members of MC5 told Fields to see their 'little brother' band, The Psychedelic Stooges.

'When Iggy came off the stage, I went over to him, gushing about the show, telling him I was from Elektra Records and was eager to get them a contract,' remembered Fields. '"Speak to my manager," he said, still walking toward the dressing room, not even looking at me. As it turned out, he didn't think I was serious.' Iggy recalled, 'So I wander off the stage and this guy says, "You're a star!" Just like in the movies. I believed he was an office boy, who just wanted to meet me and impress me. He didn't look like what I thought a record company executive should look like. He was dressed like us, in jeans and leather jacket. He told me that he was from a New York record company, but I just thought he was a fag trying to pick me up. At the same time, I was interested because I was always interested in people who liked what I did. He turned out to be genuine.' Ron Asheton said, 'After the show, he came back to the dressing room, "How'd you guys like to be stars?". I said, "Yeah, right," and just blew him off. We didn't believe him, but the next day he went to Elektra and persuaded the company's President to sign us. Fields was convinced that we would be the next big thing.'

Tuesday, 8 October 1968: The Fifth Dimension, Ann Arbor, MI

This show was a celebration for The Stooges and MC5, both signing with Elektra Records. Danny Fields and Elektra Vice President Jac Holzman brought the contracts for MC5 and The Stooges to sign. The Butterfield Blues Band opened the concert. The festivities led to a trashing of the club, making it the last show ever at the Fifth Dimension.

Iggy recalled the concert: 'The night Jac Holzman was there from Elektra, we did 'I'm Sick,' 'Asthma Attack,' and one other song about being sick. And nobody believed us; everybody thought it was this way of saying, "I'm sick of all this." I was singing songs about what I was really into. During 'Asthma Attack,' I would wheeze for real. I lost 20 pounds. I was just up in a room for about three weeks. I literally couldn't move. Couldn't do anything. But I didn't want to go to a doctor because I don't like to do those things at all, because they sap one's strength. I was so nervous that we had a big chance to play and get myself a recording contract that I made myself ill. I had a temperature of 104; there were bruises on my head because I'd had a kind of a fit, and my one ear was gone. Before I went on, I was sitting in this blanket, shivering. So we had to do a show, right in the middle of the biggest part of my sickness. The funniest thing was that when I was really sick, I had to literally, by the will, come up on stage, and when I got on stage, I was white as a sheet. It was this way we did about three jobs. It was really macabre.'

Friday, 11 October 1968: Grande Ballroom, Detroit, MI
The bill also included John Mayall and The Frost. Ann Arbor music fan Ron, who had seen the Stooges in April 1968, attended the concert: 'This appearance wasn't, for me, all that memorable. I recall telling the gal I was with that the Stooges would be "interesting" and the puzzled smirk on her face. We'd come to see John Mayall. It wasn't as loud a performance as the Union Ballroom show in April '68 (the Grande had better acoustics, so maybe that was it). The set was still short, not more than half an hour, if that. The band was playing tighter than my first experience with them. Iggy was very animated. He strolled through the audience seated on the floor in front of the stage at this show. In the end, while the audience response was warm, it wasn't over the top, like say for the MC5 or even The Frost. My girlfriend's reaction was classic: "That's it?"'

Sunday, 27 October 1968: Grande Ballroom, Detroit, MI
This was a benefit for State Senator Roger Craig. The Psychedelic Stooges performed along with MC5, Toad and Carousel. The gig was listed in *Detroit Free Press* and has been confirmed on an MC5 website.

Wednesday and Thursday, 30 and 31 October 1968: Grande Ballroom, Detroit, MI
The Psychedelic Stooges supported MC5 at these concerts, although they were not listed on the concert poster. The focus was on MC5, who recorded their debut album *Kick Out The Jams* over both nights at the Grande Ballroom. There was no entrance fee in order to attract a full house and a good atmosphere. Recording a live album for a debut was unusual and bold, considering that most bands release at least a few studio albums before releasing a live album. MC5 wanted to replicate their live set, as they considered live performance to be their strength. A Thursday afternoon performance of the songs was also recorded to make sure they had enough takes to choose from, but these tracks were not used. No recordings of the Stooges from the same nights have appeared, so it is unlikely that their sets were taped.

Sunday, 3 November 1968: Silverbell Hideout, Clarkston, MI
With MC5, Dharma and The Bottle Company. Clarkston is north-west of Detroit. This was supposedly the last gig as The Psychedelic Stooges because the band shortly afterward shortened their name to The Stooges on the suggestion of Danny Fields.

Once the Stooges got underway, Wayne Kramer of MC5 recalled, 'There was a guy who has his head on the stage. He was either passed-out or sleeping in the middle of their set. I watched Iggy. He saw the guy's head and he danced around singing. He was looking at the guy's head and he was getting madder and madder. Finally, he drop-kicked him like you would a football. He kicked this kid in the head so hard. "Oh my God, the kid's gonna die." But the kid just came to and then got into their music. At the time, I felt like he was doing it so he could establish his legend.'

An item from *East Village Other* reported an incident from this gig where 'Iggy was threatened with arrest for "indecent exposure".' According to the report, 'The club owners quickly interceded on Iggy's behalf with the Oakland County pigs when they learned that the Stooges' brothers, the MC5, would leave the club without performing if the Ig were harmed in any way. Mindful of the screaming multitudes awaiting the 5's religious ceremony, the operators of the Silverbell quickly secured the much-maligned singer's release, and the show went on.'

Friday, 8 November 1968: Henry Ford Community College, Dearborn, MI

No details about this show are known. It was held in Dearborn, just west of Detroit. Later in November, Iggy and Ron went to New York. Danny Fields took them to a club called The Scene, where they saw Jimi Hendrix jam. Fields also introduced them to former Velvet Underground singer Nico, who befriended Iggy and later came to live in the band house for a month, taking up residence in Iggy's attic room. Nico lured her friend, avant-garde film-maker, Francois DeMenil, to Ann Arbor to shoot a film of her song 'Evening of Light' with her and Iggy.

Thursday, 21 November 1968: Grande Ballroom, Detroit, MI

The Stooges performed with Blue Cheer. John Sinclair reported on the concert in his column for *Fifth Estate:* 'Blue Cheer was blown away again in their second Detroit appearance at the Grande, Nov. 21st when The Stooges unleashed their new set. The Stooges sound better every week, and that Thursday night, they were stronger than they've been since last March when I saw them for the first time and came all over myself. There were times in their show when the music passed into pure magic, rising and rising in intensity until it was felt more than heard.'

Wednesday and Thursday, 27 and 28 November 1968: Grande Ballroom, Detroit, MI

Two gigs with MC5 and The Frost.

Saturday, 30 November 1968: Grande Cleveland, Cleveland, OH

With Blood, Sweat & Tears, this Ohio gig was The Stooges' first performance outside of Michigan.

Friday, 6 December 1968: Athletic Memorial Building, Dearborn, MI

The Stooges performed with Bob Seger System, MC5, Wilson Mower Pursuit and The Frost, according to a listing in *Detroit Free Press*.

Sunday, 15 December 1968: Grande Ballroom, Detroit, MI

The Stooges played with The Frost, Dharma and Third Power. The concert was listed as a 'benefit for the needy' in *Fifth Estate:* 'WABX and WKNR FM, in cooperation with Russ Gibb, will present a charity benefit for needy blacks and whites.'

Friday, 27 December 1968: Grande Ballroom, Detroit, MI

The Stooges and Wicked Religion opened for Fleetwood Mac during their second of two nights at the Grande Ballroom. Fleetwood Mac were still very much a blues-rock group, with Peter Green, their original guitarist, still with the band.

Tuesday, 31 December 1968: Grande Ballroom, Detroit, MI

The Stooges closed out 1968 with another performance at the Grande Ballroom. They played on a bill with SRC, Wilson Mower Pursuit, Up and Stuart Avery Assemblage (not clear which act was the headliner). The Stooges were billed as 'The Stooges,' which was becoming more common.

1969

The Psychedelic Stooges evolved into The Stooges in the course of 1969, as the 'psychedelic' moniker became increasingly dated at a time when the zeitgeist that had spawned psychedelic music and the hippie movement seemed to be on the wane in the USA. 'That was the end of the Sixties and the whole high-minded thing,' said Jimmy Silver. 'All the people who believed that drugs were mind-expansive were really going downhill.' Certainly, the intense music and confrontational performing style of Iggy had little in common with the laid-back approach and peaceful ideals of the flower power culture.

The Stooges continued performing around Michigan throughout 1969, usually playing weekend gigs. Their live set was still very short – around 20 to 30 minutes – but their music developed into more conventional rock as they added the trio of '1969, 'No Fun' and 'I Wanna Be Your Dog,' which became the core of their first album, *The Stooges*. The strategy for the band was to play infrequently, as Silver explained: 'There was a point when I could have had gigs for them virtually every night, but they told me not to. They said they didn't want to overexpose themselves. Really, it was because they did the same thing every night. They didn't have a lot of musical breadth to what they could do. They had one show that they did wherever they went. I couldn't book them in the same area night after night. The concerts had to be very widely spread out. It was pop festivals, clubs, ballrooms on weekends mostly.'

The band played with unrelenting force, while Iggy mesmerized the audiences with his combination of wildly kinetic dance moves, including some quasi-James Brown footwork, actor-like facial expressions and passionately delivered lyrics. He was a bona fide acrobat, doing backbends with his head touching the floor. Other tricks included dives onto the microphone stand or pretending to be dropping face-first to the stage floor, only to catch himself at the very last moment on the bottom rung of the microphone stand, before slowly and deliberately raising himself, hand over hand, pulling himself up to microphone level.

The Stooges generated responses that ranged from devotion and laughter, to shock, intimidation, hostility and outright anger. Their uncompromising music and the performing style of Iggy, made it very difficult for the audience to be indifferent. Many saw the stage performances as something different from most other rock acts, more akin to the Living Theatre and other experimental theatre groups than conventional rock shows. John Sinclair called their performance 'psychodrama,' and observed, 'It exceeded conventional theatre. He might do anything. That was his act. He didn't know what he was going to do when he got up there on the stage. It was exciting. I'd just watch him, and I'd think, "Wow, this guy will stop at nothing. This isn't just a show – he's out of his mind!".' MC5's Wayne Kramer said, 'It was always a battle whether or not the crowd liked them. The crowd didn't know what to make of them. They didn't know if that was really any good or not. They couldn't relate to or understand them.'

If Iggy did not get the reactions he wanted, he would often verbally abuse the audience and go after any catcallers in the crowd. Sometimes he would inflict wounds on his body with drumsticks or the microphone out of frustration with the audience's lack of response. Ron stressed the importance of generating a reaction from the audience: 'Our idea was, "If you can generate anything from the crowd, it's good. If they hate you, that's great". Our idea was not to worry about pleasing the audience. If they liked it, great. If they hated us, even greater. Just to make them do something... That's what Iggy was involved heavily with, going into the audience and making things happen.' Sinclair commented, 'Sometimes it was getting too weird. I remember when he started taunting the crowd with broken bottles. He did that as early as 1969. He'd get his audience response. I think he got to where he didn't really have any respect for the audience. So he'd do things to see what would get a response.'

Taking a break from performing, the band went to New York in April 1969 to record their debut album, with former Velvet Underground member John Cale, in the producer seat. For the album, the band had worked up five numbers, 'I Wanna Be Your Dog,' 'No Fun,' '1969,' 'Ann' (which reused a guitar riff from 'The Dance Of Romance') and the free-form noise improvisation, 'Asthma Attack.' They intended the songs to incorporate lengthy passages of improvisation as per their live set and believed the songs they had would be sufficient for the album. However, the record company demanded more songs to fill up the album, so Ron Asheton and Iggy very quickly came up with more numbers in their Chelsea Hotel room in New York. They turned the existing 'Goodbye Bozos' into 'Little Doll' with some lyric changes, created 'We Will Fall' around a chant by Dave Alexander, and came up with 'Real Cool Time' and 'Not Right' on the spot.

Gigs continued after the sessions in New York. They played several concerts at another Detroit venue, Eastown Theater, which opened in May 1969. The theater was originally a 2,500-seat movie house but closed in 1967 after nearly four decades as a movie palace. It reopened after conversion into a rock venue. The seats of the once opulent movie palace had been ripped out in order to cram more people onto the cement floor; its capacity was legally 1,727, although it drew crowds of 3,000 some nights. The venue had a low stage that allowed for interaction between the performers and audience, something which Iggy took advantage of. While the Grande Ballroom had more of a hippie identity, Eastown was distinctly blue-collar. Alice Cooper has been quoted as saying that the Eastown had 'the best audience in the world.'

The Stooges was released in early August, and the band played a short East Coast tour in September 1969 to support the album, including their first New York concerts, at the outdoors Pavilion at Flushing Meadow Park, followed by club concerts in Boston and Philadelphia. The Stooges' set in the second half of 1969 remained short, comprising four or five tunes from the first album. Their normal set opener was 'I Wanna Be Your Dog,' and they used to close their shows with an extended take on '1969.' As they continued playing, new material was introduced into the set and the band gradually replaced *The Stooges* tracks with new numbers. By late 1969, they were playing almost exclusively new songs that would be released on their second album, *Fun House*.

Although *The Stooges* was not a mainstream success, the band did attract a fair amount of attention from the rock media, raising their profile considerably in New York, Detroit, and other large cities of the US. They were still a largely unknown commodity in Europe and the rest of the world. 'It was a small following,' Ron commented. 'The album didn't sell more than maybe 20,000 copies. Our biggest following was New York, Detroit, the Midwest, and East Coast, including Boston. No real Southern interest. Mostly just the hardcore Midwest, that block from St. Louis to Washington DC.' A Stooges fan club was launched by Natalie Schlossman out of Philadelphia. She published *Popped*, a fanzine which reported on all things Stooges, and she built a network of like-minded followers who traveled across the US to watch the band perform. The Stooges were building a devoted cult following. Iggy said in an interview at the time, that mass recognition was not important to him: 'What's important is individual recognition. In other words, it's not how many people recognize you; it's what the people who *do* recognize you recognize you for.'

Sunday, 5 January 1969: Grande Ballroom, Detroit, MI

The Stooges opened 1969 with a concert at the Grande Ballroom, the first of a dozen gigs at the venue throughout 1969. Amboy Dukes headlined and Frozen Sun was first on the bill. The Stooges were again billed as just 'The Stooges'.

Sunday, 26 January 1969: Delta Community College, University Center, MI – Pops Festival

The Stooges appeared alongside MC5, The Rationals, Amboy Dukes, Third Power, Bob Seger System, and Up, among others, with the 10-hour festival lasting from 2 pm to midnight. At one point during the concert, Iggy scooped a girl from her seat and started carrying her around the auditorium. Pete Andrews, the promoter of the festival, happened to be watching the performance next to the girl's father, an administrator at the Community College. Andrews hurriedly crawled across the floor of the venue to reach Iggy: 'I said, it's a bit serious, could you put her down and stop this? He said, "Oh gee, I'm sorry," put her down and went back to the stage.'

An eyewitness account by Bo White on his blog said of the Stooges' performance: 'Iggy and the Stooges stunned the crowd with a maniacal, one chord feedback-drone, nihilistic push-all-the-buttons performance. Iggy was over-the-top, spittin' at the audience and cuttin' and scratchin' himself until he drew blood. He even sang and groaned a little. Finally, he grabbed a girl from the audience, carried her through the crowd until he stumbled back, then forward, and deposited her on the gymnasium floor, where he proceeds to dry hump the hell outta the poor girl. A plant? Rumour had it that he humped the Dean's daughter.'

The story of 'the Dean's Daughter' would be repeated in many press articles about The Stooges. Iggy would subsequently claim that he had become 'obsessed with this chick' and had bit her, but 'the people dug it so much that we got paid and asked back.' Leni Sinclair (wife of John) captured a few minutes of the Stooges' performance on film (no sound), which is the earliest known live footage of the band. This concert footage has often erroneously been dated to July 1969, but the Delta concert occurred in January 1969, as verified by *The Delta Collegiate* newspaper reporting.

Tuesday, 4 February 1969: Grande Ballroom, Detroit, MI

In front of a crowd of 1,500, The Stooges appeared with MC5, Up, Denise Martin, The Oracle Ramus and Joshua Newton, in an event that was billed as 'Legal Self Defense Benefit, aka The Second Annual Tribal Stomp.' A review in Detroit's *Sun* tried to describe The Stooges' performance, 'As Pun (Plamondon, White Panther activist, also later jailed) said when he introduced them, from the 14th level of the catacombs came The Stooges! The Stooges did their thing and no one really knows if it lasted twenty mins or three hours. No one has yet written a real description of The Stooges in action and I won't even try; the words aren't available to us yet.'

A concert on 25 February 1969 at the Union Ballroom, University of Michigan campus in Ann Arbor, was advertised in *Ann Arbor Argus*. The Stooges were slated to perform with MC5 and Red White & Blues Band in a 'Benefit for Ann Arbor Argus.' However, a note in the *Sun* thanked MC5, Red White & Blues Band and The Gold for playing, implying The Stooges did not play. Thus, the 4 February gig at Grande Ballroom was likely the last gig The Stooges played before traveling to New York in late March 1969 to record their debut album, *The Stooges*, with John Cale. In New York, the band stayed at the Chelsea Hotel. Recording sessions at the Hit Factory began on 1 April. Future Stooges guitarist, James Williamson, paid the band a visit while they were in New York.

A Stooges concert on 1 April 1969 at McKenny Hall Ballroom, Ypsilanti, Michigan, was listed in *Ann Arbor Argus*, but the date clashes with the start of *The Stooges* recording sessions in New York, so it is unlikely that they played it. The Stooges were scheduled to appear with Up, Commander Cody and Sunny Hugg in The Obsidian Art Festival.

Sunday, 27 April 1969: Grande Ballroom, Detroit, MI

Having completed their debut album in New York, The Stooges returned to live work with yet another gig at the Grande Ballroom. The *Sun* reported this gig as being the first top billing for The Stooges at the Grande Ballroom, supported by Third Power and All The Lonely People.

Friday, 9 May 1969: The Crow's Nest (East), St. Clair Shores, MI

All The Lonely People supported The Stooges (listed as Psychedelic Stooges). The Crow's Nest (East) club opened in late 1967 and closed in August 1969.

St. Clair Shores is a suburban city bordering Lake St. Clair, approximately 20 kilometers north-east of downtown Detroit.

Saturday, 10 May 1969: The Crow's Nest (West), Westland, MI

Licorice (sic) supported The Stooges (still listed as Psychedelic Stooges). The Crow's Nest (West) club was only open for six months in 1969. Westland is halfway between Detroit and Ann Arbor.

Thursday, 22 May 1969: Grande Ballroom, Detroit, MI

The Stooges played with It's A Beautiful Day – a folk/country rock group originally from the San Francisco area – as the opening act.

Friday, 23 May 1969: The Grey Chapel, Ohio Wesleyan University, Delaware, OH

This concert was organized by the student union, prompted by future rock journalist, Ben Edmonds, who was a fan of MC5 and had booked them for a show during the school's homecoming weekend. He was convinced by John Sinclair to book The Stooges the night after MC5. The concert was held in a 2,500-capacity venue, but there were less than 100 people in attendance, according to Edmonds.

'I was totally mesmerized by Iggy,' said Edmonds. 'I had never seen anybody move like that before; just like the music, his movements seemed to have no precedent; made Jim Morrison's Native American soft-shoe look like silly affectation, for starters. There were these explosions of movement, but it was more fluid, and dare I say more graceful, than the spasms of herky-jerk motion you see today. Now it's all about playing off a pre-existing relationship with the audience; back then, Iggy seemed safe and complete in his cocoon of sound, lost in his own world when he danced. I sometimes wondered if his habit of hurling himself into the audience – not on display at this gig because there was no audience – was his way of re-entering ours. I must admit that I was so stunned by Iggy that I barely noticed the band. Unlike the MC5, who'd easily filled the large stage with their stars and stripes and skull and crossbones-draped Marshall stacks, flamboyant costumes and nonstop five-man assault, the three instrumental Stooges seemed dwarfed in the expanse, almost anonymous in their jeans and tee-shirts. They barely moved a muscle. I could tell right away that they weren't "good" musicians like the MC5, but it didn't seem to matter. I now know that they'd just finished recording the album, so the set probably consisted of four or five snappy numbers from that, plus their customary set-closing freak-out. At the time, I couldn't distinguish one song from another, except for one that went "No fun, my babe, no fun." The music was loud and crude but possessed of a rhythm so elemental that its source might not have been musical history, but something further back, some suppressed genetic memory. The singer was completely captivated by it, and that was good enough for me.'

Edmonds continued: 'At one point, he picked up a drumstick shard and began absent-mindedly running it across his bare chest. He apparently increased the pressure with each stroke because red welt lines soon became visible, which then discharged trickles of blood running down his torso. I was dumbstruck. Well, I was already dumbstruck; now I was somewhere beyond. I mean, what's gonna prepare you for *that*? But the singer didn't seem to notice. He finished the show without acknowledging what he'd done. Afterward, he put on a white tee-shirt and traces of red began to soak through. I don't know why, but the sight of that made me more queasy than actually watching him commit the act. It was mild compared to the damage he'd later inflict on himself, but this, it turned out, was the first time he'd ever done such a thing. Quite a first experience to have with them. Mind-destroying, just like the man said.'

The concert was an important one in Stooges lore. In attendance was Wendy Weisberg, a friend of Iggy's from university (which Edmonds learned about when Iggy told the story in his *I Need More* book). 'I was shocked,' said Iggy. 'I remembered her immediately. She was someone you always kept in your mind, maybe to encounter again. She was tomboyish, with a very, very beautiful build – a Jewish girl from Shaker Heights: a wealthy suburb of Cleveland.' Wendy attended the show with her boyfriend, but Iggy returned the next weekend to spend time with Wendy. They announced only a few weeks after their meeting that they were getting married, much to the surprise of the rest of the band, and their friends.

Saturday, 24 May 1969: The Crow's Nest (West), Westland, MI

A group called The Flow opened for The Stooges. This was the penultimate show at The Crow's Nest (West), which closed shortly afterward. Jimmy Silver commented on the concert in a letter to Danny Fields, reproduced in the *Total Chaos* book: 'We were in this dive (one Crow's Nest West) with about 100 kids, and the other band was fucked up (bass was broken), so they went on about 10 pm doing a drum-guitar duet, and after a while, Jim starts singing with them and they start playing about 50 feet above their heads and the bass player stops and starts playing 3-string bass, and after a while, they get really out there and Jim steps down, and for about five minutes they played music like I'm sure they've never played or heard before. Then we go on and play pretty good (borrowed fucked-up equipment, etc.) and finish in about 35 minutes. Pretty soon, the owner comes down to the dressing room bitching, "Too short!", "1/2 the money", etc., etc.. So Jim says, "Okay, I'll go do my Flamenco dance, who wants to jam with me?" and the band goes upstairs and John sets up the amps again and they start playing. Soon Jim's shirt comes off and the boys start really working out, Scotty right in the middle moving with the grace of some black-maned lion at the drums, and Ron and Dave on either side, twisting and writhing like madmen, perfectly erect, way up front of them, almost stock-still, bathed in this pale white light, just like some crazed body, the band moving crazed with Jim an erect hard white dick. Right there... it was indescribable...

35

perfect. And that was it. Intellectually I always knew that was it, but right then... it was. Far out. Anyway, it can't miss; it's the real thing. I'm speechless. Not by what the show was or is, but by my own realization of it. Just thought you'd appreciate it.'

Friday, 30 May 1969: Michigan State Fairgrounds, Detroit, MI – First Annual Rock & Roll Revival

The festival included local acts The Stooges, MC5, Terry Reid, Amboy Dukes, SRC, The Frost, The Rationals, as well as several visitors from outside Michigan, including Chuck Berry, Sun Ra, Dr. John and the Night Tripper, New York Rock & Roll Ensemble and Johnny Winter. A photo from The Stooges' performance attributed to Ron Richardson is featured in Bob Matheu's Stooges biography.

The Stooges performed just as it was becoming dark on the first day of the two-day festival, which drew around 30,000 people over two days. Coming on stage, Iggy addressed the audience, 'Nice to be here at this... rodeo yeah!', before launching into 'I Wanna Be Your Dog.'

Dennis Frawley, writing for *Fifth Estate*, felt the festival 'displayed to visiting pop luminaries the significance of Detroit's rock and roll scene.' He described The Stooges' music as 'contemptuous' and compared 'Iggy's bumps and grinds' with 'burlesque stripping.' The review in *The Seed* focused on Iggy: 'Stoges [sic] play minimal rock: each song has two chords, one vocal, and no technique. The open secret to the Stooges' success is Iggy, who goes through a psychodrama of grunts, postures and insults until he gets bored. Someone tells a story about how Iggy once broke a bottle on an unknown chick; tonight, he temporizes and merely boos the crowd. Half of them cheer, the others boo back.' The reporter from *Underground Flick* was not impressed: 'If you have never seen The Stooges, you haven't missed a thing. Their performance was a funny thing to watch. The singer, at one time, dove into the audience, falling on a few people who weren't too thrilled about this. He had the microphone in his mouth while he was singing. I'm surprised he didn't swallow it. It might have helped. At one point, he was cussed at; he in return, dared the cusser to come on stage. He declined. He closed "his" performance by kissing a girl for a near-record five minutes.'

The Fairgrounds, which includes exhibit buildings and a multi-purpose coliseum, were host to the annual Michigan State Fair as well as a wide variety of events throughout the year. Iggy's father saw him perform for the first time at the concert. Iggy recalled, 'My father tried to appear cool after the concert. But my mother told me that he had actually climbed a girder to the grandstand to see what I was doing onstage.'

Friday, 6 June 1969: Eastown Theater, Detroit, MI

The Stooges' first appearance at the Eastown Theater was on a bill topped by MC5 and with Illinois Speed Press as the opening act. Ron Asheton actually performed with MC5, filling in on bass for MC5's Michael Davis (who was in jail), as he recalled: 'They asked me if I'd play bass, and we just did like, I didn't know songs, but we did like four songs, real long versions, a lotta playing for almost an hour. We did a couple blues things, and we did "Looking at You," "Kick Out The Jams," stuff that I know. It was really fun; it was fun; it was a different feeling for me to hear the big double guitars; I was used to holding everything up myself. You'd have your speaker, then double up the stacks you'd have guitars; you'd have a little bit of everything. So I happened to have my ear, and I was used to it, didn't bother me at the time, but I guess double doses. I got offstage and thought it's just a ringing, but I couldn't hear out of this ear for about three days. It was like seriously heavy fingers, cotton; it was driving me nuts. I'd pound on it, stick things in it.'

Saturday, 7 June 1969: Michigan State Fairgrounds, Detroit, MI – Festival After The Festival

This was to be the second of two nights of concerts at the Fairgrounds. The first night (6 June 1969) should have been headlined by The Who supported by Arthur Brown, It's a Beautiful Day and The Stooges, but The Who postponed, and The Stooges played the Eastown gig instead. On 7 June 1969, the line-up was scheduled to be as the previous night, but with Bob Seger playing instead of The Who.

Friday, 4 July 1969: Raceway, Mt. Clemens, MI – Rock and Roll Revival No. 2

The bill included Savoy Brown, Third Power, Pentangle, Brownsville Station, The Frost, MC5, Sunday Funnies, Sky, The Bump and All Those Funny People. The headliners – Amboy Dukes – did not play due to rain. Mt. Clemens is located approximately 40 kilometers north-east of downtown Detroit.

Saturday, 5 July 1969: Pottawatami Beach, Saugatuck, MI – Saugatuck Pop Festival

Saugatuck is located in western Michigan on the shores of Lake Michigan. The bill for the Saugatuck Pop Festival featured SRC, Procol Harum, MC5, Muddy Waters, John Lee Hooker, Amboy Dukes, Rotary Connection, Crazy World of Arthur Brown, Bob Seger, The Frost and several more. The crowd was estimated at 20,000 people. According to Art Johnson in *Berkeley Tribe* (an underground newspaper based in Berkeley, California), 'Saugatuck was overrun with drunk and half-crazed greasers and organized gangs. The Highwaymen, who are the MC5's favorite gang, got in free for guarding the outside fence.' Photos from the show by Robert Matheu are featured in his Stooges biography.

W. Rexford Benoit, writing for *Creem*, felt the Stooges were amazing: 'Listening to The Stooges there (or anywhere in person) was like watching a TV set with a finger in an electric light outlet.' He singled out MC5 and

The Stooges as the high-points of the festival: 'The Stooges and 5 are the essence. Their distinctive sounds make them unlike any other bands and will undoubtedly make them famous.' The Stooges' performance was also reviewed by Art Johnson in *Berkeley Tribe:* 'Iggy was the first rock and roll star I know to use raw hamburger in his act. He rubbed it all over his body and raw chest and then ate some. Wiggy Iggy is with The Stooges, yet another macabre feature of the seamy side of Detroit, my hometown.' He thought Iggy 'is very weird and very sick, and he sucks off the microphone when he sings and does all kinds of contortions with his double-jointed body as if he were a trapezoid.'

Sunday, 6 July 1969: Eastown Theater, Detroit, MI

No details are known about this gig, if it happened; at least one local paper, the *Windsor Star*, reported the venue closed for the weekend.

Days later, on Saturday, 12 July 1969, Iggy and Wendy Weisberg married at the band's farmhouse. The wedding was officiated by band manager Jimmy Silver, who had become a minister of the Universal Life Church (an appointment which required a $1 donation), allowing him to marry them. Ron was the best man (and wore a Nazi uniform despite Wendy being Jewish) and Jimmy's wife Susan Silver catered the party. Wendy's parents refused to acknowledge the marriage, so no one in her family showed up. The marriage lasted only a few months.

Sunday, 13 July 1969: Eastown Theater, Detroit, MI

This concert was promoted as 'Legal Self-Defense Presents The People of Michigan Salute John Sinclair for his Heroic Work in the Community.' Sinclair had been sentenced to a nearly 10-year prison term for the crime of possessing two marijuana joints. Also appearing on the bill were MC5 and Up, together with film, poetry readings and 'a people's trial,' with the two federal agents responsible for John Sinclair's arrest being 'put on trial.'

Friday and Saturday, 18 and 19 July 1969: Fifth Forum Theatre, Ann Arbor, MI

The Stooges were billed with the old name of The Psychedelic Stooges on the concert poster. The advertisements in the press had them billed as both Stooges and Psychedelic Stooges. Films of old cartoons were shown at the late-night event, which started at 11 pm. Fifth Forum Theatre was a small movie theater.

Tuesday, 22 July 1969: Grande Ballroom, Detroit, MI

No details are known.

Wednesday, 23 July 1969: Grande Ballroom, Detroit, MI

MC5 was the headline act and Tate Blues Band was also on the bill. The concert was a benefit for the 'John Sinclair Defense Fund.'

Sunday, 3 August 1969: Sportsman's Park, Mt. Clemens, MI – Mt. Clemens Pop Festival

Also on the bill were Eric Burdon, MC5, John Mayall, Muddy Waters, John Lee Hooker, Alice Cooper, Cat Mother, McCoys, Up, Rush, Fruit of the Loom, Savage Grace and a few more. This was the first time The Stooges appeared with the Alice Cooper band, which would relocate to Detroit from Los Angeles in the spring of 1970 (Alice, also known as Vincent Furnier, was born in Detroit).

Rolling Stone photographer, Baron Wolman, wrote later, 'I had no idea who they were and was not prepared for Iggy's onstage gymnastics. Man, he bent over backward almost in half, still wailing into the microphone: he was hardcore. Had I known more about Iggy, understood who he was, especially in the Detroit music scene, I would have shot a whole lot more film; hell, I only took a total of ten frames or so. Unforgivable!'

Wednesday, 13 August 1969: Grande Ballroom, Detroit, MI

This was a benefit for State Senator Roger Craig, to help raise money for his race to become governor of this state. Sky and Catfish were also on the bill.

Sunday, 17 August 1969: Kenwick-on-the-Lake, Brights Grove, Canada – Canadian-American Pop Rock Festival

The Stooges appeared on the bill with MC5, Amboy Dukes, The Pleasure Seekers, Mitch Ryder, Motherlode, The Rationals, Fruit of the Loom, Frijid Pink and a few others. Brights Grove is a neighborhood on the shore of Lake Huron, Ontario. *The Windsor Star* previewed the two-day event (15–16 August 1969) by saying that it was the first and largest show of its kind in the area, costing the organizers more than $23,000 to secure the services of the bands. The newspaper also noted that The Stooges would be making their Canadian premiere. In his review of the event, Ron Bonnett from the *Times Herald Reporter* reported the concert a disappointment, with only about 800 attending the two days, when more than 5,000 had been predicted. The second day of the event (Saturday, 16 August) was washed out, and instead, bands played on the Sunday (17 August), although there is no reference to The Stooges eventually playing then or earlier at the festival.

The Stooges' appearance at an event called Festival of Life – to be held on 17 August 1969 at Speedway, Milan, Michigan – was canceled. According to a report in *Sun*, the reason was that 'the Musicians' Union forced cancelation of the whole event by telling the bands they couldn't play for the benefit, or they would be kicked out of the Union. It rained all day anyway, but we all had a party with the God's Children, Scorpions, Huns, Spokesman, White Panthers and assorted beer-drinking revelers. Some of the brothers from Milan and Jackson jammed awhile in the sun and rain. It was far-fucking out. Monroe Sheriffs put a roadblock up for a while and hassled people on the way out.'

Friday, 22 August 1969: Grande Ballroom, Detroit, MI
Support act was the group Stoney, and the Jagged Edge, the latter debuting a new line-up.

Saturday, 23 August 1969: Grande Ballroom, Detroit, MI
The Stooges headlined over The Frost and All The Lonely People.

Thursday, 28 August 1969: Ski Lodge, Mt. Holly, MI
The Stooges appeared on a bill that featured twelve acts, including Grand Funk Railroad, All The Lonely People, Savage Grace, The Rationals, Third Power and The Frost, among others. The concert in Mt. Holly, which is located approximately 50 kilometers north-west of downtown Detroit, ran from noon to midnight and was held outside and behind the Mt. Holly Ski Lodge, on the slopes of the ski area. An audience of 20,000 was expected. Half-Life guitarist Jim Nash recalled, 'In the middle of the set, Iggy called for a "cigarette break." He lit one up and stood next to Ron, seemingly to discuss the next song and how it would play out. This was hilarious to me.'

Sunday, 31 August 1969: Benedictine Stadium, Detroit, MI – Rock and Roll Picnic
Also on the bill were Light House, Keef Hartley, Mitch Ryder, Sky, Third Power, Friend and Lover, Wilson Mower Pursuit, The Red White and Blues Band, Brownsville Station and Underground Wall. The event was attended by around 3,000 people.

Monday September 1, 1969: Grande Ballroom, Detroit, MI – Fifth Estate Benefit
Also performing were MC5 and Gold Brothers. The *Fifth Estate* explained the event: 'Everyone who wants to tune in to the music of our culture should be at the *Fifth Estate benefit* to be held Sept. 1 at the Grande Ballroom from 6–11 pm. Featured will be the MC5, Stooges, and the Gold Brothers, along with Newsreel films of the San Francisco State strike and two short films from Cuba. The reason our paper had need of a benefit is due to the large number of free GI subscriptions that we have given to our brothers in Vietnam. We want to keep this policy going, but 500 free subs at $3 per winds up to be a lot of bread we don't have. Also, one thing should be made crystal clear: this benefit is not for people under 21 or under 30; it's for all *Fifth Estate* readers and no one should be hung up about coming because they don't have shoulder-length hair or they're not wearing beads. None of us are into a hipper-than-thou thing. If you dig our paper, come to the Grande. Support us and support our GI brothers.'

The newspaper also reviewed the event: '*The Fifth Estate's* Labor Day benefit at the Grande Ballroom was an overwhelming success. The bands were beautiful and so were the people. Newsreel's films turned everybody on and a good time was had by all. Special thanks to the MC5, the Stooges, the Gold Brothers, Newsreel, Uncle Russ and everyone who came. It was a real Detroit city evening. Everyone got down.'

Friday and Saturday, 5 and 6 September 1969: The Pavilion at Flushing Meadow Park, New York, NY

The Stooges' New York debut was originally advertised for Wednesday, 3 September (an advertisement appeared in *The Village Voice* with this date), but was subsequently rescheduled as two nights, Friday and Saturday, 5 and 6 September. *Variety* reported 2,200 tickets were sold for Friday, and when 2,300 had been sold for Saturday, MC5 waived their fee to allow additional people to be allowed in for free.

The two concerts in New York opened a brief Elektra-supported tour to promote The Stooges' debut album, which was released two weeks earlier. The Memphis blues band, Moloch, opened the proceedings, followed by Elektra's David Peel and the Lower East Side, then The Stooges, and last, the bill-topping MC5. The Stooges' New York debut received a mixed audience reception. Some seemed captivated and intrigued, but others were unimpressed, some even throwing drinks at the band. Regardless, Iggy, wearing only jeans cut down to shorts, and sneakers, gave it everything he had. During both concerts, he ran from the stage and leaped into the crowd, something which the New York audience had never experienced before at a rock show. The audience tossed him back onstage. The concert opened with 'I Wanna Be Your Dog,' and they also played '1969' and 'No Fun' amongst others.

The New York shows were attended by Natalie Schlossman, who had launched her Stooges fan club: 'I was blown away by the energy and the volume. I had heard stories of Iggy's stage presence, but nothing prepared me for his dancing and singing. The album was great, but I have to say that I did not fall in love with the band until I saw them live. Iggy was bare-chested, wearing tight blue jeans. He was all over the stage, dancing around, turning with his back to the crowd and shaking that cute ass. He drove into the mic stand and was swinging it around, all the time singing and not missing any words. The band was tight, and I was impressed with Ron, Dave and Scott's playing with abandon. To me, it seemed like music with no boundaries and just a bit dangerous. It was loud, free, high energy, and the music gave me a natural high.'

Natalie continued: 'I was jammed up against the stage almost directly in front of Iggy. I have read that drinks were thrown at the stage, but from my vantage point, the only wetness I felt was from perspiration. The crowd was wild, but it did not seem like an unpleasant atmosphere. The walls seemed to be sweating and I loved it. The set lasted about one-half hour. It consisted of the songs on the first LP. After the Stooges set was over, I scraped myself from the front of the stage and made my way backstage. We said "hi" to the guys, told them how blown away we were and then we stood at the back of the hall for the MC5.'

Natalie also attended the second night: 'The set was exactly the same. I stood a bit on the side so I would not be crushed again. I still wanted to be close because I needed to determine if what I felt the previous night was a one-time thing. The band played just as loud, there was just as much electricity in the air, the vibe was the same, Iggy was just as wild, and I felt the same as the first time. I knew I was witnessing something very special. I had no idea the feeling I had for the music would take me on the wildest journey of my life, or that it would take the world 30 years to catch up!'

The Stooges' New York premiere generated a great deal of press, as rock journalists were uncertain what to make of Iggy and the band. Calling Iggy 'a burlesque parody of Jagger,' *Billboard's* Fred Kirby thought the Stooges' performance was an 'erotic display.' He concluded that they would go over better in the more intimate surroundings of a small club. Karin Berg of *Rock* and *East Village Other* felt the Stooges 'can be a little terrifying – they put on a great show, but the show is not a put-on. They can shake up, intimidate, excite their audiences – they can also anger them, sometimes make them hostile.' She drew comparisons with the Living Theatre. Similarly, Mike Jahn of *the New York Times* observed that the Stooges 'probably belong Off-Broadway more than to the world of rock 'n' roll, but the group's effect is nonetheless impressive.'

Christian Hodenfield of *Rolling Stone* described some of the action on and off stage. 'The music is incessant and pounding, with usually one certain theme laid down, again and again, all loud and inane. Iggy wriggles and oozes about on stage in various sexual posturing. He makes use of the microphone stand; he does fandangos around; he sits on it, lies on it, caresses it. At one point, someone in the crowd made an obscene gesture. Iggy leaped, head-first, out onto him. Suddenly, the whole place was up on its feet, crowding around to see their fantasies being acted out. The crowd managed to get him back on stage. He ambled around while the band was keeping with the same feedback and hi-screech cachexia. He drifted to the back of the stage and then, with new vigor, ran across the stage, into the air with a set expression on his face, and onto the person again. By the time he got onto the stage again, he was drained and livid at the same time, stalking uncertainly. He started to claw at his glistening, sweaty chest, and welts that had been there began to get bloody again. Raising fresh weals, uttering one word over and over; the band working their amplifiers into a frenzied fuzz-fog. All fall down. Guitars thrown at the amplifiers; finis.'

Writing in his column for *Chicago Tribune*, Robb Baker reported, 'Stealing the show the other weekend was the violently sexual performance of Iggy, lead singer of the Stooges, a rather good Ann Arbor, Mich., version of Britain's Rolling Stones. Iggy appears on stage almost nude, except for short, short denim cut-offs. His eyes are glazed. He jumps, dances, screams, claws and digs at his own skin, hurls himself blindly into the crowd in front of the stage. It's a strangely compelling, shattering experience, surprisingly pertinent as a comment on the violent, even sadomasochistic, extremes that mark more inter-personal relationships in our present-day society than most of us are willing to admit. Not that everyone at the Pavillion was charmed. Iggy was bombarded with all sorts of paper missiles. Yet most of the onlookers stayed riveted in place thru all the short set.'

David Walley believed The Stooges, 'like a snake charming a bird, are fascinating to watch,' and he wrote in *East Village Other* about the Saturday concert: 'Stooging is a unique experience for those who can stand it. The Pavilion audience didn't really know what to do with the Ig. They had never been subjected to a band which ignored them, which didn't give a damn how cool the scene or how groovy they were. The Stooges didn't give a damn... and neither did Iggy as he crouched by the bass amp, eyes gleaming insanely, as he took a headlong dive into the crowd, only to be vomited up on stage again. Saturday night's set ended with guitarist Dave Alexander tossing his bass over his amp and stalking off. The crowd by this time was screaming for more, but Iggy had retired to his dressing room where there weren't any chicks. He couldn't care about that; he was just taking it easy, letting himself get back to himself, away from the Ig of Stooge.'

Rolling Stone's Hodenfield interviewed Iggy after the concert, wanting to know why Iggy at one point went after someone in the audience: 'The guy insulted me, so I either wanted to make it with him or embarrass him in front of everybody, which I think I did.' Hodenfield was bewildered: 'The Stooges no doubt appeal to base, broken tastes. My friends and I all just shook our heads and mumbled about the loss of civilization. But there was another guy there who really dug Iggy. He said it was really different... that was really some fine performance.'

Alan Vega of Suicide attended both the shows and was so thrilled that it inspired him to become a performer. By 1970, Suicide was playing in various spots around New York, advertising their music as 'punk music.' Vega recalls, 'What I saw that night was beyond anything I'd seen before. It was like the new art form because the separation between artist and audience was broken down. After that night, I thought if I was gonna be a real artist, I had to go where Iggy was. I never in my life thought I'd ever get up on a stage. I was totally shy, so it was the scariest place. I had no idea how I was going to make this happen. I can't perform, much less sing. I must have been out of my mind.'

The Stooges had originally been scheduled to play on 5 September 1969 at University of Davis Stadium, Davis, Michigan, as part of 'The University of Detroit Student Government Orientation Program,' with Cat Mother, Bob Seger, and Frost also on the bill. However, it is unlikely that The Stooges performed, given their New York commitments.

Tuesday, Wednesday and Thursday, 9, 10 and 11 September 1969: The Tea Party, Boston, MA

The next stop of the tour was Boston, where The Stooges opened for Ten Years After during a three-night residency at the 400-capacity Tea Party club. Jimmy Silver remembered, 'The boys were making fun of them, calling them Five

Minutes Later. They were kind of annoyed that Ten Years After was getting hype and recognition because they could play speeded-up derivative blues tunes.' Boston Tea Party operated from 1967 to late 1970. Many of the artists that played the venue also performed at New York's Fillmore East, San Francisco's Fillmore West and Electric Factory in Philadelphia. Lou Reed said it was Velvet Underground's 'favorite place to play in the whole country.'

The Stooges confronted a crowd that had little interest in them, having come for the headline act. The audience responded with near silence to each song. Natalie Schlossman was in the audience: 'The band performed the same set as the previous shows at the Pavilion. They performed the set, ignoring the negative vibes from the crowd. This was the first of many gigs that were played with a less than warm crowd reception. I attended only one of the Boston shows. I had my first real job and did not have much vacation, so I took the train up to Boston, attended the show and returned to Philadelphia and went to work the next day for half a day. I reflected on the train ride back to Philly about the distinct difference in the reaction between the NY and Boston audience. It may have been the summer of love, but there was not much love in Boston for the guys on that early fall evening.'

Friday and Saturday, 19 and 20 September 1969: Electric Factory, Philadelphia, PA

The Stooges proceeded to Philadelphia, where they opened two concerts for Buddy Miles Express, featuring Buddy Miles on drums and Jim McCarty on guitar. The 2,800-capacity Electric Factory was a big warehouse that had been converted into a music venue with state-of-the-art lighting and a decent PA. It had stalls built around the outer walls where people could climb up and stand to watch the show. At one end in the back of the warehouse, there were monkey bars and a couple of adult swings. For some shows, they would set out folding chairs for the audience, but most of the time, they left the floor open for dancing and standing about. From its opening in 1968, Electric Factory played host to many of the biggest names in rock at the time. The club later changed location and became Franklin Music Hall in 2018.

Natalie Schlossman remembered, 'This was the first time the guys were coming to my hometown. I decided to bring food as a welcome. My two friends from Elektra were coming down from NYC for the shows. I rushed home from work and baked a few chickens. I also brought a bag of fruit consisting of oranges, apples, bananas and grapes. We went to the show early because I wanted to get the food to the guys before the show. Knowing that most of the guys were eating a macrobiotic diet, I figured chicken and fruit would be acceptable. I barely had a chance to put the package down and some of the guys started digging in.'

Natalie continued: 'Before the show began, Iggy was out and about the Factory. He found a very cute, very young-looking girl and proceeded to take her to the stalls and make out with her. I knew the girl and her friend from seeing them around at concerts. The both of them were about eighteen but looked fourteen. In those days, Iggy always went for the very young-looking girls. This girl, who I nicknamed Pattie-chickie, was wearing knee socks, shorts and had her long brown hair in pig tails. She spent the time before and after the set with Iggy in that stall. I also gave Pattie and her friend another name, which was the "virgin groupies" because they told me they would go back to hotels with bands but would only strip to the waist. It gave me a good chuckle and I guess it did not bother Iggy too much because on Saturday before the show started, he was there in the same stall making out with her again!'

Referring to the Stooges' opening act, Buddy Miles told the crowd at one point; 'Okay, unlike some people, I *can* play music.' The Stooges wasted no time retaliating the next night with a full-blown feedback freak-out while Ron yelled curses against the headliner into a microphone. Jimmy Silver recalled, 'Buddy Miles' idea of a show was to pretend to fall asleep on his drum kit during his drum solo, which brought cheers and applause from the audience. The boys, of course, hooted with derisive laughter, bringing extreme bad vibes and enmity from the superstars, particularly Buddy Miles, who informed us along the lines that we were nobody, going nowhere.'

'Both nights, the show was very similar to the shows at the Pavilion the prior weekend,' said Natalie. 'Iggy performed similar moves. In my early days of seeing the band, there was no wax or cut glass or peanut butter. There was just loud music, high energy, plenty of dancing and wild screams. Although there was a bit of trouble with Buddy Miles, the audience reaction was much more positive than in Boston.'

Saturday, 20 September 1969: Philadelphia, PA – *The Hy Lit Show*

The Stooges lip-synched 'I Wanna Be Your Dog' and either '1969' or 'No Fun' on a local Philadelphia television show (on channel 48), named after its host, Hyman Aaron Lit. Natalie Schlossman attended the taping session: 'We were up in the production booth, looking down through the glass at the guys. Since it was lip-synched and not live, we were there less than two hours.'

Lit was a very popular DJ in the Delaware Valley. He was one of the first DJs to play The Beatles and introduce British rock music to the area. His son – who now has responsibility over the estate – has been contacted about the tape of The Stooges, but he has said that it cannot be found.

Saturday, 27 September 1969: Pavilion, Wampler's Lake, MI

Returning home after the East Coast tour, The Stooges continued gigging around Michigan for the remainder of 1969. The Woolies opened for The Stooges. Pavilion in Wampler's Lake, west of Ann Arbor, was established in the 1940s but did not present rock artists until 1965. It closed in September 1971. After closing down, the venue was demolished, and a storage facility was built. The Stooges played there twice in 1970 and once in 1971.

Sunday, 28 September 1969: Sherwood Forest, Davison, MI – WTAC Pop Festival

The club was run by two DJs, Peter Cavanaugh and Johnny Irons, from WTAC in Flint. The Bob Seger System, The Amboy Dukes, The Bhangs and Third Power also appeared. *Detroit Free Press* announced, 'Sunday: WTAC (in Flint) Pop Festival, Super Sunday, Sherwood Forest-Davison. Bob Seger System, Amboy Dukes, The Bhangs, Third Power, the Stooges, etc..'

Recalling the event on his blog, Cavanaugh said, 'One Super Sunday concert featured a number of Flint and Detroit-area bands and was headlined by the Bob Seger System, SRC and The Stooges (featuring the notorious Iggy Pop). Approximately 4,000 rockers attended, and this represented our first truly major turnout at Sherwood Forest for a "rock 'n' roll only" event.'

Friday and Saturday, 3 and 4 October 1969: Grande Ballroom, Detroit, MI

Both nights featured British rock band, The Move, together with Teegarden and Van Winkle. It was the start of The Move's first and only US tour.

Friday, 10 October 1969: Bursley Hall, University of Michigan, Ann Arbor, MI

The Stooges performed at a benefit for the Chicago Eight conspiracy, a group of people who were on trial in Chicago for conspiracy, inciting to riot and other charges related to anti-Vietnam War protests on the occasion of the 1968 Democratic National Convention. Also on the bill were Up, Tarantula and the Solar Wind. The event also featured poetry readings, a light show, newsreels and movies. Bursley Hall is a University of Michigan residence hall located in the University of Michigan North Campus.

Monday, 13 October 1969: Grande Ballroom, Detroit, MI

This concert with Allen Ginsberg was advertised as *Argus Obscenity Legal Defense Benefit*, encouraging the audience to 'support your community newspaper in its attempt to support you.' The Stooges were billed as 'featuring the repugnant Iggy with his latest hits.' Photos by Bob Matheu from this concert are featured in his Stooges biography.

Saturday, 18 October 1969: Silverbell Hideout, Clarkston, MI

Up opened for The Stooges at the Silverbell, which was one of a number of venues run at various times during this period by Dave Leone: a local promoter, and Edward 'Punch' Andrews, producer and long-time manager of Bob Seger.

Sunday, 26 October 1969: King Animal Land, Richmond, MI – Cosmic Circus

The show in Richmond – which is located approximately 60 kilometers north-east of downtown Detroit – was scheduled to start at 1 pm and end at 11 pm, being held in a heated tent. It featured The Stooges along with Joe Cocker, Grand Funk Railroad, MC5, Sun Ra, Milky the Clown, The Mechanical Man and others. The show was not without incident. The *Detroit Free Press* reported, 'Joe Cocker and Grand Funk Railroad did an unscheduled free show at the Cosmic Circus at King's Animal Land last Sunday. They were scheduled to appear, but they were supposed to be paid. Trouble started when the box-office was robbed, according to Grand Funk manager Terry Knight. The promoter, of course, couldn't pay the acts, so Cocker and Grand Funk played for the fun of it. The show ended abruptly when the Macomb County Police arrived during Joe's show and, according to Knight, pulled the plugs cutting off all electricity, which left the Cosmic Circus tent in complete darkness. The police gave no explanation, but it would be nice to find out why. The people remained orderly although I've been told they started a fire so they could see, then left the tent singing, "We Shall Overcome," but they obviously have a lot of work to do.'

Friday, 31 October 1969: Olympia Stadium, Detroit, MI – Black Magic and Rock & Roll Festival

Also going under the title of 'A Black Arts Festival,' the concert was advertised as featuring Pink Floyd, Alice Cooper, Kim Fowley, MC5, Arthur Brown, Bob Seger System, The Frost, SRC, Savage Grace and Bonzo Dog Band, amongst other acts. However, it turned out that the promoter falsely advertised four major rock acts he never had under contract for the event. None of the four acts, The Crazy World of Arthur Brown, Pink Floyd, Kim Fowley or MC5, appeared at the show, which was attended by a crowd of 12,300 people.

The Stooges did play, however, and Iggy spent a great deal of the show in the audience. At one point, he was pummelled by a couple of guys who wanted to protect their girlfriends. The show was cut off at 1 am – halfway through Savage Grace's set – and the lights came on two hours before the advertised 3 am end of the event, which resulted in the audience tearing up seats and creating havoc.

The Stooges were scheduled to appear at another rock festival, A Day of Peace, at the Olympia Stadium two weeks later (11 November) along with a number of other bands from the area, but it was canceled due to the riot at the Black Magic and Rock & Roll show.

Saturday, 15 November 1969: Silverbell Hideout, Clarkston, MI

With the Chip Stevens Blues Band and The Promise.

Saturday, 22 November 1969: The Borderline, Richmond, MI

The Stooges appeared at the club – which had only recently opened – with Richmond and Phenomena also on the bill.

Sunday, 30 November 1969: Forsythe Jr. High, Ann Arbor, MI – Rock 'n Roll Dance

Presented by 'The Foundation of Every State,' this show also featured Up, whose band members had been students at the school. Much to the delight of the group, Iggy cracked a hole in the stage floor with the microphone stand.

Tuesday, 2 December 1969. Canterbury House, Ann Arbor, MI

Canterbury House was an episcopal student chaplaincy, established in 1945 as the Episcopal Student Foundation to minister to University of Michigan students. In 1966, an old print shop was refurbished and turned into a state-of-the-art concert hall with a capacity of a little more than 200. The Canterbury House ministry functioned as a countercultural nexus, being both a coffee house and a hip music venue where rock, blues, folk and jazz artists would play (among them Neil Young, Joni Mitchell and Janis Joplin). In 2018, the non-profit Michigan History Project discovered professional-quality recordings made at the venue, although none with The Stooges.

Friday, 26 December 1969: Eastown Theater, Detroit, MI

The Stooges played with The Flock and Savage Grace.

Saturday, 27 December 1969: Ford Auditorium, Detroit, MI

The Stooges played with Up at the prestigious 2,920-capacity Ford Auditorium. Financed by the Ford Motor Company, the venue opened in 1956 and served as the home to the Detroit Symphony Orchestra for more than 30 years. The building was demolished in 2011. *Detroit Free Press* initially listed MC5 along with Up and The Stooges, but the listing on the day prior to the show did not mention MC5.

Sunday, 28 December 1969: Sports Arena, Toledo, OH

The Stooges were second on a bill with headlining MC5, Love Sculpture, Fruit and Haymarket Riot. It was the Stooges' first of five concerts in five years at this venue. The multi-purpose Sports Arena could seat 4,000 to 6,500 for concerts, depending on the chosen layout. The arena was built in 1947 and demolished in 2007.

Monday, 29 December 1969: Aragon Ballroom, Chicago, IL – Chicago Pop Festival

The Stooges wrapped up 1969 with a performance at the Chicago Pop Festival held at the 4,500-capacity Aragon Ballroom. The festival featured MC5, Bob

Seger, Pacific Gas & Electric, Litter, John Lee Hooker, Howlin' Wolf, Coven, Baby Huey, Alice Cooper, Mason Profit, Rotary Connection, Bangor Flying Circus, and Hot Set Up. *Chicago Tribune* wrote about the festival, 'The show is sponsored by WLS-FM and a guy named Mike Quatro who is 24 and has been putting on festivals like this in Detroit for a while now, very successfully.' Mike Quatro was the older brother of soon-to-be-famous rocker, Suzie Quatro. The article also mentioned that the festival had drawn very little attention from Chicago's radio, television and print media.

The show, or parts thereof, was shot on film by a team of underground film-makers. According to Natalie Schlossman's *Popped* fanzine, one of the tunes the film-makers shot footage of was 'I Wanna Be Your Dog.' Jimmy Silver recalled, 'Someone in the audience took the cinematographer's battery pack during the show and he was making a scene while the band was playing, which definitely annoyed the boys.'

An unnamed reviewer in *The Seed* – an alternative Chicago-area paper – described Iggy as 'an incredibly horny version of Mick Jagger on speed' and seemed fascinated by the performance. 'The technicians finally finish their endless readjusting, and Iggy Stooge enters, dressed only in a pair of jeans, so tight they seem to be squeezing his buttocks like ripe tomatoes about to burst. Coiling and bending his lithe body as he growls into the microphone, rubbing the mike stand between his arched shoulder blades, lips curled back in a perpetual snarl as he slides his hips over the bass player's ass in a lewd parody of sexual frenzy. He's convincing; wild-eyes at the mike and the chicks dig him even as the guys in the crowd sit on their hands.'

'Near the end of the set, a girl close to the stage opened her blouse and bared her breasts for Iggy, who reacted disdainfully, much to her dismay,' recalled Silver. *The Seed* reporter also noticed the girl: 'A chick in the first row, distinguishable by her outrageously false eyelashes, has been grabbing at Iggy through the whole set. Finally, he looms over her head on the apron of the stage, and, seeing her chance, she slides her hand up his leg and grabs his balls. Iggy throws her hand off with a look of frenzied contempt. He then collapses full-length into the audience and sinks below sight level, still moaning the refrain – "I AM you".'

1970

The Stooges frequently performed throughout 1970, developing into a tight musical unit that played with devastating attack and precision. 'We were playing all the time,' said Ron Asheton. 'We learned to play on the road. The whole Stooge experience was totally learning in front of people. Of course, rehearsing but also playing on stage. And we played all the time. During the short time span between the first and second record, we progressed amazingly. That comes from just sheer playing all the time. When you're young and you're hungry, that's what you do, and you love doing it. Being constantly on the road, it was a new adventure then.'

They were prolific and wrote many new songs; already in early 1970, they had replaced most material from their first album with new tunes that would emerge on their second album, *Fun House*. Said Iggy, 'If you had seen The Stooges live at the time, you would have realized that once we'd released our first album, I would never play those songs onstage. To me, they were old, and we needed new material. By the time we reached the second album, we'd got the songs ready, and we were real good by then as performers too.' At this stage, 'TV Eye' was referred to as 'See That Cat,' and '1970' was known as 'Your Pretty Face Is Going To Hell.' Meanwhile, 'Down On The Street' was played in an earlier incarnation as 'Down On The Beach,' featuring slightly different lyrics. In addition, the song 'Big Time Bum' was performed during this post-*The Stooges* period, according to reports by Natalie Schlossman in *Popped*, although it is not known whether this was the same as the song of the same title performed in late 1970 and in 1971. 'Dog Food' was also played around this time: it was later recorded for Iggy's 1980 album *Soldier*.

Iggy has said that he wrote more or less everything of the *Fun House* material: 'I shared credit with it, but it was written out of frustration that Ron was, frankly, locked in a place musically that wasn't advancing.' Iggy would later modify the claim slightly, yet it is clear that he was the creative force behind the new music. 'Most of the record I wrote on a Mosrite guitar with a 50 watt Marshall amp up in my room, and only Ron could have played it so wonderfully, but most of that, I wrote. He came up with a few ideas that I thought sounded like our first album but not quite as good.'

Before going to Los Angeles to record *Fun House*, the band augmented their line-up with saxophone player, Steve Mackay. He was much in-demand in Detroit, playing with both Commander Cody and the Charging Rhinoceros of Soul, as well as leading his own duo. Iggy had seen Steve play in 1969 and asked him to sit in with The Stooges to play on *Fun House*. Steve recalled, 'Iggy had *Fun House* written in his head and knows there's gonna be sax on it. It was like some sort of idea he had, a new direction, and he had it in mind and didn't tell me about his intentions. You wanna see if it's gonna work first, you know. But then he'd found out it did work. He called me like two days before we left (for California); I'm still in college, final exams and shit, I postponed them. That was my last term in college.'

The band flew out to Los Angeles on 21 April 1970 (Iggy's 23rd birthday) accompanied by Jimmy Silver and Danny Fields. 'We developed the songs on the road, in front of people, so when it came time to record, we were way ready,' said Ron. 'We were so pumped it was almost effortless. We were really up to snuff. Instead of being nervous or apprehensive about the recording sessions, we were happy just because it was a break from the road.' Following a few days of rehearsals, they spent two weeks recording *Fun House*, 11–24 May. The album basically consisted of the band's set at the time: 'Down On The Street,' 'Loose' (the live set opener, but placed as the second track on the album), 'TV Eye,' 'Dirt,' '1970,' 'Fun House,' 'LA Blues.' The last track was essentially a continuation of 'Fun House,' which would dissolve into a free-form instrumental piece to close their shows, often referred to as 'Energy Freakout Freeform' or simply 'Freak.' The band also cut two tracks that did not make the album: 'Lost In The Future,' and the jam 'Slide (Slidin' The Blues).' 'Fun House' became the name of the band's farmhouse.

While recording *Fun House* in Los Angeles, Silver met some friends who had gone into the natural food business. He made the decision to move to California with his wife and first child: 'We had already moved out of the farmhouse. We were living by ourselves. I had begun not to go to gigs. The boys didn't like that. Our paths were diverging. In California, I met some guys that I knew from Boston, and I used to hang around with them in the daytime because the band was asleep in the daytime.' Fields commented, 'Their manager (Jimmy Silver) was getting less and less interested in them and more interested in health food. He left them and started a health food business, which became incredibly successful. There was no management; they were hard to handle. I had a lot of trouble with them because they had their own little drug problems which were sort of starting then.'

With the loss of Silver's restraining influence, there was no one who could control the band and hold all the pieces together. Fields oversaw operations from New York but had limited hands-on influence on the band. Day-to-day administration was left to road manager John Adams – a friend of Silver – who was a former heroin addict. Ron recalled, 'When we first met Jimmy Silver, John Adams was at his house and Jimmy goes, "This is a good guy, I'm giving him a macrobiotic cure." John just laid low for a good three, four months at Jimmy's apartment. He had hepatitis from heroin, from dirty needles, and he got healthy. Of course, we immediately liked "the Fellow" (one of his several nicknames) and we were smoking a little dope and stuff, and he was just a regular guy. He was our road manager, driver, just smoking dope, but after a couple of years, he started falling back into his bad habits.'

In the summer of 1970, The Stooges played several high-profile outdoor pop and rock festivals, which were attracting huge crowds and had become massively popular in the wake of the iconic Woodstock festival in 1969. A short film clip from a festival in Cincinnati – broadcast as part of *Midsummer*

Rock – as well as photos of Iggy walking out on a sea of hands raised public interest in Iggy and the band.

A rock festival in Goose Lake on 8 August 1970 was the last concert Dave Alexander played with the band. Iggy fired him after the concert. Dave had moved out of the band house and missed many rehearsals. According to Bill Cheatham – one of the band's roadies – the main reason for Dave's dismissal was that he removed himself from the band by not taking part in rehearsal sessions and the band house activities: 'I think that more than anything was what took him out. He was never around the house. He had his room but was always at his parents.' Said Iggy, 'It had been brewing, and he wouldn't show up to this, he wouldn't show up to that. At that point, he had been leaving on a regular basis... not being in town for weeks on end. He had a girlfriend he was kind of obsessed with and (he was) just not making rehearsals.' Dave took drugs before the Goose Lake festival and 'he sort of freezed on stage and forgot all the tunes,' according to Ron. His sub-par performance is evident on the soundboard recording of the concert that was released in 2020: *Live At Goose Lake, August 8th, 1970*. Ron continued, 'After the gig, Iggy said, "Hey, you're fired. We don't want to play with you anymore". When Dave left The Stooges, that's in some ways when we stopped being a real band.' Dave died in 1975, the cause of death being pulmonary edema, brought on by inflammation of the pancreas: a condition often caused by alcohol abuse.

Dave's replacement on bass was Tommy 'Zeke' Zettner, who worked as a roadie for The Stooges. 'He was playing as much for his presence as anything,' said Bill Cheatham. 'Just a big, tall, good-looking guy. Competent. I think that's why Iggy picked him.' At the same time, The Stooges decided to augment their line-up with a second guitarist, Bill Cheatham, who also worked as a roadie for the band. Bill had played guitar with Ron in their pre-Stooges garage band, the Dirty Shames, and was playing with Zeke and Scott in a hobby band they called Rock Action (two of their songs were 'Searching For Head' and 'Out On The Range'). 'The political types loved us because we were promoting road guys into the band,' Bill commented. Bill did not always perform with the band as he did not feel comfortable on stage. According to Ron, 'Billy played just really simple stuff and a lot of times, it was like, "Bill, if you don't feel good about it, turn your guitar way down. If you feel strapped, it will be more than covered". He really couldn't take the pressure and he couldn't play that well. He just decided it was much more fun being road manager.'

The extended six-piece line-up of The Stooges – with Steve on sax, Zeke on bass and Bill on guitar, together with the original trio of Iggy, Ron and Scott – made their debut with the band at Asbury Park on 15 August 1970: a warm-up for a prestigious three-night stand at Ungano's in New York City, which coincided with the release of *Fun House*.

While Elektra had high hopes that the album would be a good seller, it was becoming increasingly evident that the Stooges' music was too radical for mass appeal. 'Elektra had it all wrong,' Iggy observed later. 'They were trying to market us to college kids, and they were too educated to appreciate the Stooges' sound. I wanted them to target the dropouts, people like us.' Despite the lack of commercial success, the album was lauded by the Stooges' many loyal supporters in the music press, and media interest in Iggy and the band was growing by leaps and bounds. Said Iggy, 'After we did *Fun House* and I'd had a taste of California for the first time, we went back to the Midwest. I was getting delusions of grandeur by that time. The shows were good, and I knew I was dabbling in something that was really happening. I felt we were ahead of everybody else and started thinking that I was semi-divine and shit like that!'

What had once been highly spontaneous became increasingly premeditated as Iggy tried to live up to the audience's expectations of him. 'Iggy began to feel a pressure to do more outrageous things and more and more live up to his billings,' commented Silver. 'He would do things that were physically destructive to him. He chipped his tooth on the microphone one night and he got more into mutilating himself, scratching himself, and he would pour hot wax on himself like he did at the Whisky. I think it was partly for effect and partly, I think, he was being somewhat driven to do more and more outrageous things.' The media focus on Iggy created growing tensions within the band. 'Iggy started believing the press,' commented Ron. 'People kept saying, "You're the one, you're the star," and he started believing it. I was sitting right there in my own apartment, and people were going, "You don't need these guys, they don't play that well, you should dump 'em and get a really good band, 'cause you're the only one anyone really cares about." He had all those people telling all that stuff and he started breaking down. It was very stressful; it was the old syndrome of "I've got to top myself every night." You can't go and play for two years almost every night, jumping into the audience, getting banged up and getting stitches. He started out doing self-destructive things because that was the way he felt. Then it got to be expected. He'd just try to top himself for the crowd. We would often say, "Give it up, Iggy." He's a different person when he gets on stage. It was expected and he tried to top himself every time. I was waiting for him to kill himself.'

However, as media and public interest in Iggy and the band increased, signs of self-destruction were becoming evident. The drug scene in Detroit had changed, as cheap imported heroin flooded the market. 'Suddenly unemployment was driving people out of Detroit,' observed Iggy. 'The whole atmosphere had changed. Around the summer of 1970, heroin was being pushed into the surrounding suburbs of Detroit by the motorcycle gangs and by a lot of assembly line workers.' Ron witnessed the introduction of heroin to the band by John Adams: 'I remember one day he (John Adams) was real excited, and he comes down and goes – I was the only one at home at that time – he goes, "C'mon here, I wanna show you something, man." I thought, "What is it?" and thought he got another pound of hash, and he's going, "Isn't this pretty?" and he's sifting through a fist-sized pile of powder. I'm going, "What's that, man? Is that coke or powdered mescaline?". He's going, "No man, it's the big one. Heroin!". I knew, right then and there, I could see it coming.

So sure enough, that night, he wanted everyone to try it. Everybody except for myself did a snort. Everyone puked, and then everyone liked it. I can't remember the transition from snorting to hitting, but that was the beginning of the end.' Adams became the band's supplier, and it did not take long before all members, barring Ron, succumbed to the drug. Bill recalled, 'At first we would say to John, "What in hell are you doing?". We'd all been smoking dope together for so long, but he said, "No, no, you don't understand. This is the best high". He literally talked us into trying it.'

Iggy was the first to fall prey to heroin, according to Leo Beattie, one of the band's roadies: 'Initially it was Iggy and John. Iggy was down there with him (in his room in the band house) dabbling in it. It seemed like Scott went along. Ron kept his distance. Heroin made a bond between Ig and John. I know that (John) Sinclair would comment on John Adams and asking what his purpose was. I'm at a loss to know why they kept him around.' Another band roadie, Dave Dunlap, said, 'I remember going down to the basement. Iggy would be down there doing heroin, saying, "Come on, guys, try a little!". I would go, 'Fuck off, I can't believe you're doing this shit.' John kind of went along with Iggy when he was in the heroin phase. He would keep him supplied, so instead of saying, "Hey, you're screwing up here," it was OK, "Whatever'll keep Pop happy."' Bill said, 'John started, I guess Jim was next, it was pretty much simultaneous. Scott and I, we started out snorting, then I remember skin popping, then going to mainlining. Eric Haddix got involved too. Then, later on, Tommy Zettner, Zeke. We were all using it except for Ron.'

Consuming most of their time and money, heroin quickly became more important than the camaraderie of The Stooges. 'If somebody wants heroin, you can't really get them interested in anything else, can you?', Fields reckoned. 'What he (Iggy) did while still having that dope priority in his life, you've got to hand it to him, how he could perform at all, do anything at all, get anywhere at all, but he did. Still, it was the great monster squashing everything else and every possibility. It was all falling apart; there was no money, the records weren't selling. It didn't help to be a critical sensation.' Beattie observed how rehearsals almost ended, as the music was becoming secondary to getting high: 'Instead they'd go down to John Adams' room, waiting for a fix, preparing for a fix, nodding off and not being motivated, depressed. Ron would be sitting up there with his guitar, starting out mild, then get into a tantrum; sit there and wonder, "What the hell, there's nothing I can do".' Ron felt estranged from the other Stooges, watching with exasperation how their drug intake got out of hand: 'It was fun when we were smoking marijuana and hash, and we had our little acid phase, but we were never into anything stronger. We enjoyed smoking some pot. For me, that was about as far as it went. Then... ba-ba-ba-boom! It was some of the worst times of my life, just to see everything you had done fall apart, only because of drugs. Once heroin was introduced into the picture, it was the beginning of the end. I saw my whole world crumble, friendships, the music.'

The Stooges' line-up underwent some changes in the autumn of 1970. Steve Mackay left the band sometime between mid-September and mid-October 1970, returning to Detroit to form the Mojo Boogie Band. 'There was never a job I ever wanted to be fired from more than that one,' said Steve. 'I could just see this shit falling apart. By then, instead of my $50 a week salary, I was getting a $15 bag of weed, $15 in cash, and a dime bag of smack. I'd got to snorting smack every day for maybe two weeks, then when I got frozen out of the band, I lost my connection. I wasn't so driven that I had to phone them up, but for about two months, I couldn't sleep through the night. I had these pains in my arms, so I went through a minor withdrawal. If they'd sacked me two months later, I'd have a full-blown habit.'

A few weeks later, guitarist James Williamson replaced Bill, who withdrew from his onstage duties as a guitarist and reverted to his role as roadie for the band. 'I had seen them at gigs and stuff, because I knew those guys,' said James. 'I didn't hang out with them that much because I was more in the Detroit area than Ann Arbor at that point, but I'd seen a few of their gigs, and they were down at the Grande and so forth. I'd see them down there and they had a very unique show that was different, really way different than anybody else. I thought they were cool. I not only knew them, but I liked what they were doing. Anyway, over the course of the next few months, I'd hang out at the main Stooge farmhouse and jam with Ron or Bill or whomever.'

Iggy immediately recognized James' potential as a guitarist and songwriter collaborator. 'At the outset, Ron and Iggy were collaborating, but then I saw (Iggy) Pop shift his focus away from Ron,' observed Beattie. 'He was just enamored with Williamson. James became Iggy's bud.' Said Iggy; 'I knew from the first rehearsal with James that I had here something I could really use stylistically. He was sort of a local legend, this misfit guitarist that no one could play with. Then I heard him play a set by himself. That was manic, and I thought, "Oh, I have to get this one!"'

James' arrival made The Stooges a five-piece unit again, with Iggy accompanied by Ron and James on guitars, Zeke on bass and Scott on drums. The Stooges' jazzier direction changed in fall 1970 as they dropped the numbers that had featured Steve's saxophone-playing: '1970,' 'Fun House' and 'LA Blues.' Instead, they began adding two new high-energy songs. Penned by Iggy, 'I Got A Right' became a new set opener. It is not known what the other new number was, but it was likely 'Big Time Bum,' although this version of the song was likely different from the early-1970 song of the same title.

There were discussions about the band going to Los Angeles in late 1970 to record a third album for Elektra, with press reporting that 'Big Time Bum' was going to be a lead-off single. However, nothing came of these plans, as the band members took a much-needed break in mid-December 1970 to try to sort out their drug problems. 'We were all physical wrecks,' said Ron. Iggy took a brief trip to Jamaica to clean up and try to write new material for the band. Fields fired Adams, while Dunlap and Beattie left to work for Alice Cooper, who had recently moved to Detroit. 'There was too much junk and we weren't getting anywhere,' commented Dunlap. According to Beattie, 'We weren't getting good gigs. I had had enough. It's a story of real regret when I speak to Ron. They were on their way, but the drugs arrived, and they were fucked. The spirit of the music was the bond, but that dissolved.'

Thursday, 1 January 1970: Grande Ballroom, Detroit, MI

No handbills or other concert information seem to exist, but Natalie Schlossman reported in the *Popped* fanzine that the Stooges played, with the Dutch group Golden Earring accompanying them on the bill. Golden Earring played other gigs in the Detroit area on 2 and 3 January 1970, so they were certainly in the area.

Saturday, 3 January 1970: The Borderline, Monroe, MI

There is a lack of information about this gig, which was listed in *Fifth Estate:* 'The Stooges are at Monroe's finest niteclub, the Borderline. Telegraph, 3 miles N. of Monroe.' Monroe is 50 kilometers south-west of Detroit.

Friday and Saturday, 9 and 10 January 1970: Ludlow Garage, Cincinnati, OH

The Stooges' first concerts in Cincinnati were held at the Ludlow Garage. They performed with Flamin' Groovies and Golden Earring. This was possibly the first time that the band was referred to as 'Iggy and the Stooges,' which was listed on an advertisement for the gig. The Stooges returned to Ludlow Garage in March and September 1970. The venue began life as an automobile shop. Rock concerts were hosted from September 1969 to January 1971.

Tuesday, 13 January 1970: Hill Auditorium, University of Michigan, Ann Arbor, MI

The Stooges appeared with Up, and Teegarden & Van Winkle at Ann Arbor's Hill Auditorium, the largest concert hall, seating 3,500, on the campus of University of Michigan. Opened in 1913, the hall is renowned for its excellent acoustics. 'It was and is a beautiful theatre,' in Iggy's words. Photos by Tom Copi from this concert are featured in Iggy's autobiography *I Need More* and Robert Matheu's Stooges biography. The bill also featured Timothy Leary, the controversial LSD guru who, just one week later, would receive a 10-year jail sentence for drugs charges. The concert was a benefit to raise funds for the legal defense of John Sinclair.

Bert Stratton's review of the concert in the *Michigan Daily,* said that the bands performed in front of a 'sizeable crowd,' finishing with, 'The Stooges were to be on next. I left.' A post on the *Ann Arbor News* website by someone who was at the gig, read, 'It was either 1969 or 1970 when the Stooges opened for Timothy Leary at Hill Auditorium. An awesome show, and in my mind, it had to be one of their best performances. The crowd was so psyched!'

Friday, 16 January 1970: Grand Ballroom, Detroit, MI
The Stooges appeared with Wilson Mower Pursuit and The Attack.

Saturday, 17 January 1970: Daniel's Den, Saginaw, MI
Half-Life opened for The Stooges. The band's guitarist Jim Nash was ill, so they put on a three-man performance. To some extent, Daniel's Den was to Saginaw what Grande Ballroom and Eastown Theater were to Detroit, showcasing many of the local acts as well as nationally famous artists. The Stooges returned there in April 1970.

The Stooges' performance at Daniel's Den was reviewed very positively by Purdie DeMercurio for *Saginaw News:* 'It was hard to decide what was more entertaining – watching The Stooges or the crowd. If you have ever seen The Stooges, you know the main reason they keep the crowd so fascinated is lead singer Iggy Pop, better known as Iggy Stooge. Iggy dances around the stage to Iggy music, singing Iggy lyrics, scaring Iggy fans. So many people concentrate on Iggy and his contortions; they don't realize The Stooges have improved 100 percent in the last year. Musically, The Stooges have gone heavily into the contemporary hard rock of today. Nevertheless, Iggy, as usual, stole the show.'

Saturday, 24 January 1970: Grande Ballroom, Detroit, MI
The Stooges participated in a two-day 'Free John Sinclair' benefit event to 'free John Sinclair and all political prisoners,' held at the Grande Ballroom and Eastown Theater in Detroit. It is not evident from the advertisements which groups played at Grande Ballroom and which performed at the Eastown Theater, although The Stooges played both nights. The first day of the event lasted from 2 pm to 1 am.

Presented by STP (Serve the People) Coalition, the bill included SRC, MC5, Up, Scorpions, Commander Cody, Bob Seger System, Mitch Ryder and the Detroit Wheels, Amboy Dukes, Virgin Dawn, Wilson Mower Pursuit, The Rationals, Jagged Edge, Richmond, All the Lonely People, Sky, Brownsville Station, Floating Circus, Sunday Funnies, Shaky Jake, Blues Train, Third Power, and a few more acts. Among the speakers were Abbie Hoffman, Ken Cockrell, Skip Taube and Ed Sanders.

Sunday, 25 January 1970: Eastown Theater, Detroit, MI
This was the second night of the 'Free John Sinclair' benefit. The event lasted from 3 to 11 pm, according to the advertisement in *Fifth Estate*. The event was deemed to be 'an overwhelming success' by *Ann Arbor Argus*, which went on to say, 'An estimated 9,000 people turned out, packing the Grande Ballroom

Saturday with the biggest crowd in its history. Likewise, Sunday, as both the Grande and Eastown were filled to capacity.'

Friday and Saturday, 30 and 31 January 1970: Eastown Theater, Detroit, MI

The Stooges played two nights at the Eastown Theater with Alice Cooper and Fruit of the Loom as the opening acts. According to Dennis Dunaway of the Alice Cooper band, 'The shows with The Stooges at the Eastown Theater always had a lot of violence. Iggy would jump off stage and pick a fight with somebody, and if he picked a fight with you, then you were the hero for the next week or two.'

Saturday, 7 February 1970: Silverbell Hideout, Clarkston, MI

The Stooges were supported by The Rationals. *Fifth Estate* previewed the concert: 'Sexy Iggy and the rest of the Stooges makes it up to Silverbell along with The Rationals.'

Friday, 13 February 1970: Woodrose Ballroom, Springfield, MA

The Stooges topped the bill over Chubby Checker and the Philadelphia rock group, Lobotomy. In a pre-show meeting, Checker advised the band not to work with John Madera, who was being considered as producer of the band's second album. Checker believed they would lose control over their music.

Stooges roadie, Bill Cheatham, remembered meeting with Iggy after the concert to discuss him joining the band on guitar: 'I'd often be up at Ron's apartment in the house, and Jim was upstairs and he'd hear me lay down rhythm lines. Jim called me up to his room after the show and said, "I want you to play the guitar for the band. I've been listening to you and Ron playing".' It would take some time before Bill joined, but he began practicing in earnest to be able to perform with the band onstage.

Saturday, Sunday, Monday and Tuesday, 21, 22, 23 and 24 February 1970: Ungano's, New York, NY

This four-night stand at *Ungano's* was The Stooges' first New York headline billing. They played one set each night, despite advertisements promising two sets nightly. The opening act was Liquid Smoke, a blues band. *Ungano's* was a small, hip, Upper West Side Manhattan club, named after its founders, Arni and Nick Ungano. The club had a capacity of barely 200 people. The Stooges performed on the floor level and had trouble squeezing their amplifiers and equipment into the small area, which was made even more cramped by the presence of mirrored columns. Natalie Schlossman commented, 'Ungano's was a very intimate club and a wonderful place to hear music. I had seen other bands perform there, so I was familiar with the setup, sound system and the stage location. At the time of the first Stooges gigs, they did not have a liquor license. There was a doorman checking people to ensure no liquor was being brought in. Of course, some people were able to sneak past and the crowd was in good spirits.'

The Stooges' set now consisted of most of *Fun House*, including 'Loose' (the set opener), 'Down On The Beach' (later became 'Down On The Street'), 'See That Cat' (later 'TV Eye'), 'Dirt,' and 'Your Pretty Face Is Going To Hell' (later '1970'). Further, a take on Nico's 'Evening Of Light' was also included on occasion. Audience members and rock journalists have also mentioned 'Big Time Bum' being featured in The Stooges' set. Iggy had added elbow-length silver lamé woman's evening gloves to his repertoire.

Natalie recalled, 'This was to be the first time The Stooges were playing live in New York City. There was an excitement throughout the audience. Most everybody there was familiar with the guys, as it was the Warhol folks and the music biz crowd, and some had been to the Pavilion, but this was the NYC debut. The club is small, and the stage is not very high. It had an atmosphere of the band playing in a rather large living room. There were tables and mostly floor space. I chose to sit directly in front of the stage on the floor. I was with a few press people and we wanted to be in the center of the action.'

Natalie continued, 'The band comes out onto the stage and starts to set up. Iggy came out and just stared at the crowd. He then let out a fierce yell and the music started. Iggy danced around and soon jumped on a table, all the while making eye contact with the audience. The concerts I had seen up to this point were great, but this new stage persona was something else. Iggy had honed his act over the five months. This was the ultimate provocateur on stage. This was theater. And this was something the New York crowd, accomplished and jaded as it was, had not experienced before. The Marshall amps were stacked against each other on and around the tiny stage. It was loud, loud, loud and mind-blowing. Iggy danced and pranced and got right into the crowd. He sat on laps and laid on the floor with the mic, singing and screaming his way through the set. He made eye contact with people around him and danced around the tables. It was new and strange and fun and just a bit dangerous at the same time. I remember Ron with his wah-wah going full force. It sounded amazing to my ears. It was much more alive than any gig I had attended.'

'They played less than an hour and left the crowd wanting more,' recalled Natalie. 'The band comes back out to do an encore. It was the first time I had seen them perform an encore. The electricity in the air was strong and the anticipation was mounting. This was a NYC crowd and they reacted like only NYC can react. The encore was loud, mostly feedback and experimental with some shrieks and yells and a bit of lyrics thrown in.'

For the encore at one of the shows, as the band generated an intimidating wall of feedback, Iggy stepped out from behind the amplifiers with his penis exposed. He touched the tip of his member to the end of the neck of Ron's guitar, the feedback stimulating him to an orgasmic high. Mouths were agape in

59

the audience, and the shock of the final moments left many in stunned silence as the show ended. Jimmy Silver said, 'Iggy was only arrested once (Romeo), but I thought they might take him away that night at Ungano's. He and Ron start moving toward each other, and Ron points the head of the guitar at Jim. So Jim takes out his dick and Ron touches the end of the guitar to it and starts going crazy on the strings, feedback, etc. The crowd who were about to contract disco fever in a few years, were not into it. It completely freaked them out.'

Natalie remembers it slightly differently: 'Iggy stands in the middle of the floor among the people. He looks at the crowd, around at us, and then he unzips his jeans and reaches in and exposes himself. He held himself out with one hand as if offering the audience a gift. The entire set was very sexual, but this again was something new, something this crowd had not seen a performer do before. There was a stunned silence. I know there were reports of simulation with Ron's guitar, but I was sitting directly in the front and that did not happen. After about 30 seconds, Iggy put himself back in his jeans and finished the song. The band walks off the stage. I remember going over to my friends after the set, and I remember Danny Fields coming over to talk. We all talked about the music, but not one word was mentioned about Iggy's penis. I was never sure if it was shock or just the fact that what could you actually say about it? Although there were many times after that night when Iggy was extremely provocative and downright sexual on stage, that was the only time I ever saw him expose himself.'

MC5 fan, Jeffrey Burdin, attended the show, although he was somewhat skeptical about The Stooges' merits beforehand: 'We got to Ungano's at quarter after ten and sat on the floor somewhere about 10 or 15 feet from the stage. I was liking all the Marshall stacks for such a tiny club. Iggy and the boys didn't start until sometime after midnight. There was Iggy, bare-chested, wearing a pair of torn jeans, black boots, a lit cigarette in the corner of his mouth, plus this stare, the stare that said, "I'm in charge tonight!". Ron plugged in his red Strat, Iggy mumbled something, and for me, a love affair musically with The Stooges began. They opened up with "Loose" – still one of my favorite Stooges compositions. Iggy danced, jumped, gyrated, spun, slid, arched his back, and became a living multi-armed and multi-legged god like you would see from Indian mythology. It was living theatre, a crazed singer, dancing, backed up by a group of thugs with guitars and drums as their weapons. All the way back to the Port Authority, my friends and myself were singing and trying to do the moves (with no success) that Iggy did. It was a very great evening of music. I still love that band.'

The press also approved of The Stooges. The *Cashbox* reviewer described the shows as 'unique' and 'groundbreaking,' as he felt the band was 'the beginning of a new concept in rock, the theatre of rock carried to its logical conclusion, *living* theatre.' Dan Goldberg of *Record World* praised the band as 'loud, powerful and throbbing, with a force that puts them in a musical category something like the old Cream stripped of its heavy blues influence.'

He felt Iggy's sexuality was 'Jaggeresque,' and that he was particularly effective in a small club environment where he could confront the audience personally. Writing for *Rock*, Karin Berg lauded Iggy as a 'very fine artist,' and the Stooges as a 'great rock group whose music just gets better and better.' She felt the impression of Iggy as 'an icon of evil, of depravity' was wrong, preferring instead to view him as a 'messenger of redemption, but in no current saintly fashion. No pacific John Lennon.' In *Gay Power,* the two drag queens: Ritta Redd and Warhol 'superstar' Jackie Curtis, debated the performance. Redd argued that Iggy 'wasn't there for the audience's benefit; the audience was there for his benefit, and he told them so. He commanded the audience exactly like the master would have done in an S & M situation.' Fred Kirby of *Billboard* was genuinely thrilled, depicting The Stooges' set as 'erotic.' He felt their act 'curiously worked as the large weekday crowd tried to anticipate Iggy's next move.'

During one of the Ungano's gigs, Iggy picked out this same Fred Kirby for his personal attention, as rock journalist and fan, Brian Zabawski, remembered: 'Probably unaware Kirby was in attendance as a reviewer for *Billboard* (and *Variety* as well, I believe), Iggy more likely was drawn to him because of his conservative dress and appearance, as well as his large frame and conspicuous glasses. Iggy sat on the critic's lap and embraced Kirby, singing to him and no doubt causing him some embarrassment, as well as amusement. On another night of the engagement, my friend James Warbritton (also conservatively dressed, and, at 6'4", a big guy) was singled out by Iggy for similar attention. Iggy performed something of a lap dance on him, crooning to him for several bars, before moving on to his next "victim." That was a pretty young-model type, whom he boldly fondled by her breast. Iggy treated the Ungano's crowd to several of his spectacular, signature stage moves. He also displayed his "peace and fuck-you" gesturing, in which one of his hands was held in a raised middle-finger gesture, while the other displayed the peace or V-for-victory gesture. He would flip his hands quickly, alternately displaying the gestures, but switching their positions from his left to right hands. A photo of this ended up in *Changes* magazine, labeled "hard hat salute." Musically, The Stooges were at peak form for these Ungano's shows, producing an unrelenting wall of sound with a dense and heavy sound mix.'

The Ungano's shows were attended by several young people who, within five years, would become prominent figures of the New York punk rock movement, including Jim Carroll, Patti Smith, Lenny Kaye, and future members of The Dictators, The Ramones, Television, Blondie and Suicide. Danny Fields brought along the Andy Warhol crowd. 'Everyone was there,' Leee Black Childers recalled. 'The whole scene, all of the Max's back room, thanks to Danny. They were screaming about how fabulous Iggy was. I was starting to become a photographer, so I went there to photograph him. I went with Wayne County, my roommate at the time. We couldn't believe our eyes! I can't remember if there were any other photographers there. Dustin Pittman was there, but he wasn't a photographer yet. He was still only a pretty boy. Geri Miller – the Warhol "superstar" – went there to become a groupie. She was sitting in the front, and during one song, Iggy stalked down to her. She was grinning up at him and he grabbed her by the face. His whole hand covered her face. He dragged her by the face, and when he took his hand off her face, she was still grinning. She became a big fan.'

Friday and Saturday, 27 and 28 February 1970: Action House, Long Island, NY

The Stooges stayed on in New York and played two shows at the Action House, a rock club in Island Park, near John F. Kennedy Airport and the Nassau-Queens border. 'Big Time Bum' is believed to have been part of the set. While in New York, Iggy was photographed by Jack Robinson for *Vogue* (featured in the Stooges biography by Robert Matheu).

Natalie Schlossman reported on the Action House concerts in the *Popped* newsletter: 'The boys are doing their own version of "Evening Of Light." It's much better than Nico's. It's a changing piece and one night at the Action House, the sounds coming out of Dave's bass and Scott's drums were so incredible that Iggy and Ron stopped what they were doing and just stared with the rest of us.'

Brian Zabawski attended one of the concerts: 'The club seemed fairly empty. The large standing-room area in front of the comparatively wide stage was dotted with only a few of the perhaps 30 or 40 people who attended, who mostly hovered near the bar or in the periphery. The Stooges hit the stage, probably opening with "Loose," and a few more brave souls ventured nearer to the stage. My friends and I, many of whom were new fans from the Northport contingent who had attended the unforgettable *Ungano's* performances, sat on the floor in front of center-stage, perhaps 20 feet from Iggy. It wasn't long into the set before Iggy zeroed in on my pretty friend Debra Schauder, singling her out for his personal attention. Standing above her as she was seated on the floor, Iggy grabbed her by her leg and pulled her booted foot up until it was resting on his crotch. He then attempted to drag her around the floor in a playful manner, twirling her a bit and causing her to laugh in shock and embarrassment. He did not linger on her, however, and resumed stalking the good-sized stage. As The Stooges pumped furiously through their set, Iggy found only a few more audience members suited for his attentions. They were tight and focused that night. Despite the small crowd, Iggy seemed in good spirits. As was their wont, they left the stage with their amps still wailing a glorious wall of feedback, the sounds continuing even as they exited the stage. Typical of the band at that time, there was no encore.'

Karin Berg, writing for *East Village Other*, attended three of the six shows The Stooges played at Ungano's and Action House. She had become quite a fan after seeing them at the Pavilion the previous year. She described Iggy's antics in detail: 'Iggy jumps up, dancing around again, there are three girls, ever, ever so cool, sitting at a table, now and then passing a remark, very relaxed. Iggy's not gonna ruffle them, no sir. But he spots one, grabs her by the leg and pulls her slowly forward (slowly, so she won't fall off the chair, contrary to hostile speculation, Iggy is not out to hurt) to the center of the stage. She looks at him. Nothing. He pushes her back in disgust. Puts his hand up against her head. As he lets go, she strikes out, but she doesn't get out of her chair. Then he's off again, casing the crowd, jumping. No words now, but it's all over his face: "Shit, you're a bunch of lumps – do ya feel it deep inside, *feel*, dammit...". Bam, he's up on a table, screaming, jumping up and down (trying to break the table?), laughs as he has fun, stops, throws the hand mic over his shoulder, grabs on to a pipe holding lights, swings back and forth, does a backflip back onto the stage, never losing the mic. Stands still while music continues. Starts semi-chant, "I am you... I am you..." Walks around, getting close, down to people's faces. "I am *you*, I *am* you..."'

February-March 1970: Sports Arena, Toledo, OH

The precise date of the show is not known, but the gig occurred quite soon after the Ungano's engagement. It was The Stooges' second appearance at the venue, after the December 1969 gig there. MC5 also played. Natalie Schlossman reported in *Popped:* 'Iggy was dancing too close to the edge of the stage and he fell off backward. He hit his spine and he winded himself. The show had to be stopped right in the middle of "I Wanna Be Your Dog." That show was going so well too. The kids were all rushing the stage, taking photos and just to get closer. It was really a shame. But we were thankful Iggy wasn't seriously hurt.'

Friday, 6 March 1970: Civic Arena, St. Clair Shores, MI

No details are known concerning this concert in St. Clair Shores.

Saturday, 7 March 1970: Kiel Auditorium, St. Louis, MO – St. Louis Pop Festival

Built in 1934, Kiel Auditorium was named after the former St. Louis Mayor, Henry Kiel. The venue could seat 9,300, depending on the chosen layout, and played host to many rock concerts from the 1950s until its closure in 1991. The Stooges appeared with Country Joe and the Fish, Chuck Berry, Steam, Rotary Connection, Amboy Dukes, Frijid Pink, The Frost and many more. The event was advertised as an 'indoor Woodstock,' promising nine hours of music. *St. Louis Post-Dispatch* reported that '8,000 young persons attended the marathon pop festival.' Photos by Craig Petty from the concert are featured in Bob Matheu's Stooges biography.

Stooges fan, Phil Natta, recalled The Stooges' performance at the festival: 'The Stooges came on toward the end, around 8 pm, and jolted the frazzled burned-out crowd wide awake. The Kiel stage was huge, and Iggy took advantage of every square inch of it, doing several head dives into the first rows (of metal folding chairs, mind you) on a number of occasions, landing on top of me and two friends at one point. He also did his old classic dive on a busted glass schtick and did some minor bleeding. And did a few self-inflicted hard microphone blows to the mouth.'

Friday and Saturday, 13 and 14 March 1970: Ludlow Garage, Cincinnati, OH

The Stooges returned to Cincinnati after the January gigs to play four shows over two nights at the Ludlow Garage. Also on the bill were Stone The Crows (both nights), MC5 (both nights) and Elizabeth (first night only). Ben Edmonds commented: 'I saw them on a fantastic bill with the MC5 at the Ludlow Garage in Cincinnati, where the ascendant Stooges pushed the 5 into giving one of their better *Back In The USA* performances.'

Friday, 20 March 1970: Met Sports Center, Bloomington, MN – 1st Met Center Pop Festival

Promising 'eight hours of continuous music featuring twelve nationally famous groups,' including the Stooges, Canned Heat, Grand Funk Railroad, SRC, Litter, Brownsville Station, the Amboy Dukes and Buddy Miles. Two bands – Sweetwater and Rotary Connection – canceled their appearances. The center was the home arena of the Minnesota North Stars ice hockey team and was later replaced by the Mall of America. *Minneapolis Star* reported that 'some 6,000 youngsters screamed their approval of musicians.'

Photos of this concert, shot by Mike Barich, were published in *Creem* and many other publications since then. Barich recalled the show: 'There was no seating on the main floor, so it was SRO, except for a small space where Iggy got off the stage and everyone moved back. The audience was a little – some a lot – surprised by the show. My musician friends, I brought several, didn't quite know what to think. One said it was vaguely similar to Mick Jagger. I found it very interesting, but I really can't say more because I was trying hard to get some representative photos.'

Saturday, 21 March 1970: Silverbell Hideout, Clarkston, MI

The Stooges played with the Red, White & Blues Band.

Wednesday, 25 March 1970: Rainy Daze, St. Louis, MO

The Stooges returned to St. Louis for a gig at the Rainy Daze club, which was a concert venue from 1967 to 1971. The next day, 26 March, The Stooges were to have played at the Cincinnati Pop Festival held at The Gardens in Cincinnati, Ohio. The 12-hour festival was attended by 11,500 people and featured, among others, MC5, Mountain, Alice Cooper and Amboy Dukes. However, The Stooges never performed, as a result of mounting delays throughout the day.

Paul Trynka states in his Iggy Pop biography *Open Up And Bleed,* that fellow Detroit musician, Cub Koda, 'witnessed Iggy being lifted by the crowd in the March Cincinnati performance,' which must refer to another concert.

Friday, 27 March 1970: Something Different, Southfield, MI
The Stooges performed with Chip Stevens Blues Band. Something Different was a small club in Southfield, a suburb of Detroit. According to *Fifth Estate:* 'Though limited capacity prevents Something Different from booking big name acts, they always provide good music in what is probably the nicest setting for hearing music in the Detroit area.' There is also inaccurate information that The Stooges performed at *The Midway*, Royal Oak, Michigan, on 27 March 1970.

Wednesday, 1 April 1970: Eastown Theatre, Detroit, MI
The Stooges performed with Savage Grace. *Fifth Estate* promoted the concert: 'Fools day! April Fool Treat: what better way to celebrate this day than with the Stooges at the Eastown.'

Friday and Saturday, 3 and 4 April 1970: Warehouse, Providence, RI
Aptly named, the Warehouse was a large converted warehouse with many pop culture posters on the walls. The Stooges were advertised as 'a Detroit phenomenon.' Their set was similar to Ungano's, with the inclusion of 'Big Time Bum' and 'Down On The Beach,' according to Natalie Schlossman, who attended the show.

'I noticed that the crowd was enthusiastic and seemed less sophisticated than the New York audiences had been,' Natalie recalled. 'Iggy was wearing what by now appeared to be his trademark silver lamé gloves. His jeans were worn a bit at the knees, but not torn, and his black, scuffed boots. Scott had a button-down dark shirt on with his dark glasses. Ron was turned out in a black, shiny jacket, and Dave was very colorful in a purple shirt and dark jeans. It was a small stage and the amps were stacked. The first song started, and Iggy gave a yelp, looked at the audience – the wah-wah was loud, the drums started the steady beat, it was louder than loud, and they were off. I could just feel immediately that this crowd was loving it. Iggy joined the audience and danced with a girl and made contact with members of the crowd. This crowd was loving it. They felt it and it was great. After the gig, kids were coming up to the band and asking for autographs. I noticed several people taking down the posters off the wall that advertised the gig. I had a chance to talk with the guys backstage, and everybody felt great and they were enjoying the successful gig.'

Friday, 10 April 1970: Palladium, Birmingham, MI
NRBQ and I-94 were also on the bill. The Stooges played six concerts in 1970–1971 at the 1,500-capacity Palladium in Birmingham, north-west of Detroit. The

venue opened in November 1969 but closed less than two years later.

Natalie Schlossman was in attendance again: 'I immediately noticed that the atmosphere of the hometown crowd was different than the other gigs I had seen. There was a familiarity and friendliness among the crowd. This crowd had been watching The Stooges evolve for two years and I could feel excitement in the air. The guys had been playing around the state for quite a while and most of this crowd had seen the act many times. The set was very similar to what was played at Ungano's. I noticed that as the songs evolved, some of the lyrics changed and the tempo was varied. For the most part, these songs were recognized by the crowd and very appreciated. Iggy was dancing and twirling around the stage. He moved with grace and abandon, shaking his butt at the crowd.'

'The stage was very low and not conducive for diving, so he jumped off into the audience, making his way through the crowd, making eye contact with the guys and sticking his tongue out at the girls,' said Natalie. 'He found a girl and dumped her handbag, all the while dancing and laughing. I noticed that the people were familiar with Iggy's antics and were not intimidated, did not back away from him, and actually seemed to enjoy participating. Another thing very apparent was that this crowd knew what to expect and actually joined in by helping bring the cable off the stage and with Iggy while he was in the audience. The vocals and shrieks and chants were not lost to this crowd. The band seemed to be enjoying themselves; the energy was high, the crowd was dancing and checking out the goings-on. I realized some people were attending out of curiosity, just to see what would happen. The reputation of The Stooges had preceded them, and the curiosity level was high.'

Sunday, 12 April 1970: Sherwood Forest, Davison, MI

The bill also featured Sonny Hugg. Previously just an outdoor venue, Sherwood Forest had opened a new indoor venue six months earlier with MC5 headlining. The co-owners – Peter Cavanaugh and Johnny Irons – were afraid of trouble, so they drafted a four-page contract which 'in addition to the "No-Saying-Fuck" clause, went on to forbid anything remotely resembling anything I had ever seen The Stooges do which might be interpreted as offensive, and plenty of things I never had seen them do but that they might think of,' said Cavanaugh. 'The Stooges were not to leave the stage during performance. No crude language, actions, conduct, behavior, or facsimile of same would be permitted. Any breach of conditions would result in double forfeiture of payment. And arrest. I wrote the riders in a way I thought would not be signed unless the group was absolutely sincere in their pledges of altered attitude. Unlike most union contracts, each member of the band had to agree to the rider provisions and stipulations by signature. The contract was returned to me. It had been signed by all. There were no changes or alterations.'

Cavanaugh continued, 'The Sherwood Forest parking lot was already full at 5 pm the day of the show. Fifteen hundred were admitted by 6:30. It was wall-to-wall once again. Their equipment had gotten there and had been set up on stage, but The Stooges had yet to arrive. They were still missing at 7:30 when the opening act finished performing. It was 7:45 and we were stalling with records. Where were they? Representatives from Electra, Diversified Management and *Creem* magazine, wanted to know the same thing. "They're here! They're here!". It was 8:05. I asked Irons to find out what the deal was. It was 8:10. John had returned ashen white and righteously rattled. His voice was barely above a whisper. "They're downstairs shooting heroin." "What?" "I think it was heroin. They're shooting something. This giant biker dude told me to get the fuck out of the dressing room." The first thing I reflected was that I had left "No Shooting Heroin" out of the contract. Wait. This is crazy. Jesus Christ. There was sudden turmoil behind me. I whirled about and saw the Stooges approaching. They looked pretty bleary-eyed and unfocused, but when hadn't they? Too late for further speculation. The group appeared ready for introduction. Well, they hadn't publicly violated any contractual provisions yet. We had a full house clamoring for their appearance. Only Irons had witnessed theoretical peculiarities in the dressing room. Might as well jump into the fire.'

When The Stooges had assembled onstage, Irons wanted to introduce next week's acts at Sherwood Forest. 'A bad mistake,' said Dave Marsh, who was present to report on the gig for *Creem:* 'Iggy suggested that he shut up. Irons responded that that was a good way not to get paid, but the show went on immediately as the first Asheton cosmic boom of the night sounded immediately thereafter, beginning the show and effectively drowning out Irons.' According to Cavanaugh, 'It was customary to begin each introduction with a quick billboard of future bookings at Sherwood. Everyone was paying attention. Advantage had to be quickly taken. There was an unwritten 20-second window in which to squeeze all extraneous information before getting on with the actual introduction. Anything past 20 seconds would make the crowd restless and prompt cries of "Let's Go!" or "Kiss My Ass!" from antsy clientele. John Irons was doing the honors this night. At about the 10-second mark, he was abruptly and rudely interrupted by Iggy. "Fuck this guy. Kick it in!" The band immediately exploded into "Down On The Street" from The Stooges' *Fun House* album, and the audience went crazy. Irons wanted to kill the show right there and then. After all, Iggy had said the magic word and he had cut John off, which was a supreme professional insult.'

The concert went well, but it ended in chaos as the club managers pulled the plug when Iggy was in the crowd. Cavanaugh described the action: 'The energy was extraordinary. Maybe they'd been shooting cocaine. Maybe they'd just been sticking needles in themselves, administering self-acupuncture to unleash karmic power flow. I thought we might just pull it off. The Stooges always liked to finish things up with their love song. It was time for their last number which, by tradition, was an extended version of "I Wanna Be Your Dog", "and lay right down in my fav-or-ite place." Iggy was pretending that he was going to do one of his headfirst falls off the stage. Heh-heh. Shit! The fucker did it! Iggy was now standing shirtless in the middle of the first few rows of floor-seated enthusiasts. He was holding his microphone in his mouth and breathing into it heavily. He was barefoot. He started dancing and twirling and spinning around. Several roadies starting feeding foot after foot of microphone cable in his wake. He stopped, suddenly attracted by the heaving chest of a strikingly-well-endowed female fan directly before him. He extended one bare foot forward and started vigorously massaging her breasts with his toes. Maintaining the overall theme of his closing selection with instinctive grace, Iggy nevertheless chose to depart from normal lyric content and yelled into his microphone: "Dogs lick asses and chew big titties!!". That's it!!!!! The police were already wading through the crowd in Iggy's general direction. The quickest way to kill the music was to unplug the band. Irons moved like a flash. Everything on the stage was rendered silent in under five seconds. Except Iggy. He was on the floor, and his microphone operated separately off a sound system, which was wired behind and under the stage. It was out of immediate reach. Iggy wasn't. Iggy was now a good 50 feet in front of the stage and, in all of his swirling and twirling, had wrapped the microphone cord six or seven times around his neck. The long attached cable ran straight through the crowd to a sound mix amplifier set upon the very edge of the stage. Iggy noticed that the music had disappeared. His band had stopped playing. He was alone on the PA system. "What the fuck's wrong? Where's the music? What's happening? Where the fuck is the Arrrgghh!"'

The concert ended chaotically as Irons grasped the microphone cord twined around Iggy's neck. 'Iggy was almost garotted, then spun into several almost perfect pirouettes,' said Cavanaugh. 'He was then slammed to the floor and dragged through the crowd toward the ferocious John Irons, who was reeling him in, hand-over-hand, fist-over-fist. Chairs were flying. People were shouting. Mayhem reigned. I took a still-active stage microphone and ran a play-by-play: "Ladies and Gentlemen! Only here at Sherwood Forest! You'll never see the likes of this again. Never again! Anywhere on the planet! Iggy went hazy! Irons went crazy! What great Rock 'n Roll! Stand back! Step Aside! It's a life and death struggle before your very eyes! No prisoners will be taken! Iggy is done for! Iggy's good as gone! Iggy will die for Rock 'n Rollllllllll!!". It was a completely appropriate end to the performance. As Irons reached down and yanked a very groggy and confused Iggy onto the stage, I concluded: "Ladies and Gentlemen, The Stooges!!!". Wild applause thundered for a full five minutes as several police pulled Irons off Iggy and escorted everyone backstage. The hall lights went on and cheering continued as the crowd peacefully departed.'

Backstage after the concert, Iggy was arrested and charged with obscenity, although he was immediately released on his own recognizance (i.e., a written promise that he would show up for future court appearances). The following day, the Genesee County Prosecutors Office stated they had no interest in pursuing the matter and that such charges would never hold up in court. The Stooges did not receive the contracted sum of $1,000, but months later, the Musicians Union demanded that payment be rendered. 'I refused,' said Cavanaugh. 'Picketing and "blacklisting" was threatened, then delivered. I paid.'

'Stay away from Sherwood Forest in John Sinclair's hometown, Davison,' *Fifth Estate* admonished in response to the treatment of Iggy and the band. 'The Stooges played one of their better sets there, and club-owner, Johnny Irons (also a top man in Flint radio), refused to pay the group, citing reasons bizarre for not doing so. Incidentally, Davison is the town that MC5 lead singer Tyner got his wrist broken last summer by some local punks who thought that a tire iron (or was it a Johnny Iron?) would look better in Rob's mouth than in the trunk. Nice place to visit.'

Friday, 17 April 1970: Daniel's Den, Saginaw, MI

Footage was shot at this gig, and a snippet was later used in the VH-1 *Behind the Music* documentary on Iggy. The clip is readily available on YouTube with 'Gimme Some Skin' dubbed onto the visuals.

Saturday, 18 April 1970: Factorie Ballroom, Waterford, MI

The Stooges topped the bill over The Rationals and John Drake & the Atlantic Train. The venue was short-lived and situated in Waterford, a suburb approximately 50 kilometers north-west of downtown Detroit.

Mid to late April 1970: The Octagon, Jackson, MI

This was The Stooges' last gig before going to California to record their second album, *Fun House*. It is likely that saxophone player Steve Mackay guested on a few numbers at this show, as he participated in at least one gig before traveling with them to California. Jackson is near Ann Arbor. The band flew to Los Angeles to rehearse and record their second album for Elektra – *Fun House* – on 21 April 1970.

Thursday and Friday, 7 and 8 May 1970: Whisky A Go Go, Los Angeles, CA

Before embarking on the recording sessions for *Fun House*, the five-piece line-up of The Stooges with Steve Mackay on saxophone, performed two nights at the legendary Whisky A Go Go on Sunset Boulevard in Hollywood: a 500-capacity club which had been home to a who's-who of 1960s rock, having been opened in 1964 by Elmer Valentine and Mario Maglieri. The club has a small dance floor in front of the stage, behind which are small round tables with chairs and a bar to the left of the stage. Rather than the standard two sets a night at the club, The Stooges did only one show, starting at midnight.

Iggy spent a great deal of the Whisky concerts in the audience, standing on tables and pulling people out of their seats. Andy Warhol was among the celebrities in attendance. John Mendelsohn gave a comprehensive report on some of the action in *Entertainment World:* 'For this ridiculously typical young swinger doing the whole, you know, number right there in the center of the Whisky dance floor, the last 45 minutes have been quite gratifying. Who cares if there's been no group on stage three-quarters of the evening – what could be groovier, after all, than getting it on for all to see, right there in the mythical center of hip-posh Hollywood in one's colorful Broadway scarf, Harris & Frank shapeshift, and Florsheim boots? Yes, this swinger, this 26-year-old Firebird-driving, Encino-resident, fast-rising employee of a West Hollywood public relations firm, has ample reason to bare his perfect MacLean teeth self-assuredly as he sveltely leads his date, a slightly bouffant Summer Blonde number in last year's see-through blouse, from the dance floor and back to their excellent table right beneath the corner of the stage. He lights and draws suavely on a Benson & Hedges, winking devastatingly up at this flash little nifty now undulating expressionlessly right above them. "What's this group called again?" his date inquires, "The Three Stooges?". He smiles with amused superiority. "No, just The Stooges. By the way, they're supposed to be a little, uh, wild", he corrects teasingly.'

Mendelsohn continued: 'Three Stooges finally appear, and none of them looks even a little wild – the guitarist is even wearing rose-pink goggle-glasses of the sort the *Playboy* attire edition endorse a few issues back. "You know, hard rock really turns me on," our sharpie ventures daringly as they plug their instruments in. At which point he and everybody else in the Whisky is jolted into terrified rigidity by these three not-so-wild-looking Stooges' first homicidal chord. Reflexively, he and they throw their hands up over their ears. He grimaces broadly and yells to her something disapproving about this development, which she, of course, cannot hear. Then this skinny, bare-chested kid in ragged blue jeans that hang only silly millimeters above indecent exposure, absurd ladies' evening gloves that cover his arms up to his elbows, and psychotic bugged eyes, swaggers onto the stage and – oops! – suddenly contorts hideously, his limp wrists flapping against his chest, his knees slamming together, and his feet jutting out at a 120-degree angle, as he grabs his microphone stand and the band grinds out its tenth consecutive three-chord run to nowhere.'

Mendelsohn resumed: 'The singer – Iggy! The Ig!, with a capital T – frees his mike from its stand, screams something about sticking it inside, and, his right hand reaching up and over to caress his right shoulder blade, writhes like a suffocating fish with legs across the stage, looking as if he'll fall from it at any moment. He does, banging his head against it as he goes down vertically, into the center of a semi-circle instantly ceded him by the frantic photographers and stolid groupies present. If his head is hurt, he doesn't let on but instead continues to flail about grotesquely. Burning everyone he looks at with his madman's stare, he keeps slamming his mike against his mouth, eventually drawing blood from his lower lip. He climbs back up on stage; his expression suddenly changed from a lunatic grimace into a sweet-little-boy pout that manages to whine, "Gee whiz, I'm trying so hard for you people", at the same time that it accuses, "You miserable bunch of unsympathetic assholes".'

Mendelsohn continued: 'He moves from one table to another like a Las Vegas shlock-monger gone berserk, screaming in people's faces, sticking his tongue out at them an instant before gracing them with his cutest little-boy smile, before grinding his pelvis four inches from their noses, before dropping his mike down his pants. Hard rock may be outtasite in moderation, our sharpie decides as Iggy approaches his table, but this is going just a little bit overboard, wouldn't you say? He gets up and reaches for his date. Too late, the Ig has spotted him and has placed his swaybacked little body in between him and the aisle. He whips his mike back at his own mouth, smashing himself hard in the lip again and drawing more blood. Then he sticks it right in the trembling fellow's face. The sharpie doesn't know quite what to do. Iggy takes the mike back and shrieks "Aaaugh-aaaugh!" into it at the top of his lungs. Then he sticks it back in the sharpie's face. "Aaaughaaaugh," the fellow manages, not exactly wholeheartedly, "Aaaugh." Iggy turns his back and focuses on someone else. The sharpie scoops up his date and wrenches her toward the club's exit, both their faces ashen white.'

At one point during the concert, Iggy grabbed a candle off a table, returned to the stage and proceeded to pour hot wax on his chest. 'That was the first time I ever saw Iggy pour hot wax over himself,' said Jimmy Silver. 'He had no shirt on. He picked up one of the big candles inside a heavy glass candleholder from one of the tables and poured it on himself. It ran down his chest and congealed. As always, I thought, "Oh, my God, he's gonna hurt himself; what am I gonna do?"'

According to Mendelsohn, half of the audience walked out, but those who remained were entranced: 'What they've been saying about Iggy all these years is true – he does make Jim Morrison and very nearly any other rock and roll schlock-monger look like a simpering puppy in comparison, and he has extended the idea of physical liberation through rock and roll performance light-years past where he found it.'

Iggy had given himself an image overhaul, chopping his long locks schoolboy-short, which was an unusual haircut at a time when most rock artists had very long hair. Photos by Ed Caraeff from the Whisky gigs are featured on the *Fun House* sleeve, in Bob Matheu's Stooges biography, and in Caraeff's book *One Night At The Whisky 1970*, published in 2017.

Friday and Saturday, 15 and 16 May 1970: New Old Fillmore, San Francisco, CA

The band again took some time off from the *Fun House* sessions to go to San Francisco to perform two concerts at Bill Graham's Fillmore West, a 2,000-plus theatre that had been one of the leading venues for the West Coast rock revolution. The Stooges played two shows, topping the bill over the Flamin' Groovies and Alice Cooper. Also on the bill were Commander Cody and Heavy

Water. A photo by Kurt Ingham from one of the shows was featured in Bob Matheu's Stooges biography.

In the audience were The Cockettes, a gay drag theatre group, who invited the band to their house after the gig. Iggy said, 'During the gig, there had been all these people in the front row dressed in strange Arabian garments – quite fascinating – with bananas on their heads. After the gig, I went over to the house of these people from the front row, and they turned out to be from The Cockettes – a bunch of drag queens. I had no idea what it was going to be like. I'd never been to a gay home. I remember how penetrating and strange the house felt, and how three of them were peering at me – very strange.'

Elektra's Jac Holzman and Steve Harris flew in from New York to catch the San Francisco show. Ron Asheton recalled, 'We went up to our dressing room (at the Fillmore) and there is Holzman with shades and a T-shirt and jeans. He's trying to be cool – getting close to the guys. We were smoking dope and we brought three black kids with us to the dressing room. They were about 11–12 years old, stoned out of their minds on marijuana. The next thing I hear is a girl screaming. We went out and there are these kids – they have knives and they had a girl up against a wall. 11-year-old kids! And here is Holzman. He is so insulted from all this. He had his limousine brought by and he disappeared as quickly as he could!'

The Stooges were listed in early advertisements for a concert on 22 May 1970 at the Aragon Ballroom in Chicago (along with Bob Seger System, Mountain, among other acts), but their appearance was canceled. They were not featured on advertisements closer to the date. The band finished recording *Fun House* on 24 May and flew back to Detroit the next day, except for Iggy, who stayed in Los Angeles a few days to oversee the final mixing of the album.

Friday, 5 June 1970: Palladium, Birmingham, MI

Back from California and the recording of *Fun House*, The Stooges continued playing mostly weekends in and around Michigan. Iggy added a red dog collar to his attire, which still featured silver elbow-length woman's evening gloves. This concert also featured Mighty Quick and Ormandy, the latter being a spin-off group from Question Mark and the Mysterians. Natalie Schlossman reported in *Popped* that Iggy had gotten a tan in California: 'He looks almost black. His hair has gotten sun-bleached, and with the tan, his eyes look even bluer and more crazed than ever. He looks so nice and healthy, it was a joy to see him. He's cut his hair again; it's almost in spokes. Iggy looks like something out of a planet the science fiction movie producers have not even thought about yet.'

Natalie continued: 'What a great welcome back they got. It was really nice to see other people taking photos with an Instamatic camera. Instamatics are a fans' best friend and status symbol, and there were certainly a lot of flashcubes used on The Stooges that night. When there is a great time-lapse between Stooges concerts, for me, it is always extra special to see them again. I forget what dynamic performers they are. I don't actually forget, it just amazes me each time just how marvelous they are. And Iggy's energy will always be a source of wonder to me.'

Saturday, 6 June 1970: Pavilion, Wampler's Lake, MI

The Toby Wesselfox Band opened for The Stooges. Natalie Schlossman wrote in *Popped:* 'A lot of people from Ann Arbor and Detroit showed up and that was quite a distance to travel. The boys put on a really killer show with Iggy throwing his silver gloves to the audience and Ron using a drumstick to make even stranger feedback. Iggy had everyone rising to their feet by the end of the show. Good for the Ig! Everyone was so crazed by the end of the set. Since The Stooges use all their energy for the entire set, I've yet to see them do an encore. However, I got the feeling that had they stayed on stage until 6 am and done ten encores, the people would have stayed. And they were just that good.'

Saturday, 13 June 1970: Crosley Field, Cincinnati, OH – Cincinnati Summer Pop Festival

This was one of the biggest rock festivals of the summer of 1970, featuring Traffic, Ten Years After, Grand Funk Railroad, Mountain, Mott the Hoople, Bob Seger, Alice Cooper, Bloodrock, Zephyr, Savage Grace, Sky, Mighty Quick, Damnation of Adam's Blessing, Third Power, Brownsville Station, Cradle, Mike Quatro Band, and many more. Newspapers reported a crowd of around 25,000.

Photos by Tom Copi of Iggy walking out on a sea of hands and smearing a jar of peanut butter on himself, became iconic (later featured in Iggy's autobiography *I Need More* and almost every book ever published on The Stooges). Iggy said, 'It was just a hand in the crowd. They said it was Stiv Bators (later to become the vocalist in the band The Dead Boys). It broke the ice at that particular show and brought all the comedy into the thing, which again is a recurrent theme. Most of it was coincidence, just things that would crop up, and I always felt that performance should be part of the moment.' Ron Asheton commented, 'Usually Iggy would dive in, but the crowd just held him up. It was amazing; their hands were supporting him. He went into the crowd, but instead of being in it, they lifted him. He was on acid. If he wasn't on acid, he couldn't have done it.' Photographer, Tom Copi, said, 'I took that shot of Iggy walking on hands from the apron of the stage. We had great access. I got that shot; then someone handed Iggy the peanut butter that he smeared all over himself and on the crowd. When Iggy came off stage, he had the peanut butter all over his hands, and there was a local DJ standing on stage near the edge, wearing a powder-blue silk shirt. Iggy just wiped the rest of the peanut butter on his shirt. The guy was laughing, but you know he wasn't happy.'

Roadie, Leo Beattie, considers the festival performance the zenith of The Stooges: 'It was like nothing you'd ever seen. He had the peanut butter and he was walking across the crowd. There was no performer that could capture a crowd and do that. No one had ever done that. He was unique, the way he could tap in and connect.'

Cincinnati Summer Pop Festival was the first nationally-televised rock concert. Snippets of two songs with The Stooges – '1970' and 'TV Eye' – were broadcast in the US as *Midsummer Rock* by NBC on Sunday 30 August, marking The Stooges' first major television exposure. According to Ron Asheton, 'It was actually no fun, because the TV camera guys at that time were carrying big units, had a lot of cables, and they were just on stage and just walking through my stuff. They actually stepped on a fuzz tone, turned it on. I was pissed off, actually and having to concentrate on what I was doing. I was totally unaware of what Iggy was doing out there 'cause I was trying to hold it down on stage.' Still, Ron's most persistent memory of the festival was police overreaction: 'After we were done playing, I was sort of milling around in the back and this cop had just dragged this kid in; he was obviously all fucked up, but you don't have to treat somebody that rough. His pants were falling down and stuff. And I'm going, "What did he do?", and he said, "Shut up, you're going with him!"'

June 1970: Goddard College, Plainfield, VT

No details are known about this unconfirmed concert, which supposedly was held at a venue on Goddard College, Plainfield, Vermont (The Stooges' first and only concert ever in Vermont). In mid-June, Iggy, Ron Asheton and Jimmy Silver flew to New York to meet with Elektra representatives to discuss the promotion of the *Fun House* album, which was being readied for a late summer release by the label.

Friday, 26 June 1970: Michigan State Fairgrounds, Detroit, MI – Midsummer Night's Rock

This event was promoted as an 'Outdoor Summer Rock Festival' with a series of concerts over several nights. The Stooges headlined the first night, with the Toby Wesselfox Band and Tackle Box also featuring on the bill. Alice Cooper played on the second night (27 June 1970).

Saturday, 27 June 1970: Steven's Point, WI – People's Fair

This three-day festival (26, 27 and 28 June) was held on the Portage-Waupeca County line (near the present-day Iola Winter Sports Club). Acts included Chuck Berry, Johnny Winter, Steve Miller, Buddy Rich and Buffy St. Marie. The Stooges were a late addition to the bill. The 200-acre festival site was partly wooded, with a long, sloping field that created a natural amphitheater. The only building on the site was an old barn with a lily pond nearby. The promoters set up a system of checkpoints to keep out those without tickets. A high wire fence encircled the site. Although the festival was announced only ten days prior, it still attracted a large crowd of between 40,000 and 60,000 people at the festival's height.

A Saturday report in *Capital Times* made the festival sound like a hippie paradise and portrayed the event in a largely positive light. The police claimed to be surprised: 'Everything has gone real well,' a Waupaca County deputy told the *Capital Times*. Steve Mackay remembered the site: 'We took a little commuter plane from Chicago to Steven's Point and we drove out to the gig in two airport limousines, big stretched Cadillacs that said "Limousine" on top of them instead of Taxi. Ig rode with Buffy St. Marie and the band in the other Cadillac. We get there and it was bizarre, 50,000 people camped in the land, smoke from their fires thick as shit. We come driving in through this encampment; people were shouting "Fuck you, pigs" and throwing rocks at the airport limos. It was just, "Oh, somebody thinks they're important."'

However, the event soon turned into a debacle, with plenty of alcohol, LSD and any other drugs readily available. Police had taken knives and guns from some attendees at the gate. A motorcycle gang from Milwaukee had been hired as security. However, they were intimidating, with knives and firearms openly displayed, and did anything they wanted. On Saturday night, a group of bikers got on stage while the Amboy Dukes were playing and scuffled with a security guard. The bikers tossed the guard off the stage and he broke his collarbone. Promoters eventually asked some of the bikers to leave, but with police involved mostly in controlling access to the area and no uniformed force on the grounds, there was no way to make the bikers leave the site. Shots were fired, resulting in three people being wounded. Angry attendees threw bottles and rocks at the bikers, who fled, a few leaving their bikes behind, which were promptly set on fire by the crowd. A total of 23 bikers were arrested on the road outside. After the shootings, people started leaving.

The Stooges played a memorable set shortly before sunrise on Sunday morning. Steve Mackay watched Buffy St. Marie's set, which preceded The Stooges' performance: 'Her set was delayed because there was a guy on stage with a knife. They took the knife away and then had to negotiate to give him the knife back. She went on before us. You could see the tents and stuff on fire on the hill. And there is Iggy again; they passed him around in the audience. Out in the crowd again, the longest mic cord in the world. He never seemed to have that sucker come disconnected. Always got onstage by the end of the tune. We got out of there and it turns out there was a war. Three people were injured. It was a war between the bikers and the rest of the hippies. Somebody got tied to a tree and was tortured; we heard about it the next day. We stayed up all night; I think I took some acid; I was with Jim (Iggy), he was high.'

By Sunday evening, only 5,000-6,000 remained to see the last few bands. Charges filed against the bikers included causing injury by conduct regardless of life and carrying concealed weapons. Those wounded in the Sunday rumble were reported to be in good condition on Monday.

Friday and Saturday, 3 and 4 July 1970: Eastown Theater, Detroit, MI

The Stooges topped the bill over Blodwyn Pig and John Drake's Shakedown. Natalie Schlossman was in Detroit on a three-day visit: 'This was the first time I would see the band at this venue. It was a beautiful building with lots of artwork incorporated into the building's design. It had taken over from the Grande Ballroom as the place to see bands, and I had heard many nice things about it from the guys and from Danny.' She felt the band delivered 'two absolutely killer shows.'

'Once again, the hometown crowd greeted the band with enthusiasm,' said Natalie. 'Iggy was wearing the silver gloves and jeans, but this time they were ripped at the knees. The set had changed since I had seen them in the spring. Now the set was all material from *Fun House*. The crowd went wild when they recognized the beginning riff of "TV Eye." By this time, Iggy had been honing his act, and he was down in the audience, rubbing up against people, dumping handbags, and even taking off a girl's boot. There was stomping to the music, yelling and singing-along happening in the crowd. The Stooges were home and I felt like I was home also.'

Natalie said, 'The Eastown had an orchestra pit, and Iggy took off his red shoes before he climbed down and back out into the audience. He smiled and laughed and teased the crowd. He flirted with the girls and sang and danced and yelled his way through a song. Again, this hometown crowd knew his antics and knew that 'they' too were part of the show. They helped feed his mic cable after him as he gyrated among the people, singing and dancing and just being Iggy. The music coming from the stage was loud and great. It felt like the walls were vibrating and I loved the show. Iggy did not display as many theatrics, as the crowd was much bigger and he got lost in the middle, and only the folks surrounding him could see what he was doing. When he returned to the stage, the red shoes were gone. A fan must have taken them right off the stage. After the gig ended, the band, minus Iggy, came out and hung around the back of the theatre, saying hi to old friends and fans alike.'

Tuesday, 14 July 1970: Rainy Daze, St. Louis, MO – Summer Dance Concert

The Stooges returned to the Rainy Daze for a second gig at the club, following their performance there in March 1970. A girl was injured after Iggy's microphone stand snapped, causing the broken end of the pole to come down on her arm, cutting it open. The show was stopped, and the girl was taken care of. Photos from this show by Craig Petty are featured in Robert Matheu's Stooges biography (erroneously attributed to the March 1970 gig at Rainy Daze).

Saturday, 18 July 1970: Soldier Field, Chicago, IL – Big Ten Summer Music Festival

The bill included Chicago, Illinois Speed Press, Illusion, It Doesn't Matter,

Happy Day, Pig Iron, Dreams, Leon Russell, MC5, Funkadelic, Joe Kelley Blues Band, Mason Proffit, Bloomsbury People, Bush, and more.

The Stooges' 30-minute performance was taped by an audience member: 'Loose,' 'Down On The Street,' '1970,' 'The Shadow Of Your Smile' – briefly, as an a cappella by Iggy (a 1965 song by Johnny Mandel and Paul Francis Webster, popularized by Frank Sinatra and Tony Bennett amongst others) – 'Fun House' and 'LA Blues.' The performance was released in 2010 on *A Thousand Lights*. Pictures from the concert – showing the band spread out on the broad stage and Iggy being lifted up by the audience – have been published on the Internet.

Lynne Van Matre reviewed The Stooges' performance for *Chicago Tribune*: '...and the antics of the Stooges, whose lead singer pranced around in white, elbow-length formal gloves. It was during the Stooges set, when Mr. White Gloves had coyly peeled off one glove and had moved out, still singing, into the crowd on someone's shoulders, that the nudity so requisite at these exercises in "alternative culture" was realized. But you had to look fast – the individual who made his way up on the stage to show that black is beautiful all over was quickly hustled away.'

On 19 July 1970, the Stooges were advertised to appear together with MC5, Savage Grace, Catfish, and the cast of *Hair*, at Tartar Field, Wayne State University, Detroit, Michigan. However, based on local newspaper reviews, The Stooges did not perform. Detroit radio station, WABX, organized free Sunday concerts starting at noon on the campus of Wayne State University in Detroit. A 10-minute film (with sound) of MC5's performance was broadcast on WABX's *Detroit Tubeworks* television show.

Friday, 24 July 1970: Palladium, Birmingham, MI
The Stooges played with The Rationals and White Light. *Fifth Estate* wrote, 'Come down and help support this club before another one goes under. Free popcorn too.'

Saturday, 25 July 1970: Pavilion, Wampler's Lake, MI
The Stooges performed again with White Light. Following this show, The Stooges were scheduled to play on 26 July 1970 at the Newport Festival, held in Chester County, Pennsylvania, 24–26 July, but the event was canceled due to critique from county officials and residents in the area. Alice Cooper, Zephyr, Cactus, Amboy Dukes and Bob Seger System were among those slated to appear at the festival, which was expected to draw 30,000 people. The Stooges were also going to appear at the Harmonyville Festival in Delaware River, New Jersey, 4–9 August 1970, but this festival was also canceled.

Saturday, 8 August 1970: Goose Lake Park, Jackson, MI – Goose Lake International Music Festival
The Stooges' biggest crowd yet was at the three-day Goose Lake festival, where

they played to an estimated audience of 100,000 people on the second day of the event. The festival, nicknamed 'Detroit's Woodstock,' drew a total crowd of over 250,000. According to *Detroit Free Press*, 'Goose Lake Festival grossed somewhere close to $4.5 million, according to a quick estimate made on Sunday evening.'

Acts at the festival included Joe Cocker, Small Faces, Jethro Tull, Mountain, Chicago and Savoy Brown, as well as Detroit bands such as Alice Cooper, Bob Seger System, Detroit featuring Mitch Ryder, and SRC. The band's roadie, Leo Beattie, recalled the atmosphere: 'People were out of hand; it was out of control. A guy fell out of the PA tower (during Brownsville Station's set), bounced off the ground, got up and started dancing.' Still, the event was run with efficiency. Each band played for 45 minutes, using a revolving stage so one act could play while the next prepared their set to make it possible to begin without any delays.

Separating the stage and the audience at the Goose Lake festival was a large paved strip that was off-limits to everyone except the press, security, promoters and a crew that was filming the event. Separating the neutral zone from the audience was a huge double fence, which the audience called 'the Berlin Wall.' It consisted of a 10-foot high chain-link fence backed by another solid fence made of wood. Police officers on horseback controlled the area.

The crowd's frustration with the fence came to a head during The Stooges' set. When Iggy tried to climb the fence to mingle with the people, he was roughly grabbed by several security guards and thrown to the pavement of the neutral zone. The crowd was outraged and began to shake the fence, encouraged by Iggy, who made small gestures. Ron Asheton said, 'As the song ("Down On The Street") hit its groove, where the band holds the groove, Iggy raised his arm and beckoned to the crowd that was now smashing against the fence. When we got to the chorus where Iggy wails, "the wall," those kids must have thought we were talking to them, because they pushed the fence down and rushed the stage, which pretty much ended the festival.'

Seemingly as punishment, the power was cut off several times during The Stooges' set. Steve Mackay remembered, 'It was a big monster festival, it was really kind of Mad Max-ish. What happened in our set was a big element of the show, was Jim would dive off the stage and go out into the crowd. He couldn't do that here, so he scaled the goddamn fence and the security guys were trying to pull him down. Then at one point, maybe halfway through the set, we blew the circuits out and the power went dead. When the power went dead, Jim said, "C'mon keep going!". So Scotty could play, and I could play, and me and Scotty were playing, drums and saxophone, and I was going way out there, playing this frantic desperation. Then when the sound came back on, there was drums and insane saxophone coming out.'

The festival organizer tried to get The Stooges off the stage by revolving the stage so they would not face the crowd. Said Iggy: 'They tried to revolve us offstage and simultaneously shut off all the lights and power. Thirty seconds later, Bernie, our roadie, is up the light tower after the psychedelic ranger – he just throttled the guy, throttled the fucker, man, knocked him cold, and turns the lights back on. Meanwhile, Dogman (another roadie) had had it and just whaled three guys backstage. They weren't huge muscle guys, but they weren't bad. We were halfway revolved off, and he pushed the reverse button and we were back on.'

Photos of The Stooges by Charlie Auringer are featured in the Stooges biography by Robert Matheu. A brief film clip of '1970' from the performance has emerged and was also released in 2010 on *A Thousand Lights*. A soundboard recording of The Stooges' entire 40-minute concert was discovered many years later and released in 2020 as *Live At Goose Lake, August 8th, 1970* by Third Man Records: 'Loose,' 'Down On The Street,' 'TV Eye,' 'Dirt,' '1970,' 'Fun House,' and 'LA Blues.'

Goose Lake was the end of the road for Dave Alexander. He had taken drugs before the concert, being approached backstage by a roadie from one of the British acts who had a plastic bag with an unknown substance. Dave's girlfriend, Esther Korinsky, said, 'We didn't ask what was in the bag; we just snorted it. We laughed at the time, saying, "I wonder what that was." Before that, I remember everything. Afterward, it's just a blur.' According to Beattie, 'He was blotto! I never saw him in that state after drinking at the house – mostly just beers and hash. But that day, if he was a cartoon character, he would have had little X's over his eyes.' The drug-impaired Dave's bass-playing as he dropped out of songs and missed verse/chorus cues. 'I could tell Iggy was livid,' said Beattie. 'He kept looking at Dave, shooting him looks, beating his hip with his mic in frustration.'

Dave's replacement on bass was Tommy 'Zeke' Zettner, who was working as a roadie for The Stooges. At the same time, The Stooges decided to augment their line-up with a second guitarist, Bill Cheatham, who was also working as a roadie for the band. The debut for the newly expanded six-piece line-up of The Stooges was intended to be at the Boston College Eagle Rock Festival, planned as a 13.5-hour marathon held at the Boston College Stadium on 14 August 1970, with Led Zeppelin headlining. Also on the bill were the Allman Brothers, MC5, Junior Wells and Buddy Guy. The Stooges traveled to Boston, but the festival was canceled after objections from residents in the affluent suburb of Chestnut Hill, near the proposed site. Aware that pressure from the city's wealthier districts could jeopardize his campaign for governorship, Mayor White revoked the license only two days before the event, on the grounds that there would be no effective means for controlling the crowd, estimated to go as high as 30,000. Over 10,000 tickets for the festival had been sold. According to Steve Mackay, 'People tried to put on or did put on, a huge series of rock concerts and festivals: about half of them got canceled at the last minute because of the authorities. The one in Boston where we went but didn't play, the representative from the city of Boston came to our hotel and paid us the money.'

A few days after the Goose Lake show – 11 August – Iggy was interviewed by DJ Dan Carlisle's WKNR radio show.

Saturday, 15 August 1970: Sunshine-In, Asbury Park, NJ

The new six-piece configuration of The Stooges – with Zeke Zettner on bass and Bill Cheatham on guitar accompanying Iggy, Ron Asheton, Steve Mackay and Scott Asheton – made its debut at a gig at Sunshine-In in Asbury Park. The 'Far out rock concert,' according to advertisements, was headed by Chuck Berry, who was promoted as the 'king' of rock 'n roll in the advertisement. It also featured MC5 and Amboy Dukes, among others. The Stooges' performance on the first day of the two-day event was canceled because the band arrived late to the venue, according to a newspaper report. They finished the event, playing last on Sunday morning.

Bob Rudnick described the performance in *Earth Magazine* as a 'musical psychodrama,' and he observed that 'the stark reality of the performer's presence, unprogrammed, spontaneous, turns a mass audience into a congregation of individual zealots.' Joan Pikula reviewed the concert for *Asbury Park Evening Press*: 'The first show did go on, but without The Stooges, who were late. So almost everybody stayed on, at the invitation of the club's owner, Bob Fisher, until the music ground to a reluctant halt around 3 am yesterday. By that time, Iggy had thrust himself into the audience – which was seated on the floor beneath the stage – several times, sending some astonished youngsters scurrying out of the way while others moved closer "getting into the act," which is what he wants. Iggy Stooge is a small, muscular boy-man who appears onstage in variations of "stimulating" attire and who then usually proceeds to torture himself, while his band, The Stooges, plays wildly behind him. Well, Iggy didn't mutilate his person Saturday night, but that may be simply because the concert was stopped in time by the club's owner. By 3 o'clock, Iggy had thrust his nimble body among the throngs a whole lot of times, discarding the feather boa he wore for his prancing entrance along the way, along with a red leather choker. All that remained on Iggy's sweating body as he offered it up (or, rather, down) to an audience that didn't seem to know just how to react, were a pair of boots and the remains of incredibly shredded jeans.' She was captivated by Iggy, but seemed uncertain about the band's future: 'It could be The Stooges will make it big someday. But chances are they won't, despite the musical potential they show. The fact is, Iggy is just too freaky for most of today's audiences and too unsubtle.'

The Stooges rented a studio to rehearse their set in New York. Natalie Schlossman reported in *Popped* that Scott Asheton missed a rehearsal, but Steve Mackay sat in on the drums. According to Steve, 'They had booked a night of rehearsal, Scotty didn't show up. I knew all the drum parts for the show we were playing at that time, so I played the rehearsal on the drums. I guess I did okay because somehow they remembered, as they called me up the next year' (when he replaced Scott at Eastown Theater). While in New

York, The Stooges checked out the Velvet Underground, which played at Max's Kansas City during the New York stay. Lou Reed's final appearance with the Velvets was on 23 August (later released as *Live at Max's Kansas City)*.

Tuesday, Wednesday and Thursday, 18, 19 and 20 August 1970: Ungano's, New York City, NY

Coinciding with the release of *Fun House*, The Stooges played a three-night stand at Ungano's in New York. Support act was Fat Water. Although two sets (at 10:00 pm and 12:00 pm) were advertised, The Stooges only played one set each night. The Stooges drew large expectant crowds. The media and celebrity-packed audience included Miles Davis, Johnny Winter, Todd Rundgren and Genya Raven, as well as miscellaneous scene-makers, including the Andy Warhol crowd.

Before the first gig, Iggy managed to persuade Elektra's Vice President Bill Harvey into giving him $400 for cocaine, explaining that he needed it to get through the punishing gigs. The band met the dealer at Ungano's. Ron Asheton remembered: 'So we're sitting backstage with Miles Davis, and this guy finally arrives and just throws down a big old pile. We already had the straws ready. Imagine the great scene – Miles Davis' head right next to all the heads of The Stooges going "snnorrt!" We all just devoured that fucking pile, man. Later, Miles Davis said, "The Stooges are original – they've got spirit," or something like that. It was great. My head next to Miles Davis, man.'

The Stooges' Ungano's set featured the entire *Fun House*, barring 'LA Blues.' They closed their set by extending 'Fun House' into a jam-filled number called 'Way Down In Egypt' (also referred to as 'Going To Egypt'). The 40-minute set on the first night was captured by Danny Fields on reel-to-reel tape and was released in 2010 by Rhino Records as *Have Some Fun: Live At Ungano's*. The set featured 'Loose,' 'Down On the Street,' 'TV Eye,' 'Dirt,' '1970,' 'Fun House' and 'Way Down In Egypt' (referred to as 'Have Some Fun'/'My Dream Is Dead' on *Have Some Fun: Live At Ungano's*).

One of the nights saw Iggy singing (or reciting) lyrics from Nico's 'An Evening Of Light.' Another number had the band providing an instrumental backing for an Iggy monologue about wanting to get 'the buzz.' He sat on the floor and told about his youth, the lack of attention, inferiority complex, and the feeling of being a nobody: 'When I was younger, I always wanted to get a buzz from you. I couldn't get a buzz. Now I feel a buzz through and through.' The music climaxed as Iggy slowly stood up and walked off stage.

'That was the best I ever saw them,' said future Stooges soundman, Bob Czaykowski, of the Ungano's concerts. 'Ungano's was the super-power one. Even for me, that was a scary show. They were intense. There was a lot of high theatre going on in rock shows, which is part of their appeal of why we'd go and see it because they were really on the outside compared to when you saw the Grateful Dead. It was kind of scary because you didn't know what would happen.' Brian Zabawski was in the audience: 'Iggy was in his element at Ungano's. He spent a lot of time in the audience. At one point, he used the microphone as a pendulum to hypnotize a victim in the crowd, then took him out of the "trance" with a bop on the nose. He also got down between the legs of a guy and bit him.'

'This was a more rehearsed-seeming performance than the February '70 Ungano's stint,' according to Brian Zabawski. 'Performing *Fun House* virtually in its entirety, the band brought out Steve Mackay to join them on sax for "1970", "Fun House," and a set-closing feedback extravaganza. That was their most radical departure from their set of earlier that year. The club was filled with the dense, throbbing mix that would go on to be so envied and imitated by other bands when, over the years, *Fun House* would attain classic status. Mackay's sax treatments revealed a new psychedelic-jazz direction to their already formidably potent attack. Iggy interacted with the Ungano's audience with free abandon, as in February. At one point, someone in the audience called out, "Where's Dave?". Iggy stared back threateningly and replied, "Where are you?"'

The rock writers were intrigued by The Stooges' Ungano's performances. Bob Moore Merlis of *New York Times* observed, 'They play excruciatingly loud music as Iggy screams, sings, beats himself, jumps and (invariably) falls. Their sound is the sound of frustration and children's rage; their sound is also incredible.' Allen Richards of *Zygote* described Iggy as an 'impromptu performer, doing whatever makes him happy at the moment. In his efforts to live his fantasies and pursue his desires, he becomes totally immersed in the act he displays. Maybe too much.' Fred Kirby of *Billboard*, a firm believer in the band's potential, felt the group was 'as intense and erotic as ever' and 'even more overpowering than before with the addition of Steve Mackay on saxophone.' The review by 'k. k.' in *Cashbox* was more critical: 'Iggy is sensational – as a performer and as an acrobat – but he is supposedly a rock vocalist, and at that profession, he is anything but sensational. Iggy Stooges is in a class by himself, and the other four Stooges – in another class. As a performer, Iggy is breathtaking. As an acrobat, he is as agile as a cat – but as a vocalist, he lacks in voice quality and frankly can't sing at all. His stage act is an exact copy of Jagger's, and as a result – Iggy lacks originality.'

Circus' Tony Glover had never experienced anything like Iggy before, which prompted him to ask, 'What does it all mean? Is it just a hype, an exercise in theatric weirdness? Is it an act, designed to draw attention that the music alone wouldn't? Or is it a "real" stage madness designed to make the audience ask questions about themselves and the nature of what they want from rock groups?' He attempted to answer the questions: 'People either dig or hate The Stooges, and you can write them off very easily if you're only looking for surface depth. But if you can dig funky simplicity in its easy depth and enjoy the play, you'll dig The Stooges. If you can see them live first, then dig the record as a soundtrack.' *Zygote's* Richards questioned whether it was an act or for real: 'I was dumbfounded at the way he was driven furiously by his pursuits. How well he controlled the bourgeois middle-classers, I thought. His antics had them petrified, astounded, entertained and thrilled. Most of them feared his intrusion into their privacy. Most of them awaited what they thought were premeditated actions. They loved to see the freak go amuck, the nutty kid trespass propriety. But this performance was not an act. I fully believed that no one could take the stage and willingly turn himself from a reserved individual into a screaming hedonist. This was not a put-on.'

Later in August, The Stooges were scheduled to play at Aragon Ballroom, Chicago, 27–28 August 1970, and participate in the Spoon River Rock Festival at Big Country Ranch Resort in Washington County, Pennsylvania (with SRC, Alice Cooper, MC5 and others), 28–30 August, but both events were canceled.

Friday and Saturday, 4 and 5 September 1970: Eastown Theater, Detroit, MI

Fleetwood Mac headlined the two shows over The Stooges. The Saturday concert also featured Springwell. *Detroit Free Press* previewed the gigs: 'Eastown Theater Friday and Saturday England's Fleetwood Mac returns after an absence of many months. Along with Mac are the incredible and bizarre Stooges, Springwell and, of course, the Magic Veil Light Show.' A Fleetwood Mac fan, Randy Foley, described The Stooges' performance as 'a bit erratic' on a Fleetwood Mac website. He claimed that Iggy 'walked off the stage several times, and the set was eventually aborted.'

Sunday, 6 September 1970: Band Shell, West Park, Ann Arbor, MI

This outdoor concert was part of the 'Ann Arbor Free Concert Series' given at West Park, located close to downtown Ann Arbor.

The next day – 7 September 1970 – The Stooges were scheduled to play the First Annual Central Texas Music Festival. This was planned as a three-day festival, with Alice Cooper, MC5, Amboy Dukes, Ike & Tina Turner, Jerry Lee Lewis and many more. It was to be held on a 700-acre site between Bastrop and Elgin, near Austin, Texas. However, it was ultimately canceled. The festival was looking like being canceled in late August when the promoters ran into both financial and logistical issues. It is thought that only around 5,000 tickets had sold out of an expected 100,000. In any event, a judge granted an injunction a few days before the festival against holding 'any' such events in the area, on the grounds that it would constitute a 'public nuisance.'

Stooges concerts scheduled for 8 and 9 September 1970 at Whisky A Go Go in Los Angeles were never played for unknown reasons.

Friday, 11 September 1970: Recreation Center, Wheaton, MD

The Recreation Center in Wheaton – a suburb of Washington DC – held only a few hundred people. By now, Iggy had replaced his trademark red dog collar with a two-piece leather collar and tie that looked like some S&M gear, and he ceased wearing the silver elbow-length woman's evening gloves. Natalie Schlossman wrote in *Popped:* 'One of the regulations was no bare chests. I had small doubts about them letting Iggy on. The kids were really responsive down there and I've since gotten letters from kids wanting to know when the band will be back. About two weeks before they went, they showed the Midsummer Rock show and that is what got all the kids' appetite up for the boys.'

Richard Taylor, a musician and film-maker in Carroll County, MD, remembered the show in an interview published in *Vinyl District* on the internet in 2017 (his photos were also published). 'It was like a little gym stage, a couple of feet off the ground. When he came out, they were so loud, and I think the band started playing and Iggy came out, and he looked like an animal – he looked like a wild animal that somebody had just let out of a cage. His eyes were darkened, and I don't know if that was from drug-use or it was make-up or some combination because his eyes were sunken and darkened. He just stared at the crowd and he didn't talk to the people at the beginning. And they started doing their stuff. There was a girl sitting on the stage to his right, I believe, looking at the stage to his left, and during one of his gyrations, he picks up the microphone stand and almost hits her in the head with the damn thing. And I'm like, "Wow," this is more intense than I was really expecting! You wanted to see him, but you were also afraid because he almost hit this girl in the head with the microphone stand and he didn't care. So you didn't want to get too close, but you wanted to get close enough to see him.'

'If I recall correctly, he did a stage dive, and nobody caught him,' said Taylor. 'He landed on the concrete floor or the tile floor because that was before body-surfing. Nobody caught him and he just landed on the floor, and then he is crawling around, slithering around on the floor. And you don't know where he is, and the band is still playing, and we are watching him slither on the floor. And you don't want to get too close to the guy because, like I said, he was dangerous – real-life danger, not pretend danger. It wasn't an act. So anyway, the concert was fantastic … loud, blaring rock and roll. They just came on – and then they were gone. Then we found out they were playing at the Falls Church Community Center the next night, so we went to that show as well. And I had my camera for that show.'

Saturday, 12 September 1970: Community Center, Falls Church, VA

The Stooges appeared with a group called Summer. Richard Taylor was in attendance again: 'Somebody started throwing peanut butter at him and it pissed Iggy off. Someone must have seen it at the Cincinnati rock concert. In Cincinnati, Iggy went into the jar with his hand and smeared it on himself, but at the Falls Church Community Center, someone was throwing chunks of peanut butter at him, and it aggravated him. I was next to the guy, or a couple of people over, and he was throwing it at him, and it was irritating Iggy. I would have been irritated too. But I'm telling you, Iggy was scary. And you know, I had never seen anything like that. It was just amazing. This was way before punk rock started. I mean, he was obviously one of the first people to do that.'

Natalie Schlossman reported in *Popped*: 'Someone had peanut butter and Iggy did a repeat performance (of *Midsummer Rock*) for us. This time the peanut butter was just regular and not the organic kind, so it wasn't so sloppy. It still got all over everything and after the set, Iggy kept saying he wanted to go back to the hotel and wash his hair.'

Friday, 19 September 1970: Warehouse, New Orleans, LA
The Stooges appeared on a bill with Alice Cooper and MC5. Photos of Alice Cooper and MC5 have been published on a website devoted to documenting gigs at the Warehouse. There are no pictures of The Stooges, but one of the people behind the website claims that they played, and an Alice Cooper website says the show was with The Stooges.

Sunday, 20 September 1970: Windsor Arena, Windsor, Canada
The Stooges were billed as 'Iggy and the Stooges' on the poster for the concert, which was labeled 'Super Session.' The concert also featured Amboy Dukes, SRC, Brownsville Station and Blues Train. *Windsor Star* reported: 'About 2,000 attended. Leone (the concert promoter) admitted the program was hurt by dreary delays between acts. The Michigan bands – Brownsville Station, Amboy Dukes, SRC and The Stooges – all were late.' This was The Stooges' first concert outside the US (unless they played the Canadian-American Pop Rock Festival in August 1969).

Saturday, 26 September 1970: Ludlow Garage, Cincinnati, OH
The Stooges visited Cincinnati's Ludlow Garage for the third time in 1970. They appeared with a local rock band, Whalefeathers.

Sunday, 27 September 1970: The Frut Palace, Mt. Clemens, MI
This is an unconfirmed concert, as the first advertisements for this club started appearing in early October 1970. The Frut Palace was a club run by the local band, The Frut.

Saturday, 17 October 1970: Palladium, Birmingham, MI
Also on the bill were Bob Seger System and Julius Victor. Stooges were again billed as 'Iggy and the Stooges.' The concert was advertised in *Detroit Free Press*. However, the *Windsor Star* advertised a concert at the same venue with the same line-up of acts for 10 October. It is unlikely that both concerts were played. This was likely Steve Mackay's last concert with the band, as he did not participate in the subsequent New York gigs.

Friday, 23 October 1970: Electric Circus, New York City, NY

The Stooges were back in New York for a gig at the Electric Circus: a 600-capacity psychedelic-influenced rock club in Manhattan's East Village (St. Mark's Place). The club was in the building that had housed Andy Warhol's Exploding Plastic Inevitable. The light show was a leftover from the Warhol days and featured oil slides, which were manually manipulated in order to create throbbing bubbles of colored lights.

Scheduled to begin at 10 pm, the concert was overdue and did not start until after midnight. The band had trouble getting to the show because their American Airlines aircraft had to return to Detroit after engine problems halfway to New York. The band boarded another plane at 7 pm, which left little time for a planned radio interview Iggy was going to do before the concert. After Steve Mackay's departure, the band now featured Iggy, Ron, Scott, Zeke Zettner and Bill Cheatham.

Iggy threw himself into the crowd several times during the show. Natalie Schlossman reported for *Popped*: 'The crowd loved Iggy so much that every time he'd try to get down in the audience, they'd raise him above their heads, and he'd wind up singing up there. It was killer to watch and the kids were really flipping out.' Ed McCormack commented in *Changes*: 'Again and again, he climbs back onto the stage, then sails back into the crowd, until the event takes on the look of an epileptic street accident on St. Marks, and the Stooges sidemen, without interrupting their churning, shrieking sound, come to the edge of the stage and crane their heads down into the crowd and see the torn leg of his black Levis rising out of a dense black sea of shoulders, his scruffy black high-heeled stiletto boot waving limply on the end of it like a shredded pirate flag.' Natalie recalled, 'Several people were wearing little Iggy stamps given to them by Mark Mitchell, a friend of mine through the club. I asked Iggy if he saw them later, and he said that he was really freaked to go out in the audience and have his own face stare back at him.'

Stooges fan, Chaz Miller, attended the show: 'My friends and I spent the many hours waiting. Meanwhile, the music that was being pumped into the discotheque was typical late-'60s hippie fare, with "Stand" by Sly and the Family Stone being played at least twice per hour. The place was abuzz with commentary about how great they were when they appeared at the venue in very recent history. Finally, sometime past midnight, increased roadie activity on and around the stage indicated the show was about to start. The silencing of "Stand" in the middle of the track was further proof the concert was about to begin. The light show stopped, and white lights went full on the stage. The band was already standing there as a "trapdoor" opened in the center of the stage from where Iggy slowly arose. He hissed and growled, which startled the majority who had been attuned to the previous hippie music. It was obvious that most of the people in attendance had never seen or heard anything like this before, and by the end of the first song, the majority of audience members had backed away from the stage, leaving only a few (including myself) up front.'

According to Miller, 'The Stooges' entire show lasted a mere 25 minutes. While the band was incredibly tight, Iggy was slurring some of the lyrics, making identification of the songs-played even more difficult. In the middle of the last song, Iggy – who was talking/singing his way through this particular number – included the "lyric" "I feel like puking!" and did so immediately upon uttering the words. Then he jumped up, spread his arms and legs out, and intentionally came crashing down, face-first, into the vomit. As the band played on, he rolled onto his back and made "snow angels" (waving his arms and legs while lying there), which at this point, pretty much had him covered in it from the waist up. Then, he launched himself into the audience, where the few brave souls who remained close to the stage caught him and brought him back to the stage. This wasn't the first time he had jumped out into the audience, but it certainly was the most memorable one. When the song came to a close, The Stooges ramped up the noise into what I did think was "LA Blues" or a similar freak-out. The Electric Circus was filled with screaming feedback, probably for the first time since the Velvet Underground had played there. The feedback continued, eventually becoming a drone, which eventually faded to near-silence a full 5 minutes after their departure.'

Miller noted, 'The bright lighting for the stage during the performance was never extinguished, even after the show was obviously over. The handful of audience members who were pressed up to the stage, including myself, screamed for an encore, but our voices were few compared to the total number of attendees that night. There was no encore. Most appeared to be glad it was over, and after-concert chatter was mainly neutral or negative. Nearly everyone seemed to be in some state of stunned silence. I recall being really satisfied with the performance but was disappointed by its brevity and lack of an encore, having waited over five hours to see them.'

The band's many loyal New York supporters turned out for the gig, including Natalie, Danny Fields, Steve Paul and Josephine Mori, as well as writers like Lenny Kaye, Lisa Robinson and Karin Berg. Lillian Roxon, reporting for the *Sydney Morning Herald* (Australia), called Iggy 'America's newest rock idol,' and was fascinated by the performance: 'His whole idea is to jolt the audience into a state of fear and shock. When he sings to a girl or to the audience, he does not do it caressingly but with anger and violence. The girl doesn't know whether she wants to mother him – or back away. Watching the indecision is part of the sadistic thrill of being in a Stooges audience.' McCormack concluded in his *Changes* piece that 'the Stooges are rock and roller derby – the roughest uncut dynamite available, owing to the raw unschooled vitality of their music and the fantastic stage presence of their lead singer and songwriter, Iggy Stooge.'

Sunday, 25 October 1970: Boston College, Chestnut Hill, MA

The Stooges played a short set at an unspecified venue on the Boston College campus for 'only about one hundred "fans,"' according to the report by Curt Naihersey in Boston's *Mass Media*. The reviewer was surprised by the band's 'super tightness' and lauded Iggy as a 'showman' and 'theatrical genius,' although his audience visits polarised the audience: 'Iggy sings in any position, anywhere: lying down, kneeling before you, sitting smugly in a lap or around someone's head, somersaulting, etc.' The Stooges finished the set with '1970,' as 'Iggy dove into the audience again, whereupon he wrestled with some people, slithered along the floor, stared into people's eyes (shit, that was a crazy, crazy feeling), and literally died among his audience.' Iggy finished off by singing an a cappella version of 'The Shadow Of Your Smile' as the lights came on. 'We were cut off,' Iggy said as he left the hall.

Saturday, 31 October 1970: The Ritz Theater, New York, NY

Billed as 'Iggy & the Stooges,' the band returned to New York for a Halloween show at the Ritz Theater: a converted, large old movie palace in Staten Island that had attempted a few rock concerts. Ed McCormack described the Ritz in *Changes* as 'dark and gloomy, laden with the gothic dank of all the dumpy movie houses that nurtured and nourished all of our youthful fantasies of violence in all the outerlying provinces of this violent land,' and complained of 'the smell of urine marinated in marijuana' in the 'smoky, stagnant air.'

MC5 opened the Ritz show for The Stooges – one of the few times The Stooges headlined over MC5, a clear indication of The Stooges' strong New York status. 'For the MC5 to be opening for their little-brother band, was a huge comedown,' said Ben Edmonds who was in attendance. McCormack detected tension between the two bands, as he felt MC5 were 'sullen and mean backstage' and stumbled out drunk to take uncharacteristically long to set up. They played 'an overlong and spitefully loud set,' according to McCormack.

At one point during The Stooges' set, Iggy charged into the crowd to confront a person who had been giving him the finger since the show began, but the guy avoided a confrontation by moving away in embarrassment. However, the performance did not go well, ending prematurely when hostile audience members began throwing eggs at the stage.

Iggy was hit by several eggs and promptly walked off the stage halfway through '1970.' His bare chest covered in slimy egg yolk and broken eggshells, Iggy raised his hands up in a dual middle-finger salute to the rude audience members and led the band off stage. As they left the stage to the bafflement of the crowd, the audience soon realized there would be no more of the performance and pelted the band with even more eggs.

The band (Iggy, Ron, Scott, Bill Cheatham and Zeke Zettner) remained in New York to do a photo shoot with Peter Hujar, as featured in Robert Matheu's Stooges biography (where these shots are erroneously dated to August 1970). A concert on 31 October 1970 at Delta College, Saginaw, MI, was advertised in *Saginaw News* but was not played.

Friday and Saturday, 13 and 14 November 1970: Eastown Theater, Detroit, MI

Following a two-week break after the New York gigs, The Stooges were back in action for a few weeks of gigs. The Eastown Theater concerts were James Williamson's debut with the band, replacing Bill Cheatham. The Stooges headlined both nights on a bill that also featured Skid Row, Illusion, Allman Brothers and Mott the Hoople, although the latter band canceled. *Fifth Estate* billed the Stooges' concert on 13 November as 'Iggy Pop and the Stooges,' and the second night as 'Stooges.'

Sunday, 15 November 1970: Ole Zim's Wagon Shed, Fremont, OH

A poster advertised Up, SRC, Brownsville Station and The Stooges playing Ole Zim's, but on separate dates: Up (supported by Dog) played 25 October 1970, Brownsville Station 1 November, and SRC (supported by Rail) on 8 November. The Stooges were in the fourth of the four Sunday night slots that had been allocated. The Stooges were also advertised to appear at The Frut Palace, Mt. Clemens, on 15 November, but this Fremont gig exists on an advertisement for the concert and is part of Danny Fields' handwritten list of Stooges gigs in November-December 1970.

Saturday, 21 November 1970: U of D Memorial Building, Detroit

The Stooges appeared with Alice Cooper and Damnation. The ad for the gig stated that 'Jane Fonda presents' the bands, and the concert was part of her controversial 25-date 'anti-Vietnam war' speaking tour of America. The U of D Memorial Building was an 8,000-seat multipurpose arena, the home to the University of Detroit Mercy Titans basketball team. The name was changed to Calihan Hall in 1977.

Sunday, 22 November 1970: The Frut Palace, Mt. Clemens, MI

This gig was advertised in *Detroit Free Press* and was included on Danny Fields' list of late-1970 concerts. A concert at the Borderline, Detroit, has also been listed for 22 November but was probably not played.

Monday, 23 November 1970: Dewey's, Madison, WI

This concert was mentioned in a Detroit-area gig listing and was included on Danny Fields' list of November-December 1970 Stooges gigs. Fields' list included a concert on 25 November in Salt Lake City, Utah. However, Salt Lake City had very few concert venues in 1970. The last established venue, Terrace Ballroom, ceased having rock concerts in the summer of 1970. A new venue had just started staging rock concerts – The Fairground Coliseum – but on 25 November, Alice Cooper with Wishful Thinking played there. There is no reference to The Stooges playing anywhere in Utah at this time. Fields' list has a gig planned for Birmingham Palladium on 25 November, which suggests that it never occurred.

Thursday, 26 November 1970: Sports Arena, Toledo, OH

This Thanksgiving Day concert featured several acts along with The Stooges, including Catfish, Amboy Dukes, Damnation and Mutsie, as well as local acts Renaissance Fair, Magic Theater, Jim Stein, and Kevin and Jean. The show started at 5 pm. The gig was included on Danny Fields' list of concerts planned for November-December 1970. 'We played a sports arena with The Stooges, and Iggy was wild and jumping around,' recalled Jim Quinn, guitarist of Damnation. 'And then we're talking backstage and he just passes out... it was all the drugs.'

Another Toledo gig (at the State Theater), on 20 November, was included on a Detroit-area gig listing but has not been confirmed.

Friday, 27 November 1970: WF Herman Secondary School, Windsor, Canada

Up, Frut and Dorian also appeared on the bill. Photos from this gig – referred to as 'Herman's Big Dance' – were featured in the school's yearbook, which found its way onto the internet in 2010. The photos were accompanied by a text: 'The dance was a smash, so was everything on the stage. Kids from all over Windsor and Detroit packed the gym; sitting on the floor, the bleachers, and each other. There was a loud silence as the band came out to get ready. Then out of the wings came the "Prince Charming" of the rock acid sound – Iggy Stooges. Iggy was clad in a freckled-skin shirt, a belt, bits and pieces of Levi's and a wild pair of red silk shorts from Louis the Hatter, clearly visible through the small 14-inch rip in his Levi's. Then the audience thought they heard a buffalo stampede, being chased by something that sounded like King Kong, but it was a mistake – it was the band starting up. Then Iggy joined in and started to sing, or bark, or squeal, or something.'

Saturday, 28 November 1970: Gilligan's, Buffalo, NY

No details are known, but the concert was listed on Danny Fields' handwritten list of gigs planned for November and December 1970.

Friday, 4 December 1970: Monroe Community College, Rochester, NY

The Stooges played with six bands at this 'A Holiday Festival' concert: Catfish, Alice Cooper, Buddy Guy, Damnation and Junior Wells. The date of the show has been listed elsewhere, mistakenly, as 7 December.

At Monroe Community College, Natalie Schlossman met James Williamson for the first time. She attended a band rehearsal at the venue and reported in

Popped; 'Ron and James have this incredible rapport between them and it's totally amazing to watch.' Danny Fields also checked in with the band. Jan Hodenfeld interviewed Fields, band members and Natalie, for an article in *GQ*.

Iggy guested during Catfish's set, as reported by Hodenfeld: 'In the gymnasium of Monroe Community College on the fringes of Rochester, the group Catfish is carrying on to little effect and less response, until lead singer Bob Hodge calls this kid from the audience onto the stage. The kid, identifying himself as Jim Osterberg, is small and shrugs shyly into his nylon fleece jacket, when Hodge – all show-business hip – asks if he wants to boogie with the group. The kid starts coughing into the microphone; and humming; and jiggling around. Right into what looks like an epileptic fit. It's getting very strange. Suddenly, he rasps maniacally, "Are you nice and loose now?" and goes jerking across the stage like some faggy brain-surgeon-turned-truck-driver, belching out a song. It's Iggy.'

The show ran late, and The Stooges never actually got to play the gig due to a curfew. The *GQ* report mentioned the performance of 'Dirt' and 'Loose,' but they were not played at this non-show.

Saturday, 5 December 1970: High School, Farmington, MI

This concert in Farmington, a Detroit suburb, was advertised as 'Holiday of Rock' and featured Mitch Ryder and The Coming. Photos taken at this concert were posted by Jim Edwards (singer in Michigan-based The Rockets) on the Internet in 2011 (slides were given to him by an unknown photographer). Iggy talks in *Total Chaos* about how he shot up heroin before this concert. An account of the gig was given on an internet site by a fan who attended the concert, which tells of the band not starting until midnight due to Iggy apparently being arrested earlier in the evening, and then only playing four songs before he collapsed in the middle of the gym floor on the lap of someone in the audience.

Saturday, 12 December 1970: Palladium, Birmingham, MI

Also on the bill were Catfish and Jam Band.

Friday, 18 December 1970: Grand Valley Armory, Grand Rapids, MI

The Stooges – billed as 'The Stooges featuring Iggy' – and MC5 were joined on the bill by Riverun and Cirrus. Grand Rapids is located in western Michigan.

Saturday, 26 December 1970: Pirates World, Dania, FL

This was most likely the last concert The Stooges played in 1970. Opened in 1967, Pirates World was a pirate-themed amusement park in Dania, just north of Miami, Florida. It closed its doors in 1975. *The Miami News* reported, 'The very popular and most exciting group to come out of Detroit, The Amboy Dukes will appear at Pirates World, 613 Sheridan Street, Dania. Also on the bill are the Stooges, another vocal group to come out of the Woodstock. Showtime is 8:30 pm.'

The Pirates World gig was included on Danny Fields' list of gigs in *Total Chaos*. Further concerts from 27 to 31 December mentioned on this list were most likely never played: Jacksonville, Cocoa Beach, Orlando, Atlanta, Houston and Chicago. Two of the Stooges' roadies – Dave Dunlap and Leo Beattie – left around Christmas time 1970, indicating that there were no gigs in late December or early 1971.

1971

The Stooges went on hiatus in the early months of 1971 to deal with some
of the members' drug addictions. During this time, Zeke Zettner left the
band to be replaced by Jimmy Recca, who was a friend of James Williamson.
Zeke died of a heroin overdose in 1973. Jimmy struck up a close friendship
with Ron Asheton, both staying away from the heroin scene. Causing further
estrangement, Iggy – together with James and Scott Asheton – moved out of
Fun House to live in University Towers, a newly built high-rise building in
the center of Ann Arbor. 'They had to be in the city to be closer to their dope
connection,' said Ron. 'Fun House was too far on the outskirts of the city
for Iggy and Scotty because nobody had cars.' James maintained the move
was not prompted by drugs: 'While Scott and I did use heroin, we weren't
junkies. Iggy was the only one who was really strung out. Maybe Scott was
getting there, but frankly, we never could afford the habit to get too bad.'

Determined to return to live work and generate some income again, the
band asked Danny Fields to take over the managerial duties. The band
hooked up with a local booking company: Diversified Management Agency
(DMA) – Detroit's biggest concert promoter – which booked many Michigan
bands at the time. Fields managed the band long-distance from New York,
where he was working for Atlantic Records. 'From a professional point of
view, I wasn't very much of a manager at all,' noted Fields. 'I was really just
a friend in the right place and the right time, but I didn't really do what a
manager is supposed to do. I didn't go out there and whip them into shape
and put their affairs into order. I just did patchwork repairs. Their affairs
were a mess. I was called a manager for lack of something else. I was more
like a supporter.'

Following a four-month break from live performances, The Stooges did a
six-week tour in 1971. DMA lined up a number of mostly Midwestern gigs
from mid-April to late May of 1971. For their return to the stage, The Stooges
completely overhauled their repertoire, avoiding everything from *The Stooges*
and *Fun House* in favor of mostly new material: 'I Got A Right,' 'You Don't
Want My Name,' 'Fresh Rag,' 'Black Like Me,' 'Big Time Bum,' 'Do You Want
My Love?' (tentative title). 'Black Like Me' (also referred to as 'Dead Body')
used lyrics from Bo Diddley's 1957 classic, 'Who Do You Love?'

Aside from 'I Got A Right' – which was recorded in London in 1972 and
released in 1977 as Iggy's solo career took off – the 1971 material never
saw the light of day during the Stooges era. Their first official release was
in 2009 on Easy Action's *You Want My Action* box set. It has never been
clarified who were behind the songs, although 'I Got A Right' was an Iggy
solo composition. Iggy has claimed credit for writing 'You Don't My Name'
and attributed key elements of 'Fresh Rag' to James because it was one of
the first tunes he heard James play. Some musical elements of 'Fresh Rag'
were revisited for 'Consolation Prizes' (recorded in 1975 and released on
Kill City). 'Big Time Bum' was a musical prototype for 'Gimme Some Skin'

(recorded in London in 1972). It is likely that James came up with the music of 'Black Like Me' and 'Do You Want My Love?'

The Stooges' 1971 concerts were marred by Iggy's increasingly erratic and confusing behavior due to his heroin addiction. The band's business affairs were in shambles, with several delayed or canceled concerts causing the band to lose money. Fields' patience with the band was running out: 'I'd sit and watch them calling dealers. I could deal with the hatred of Bill Graham, but not the challenge of drug dependency. There was really nothing much for me to do anyway. I think their own personal and internal affairs were at such a runaway momentum at the time that, from where I sat, there was very little that I could do to control it. It was out of hand. I never made a penny. I lent them money. My life's savings went into the band and I was getting nothing out of it.'

Although the Stooges' concerts dried up, Fields managed to get Elektra's Vice President Bill Harvey and *Fun House* producer Don Gallucci, to come to Ann Arbor in June 1971 to attend an audition at the Stooges' band house to appraise the commercial potential of a third album for Elektra. 'While we were falling apart, we came up with some good riffs,' Iggy noted. Said James; 'I would say that our style at the time was super frenetic so that the Elektra guys could not really relate to it. Unlike *Raw Power*, which nobody could relate to, this stuff was not fully formed yet. It was a blast of high energy stuff.'

Attending the session, Fields was enthusiastic and felt the new material showed promise, signaling a new musical direction towards higher energy: 'They sounded great. I was delighted. We went back to the Glockenspiel Hotel. We didn't say a word on the way back and I was just driving with a big smile on my face. I remember saying to the Elektra people; I think it was back at the hotel, "Well?". Bill said to me, "I didn't hear anything at all." So I went to my room and called Iggy and said, "You're going to get dropped." He said, "Why? We were really good". I said, "I thought so too, but our arch-enemy did not." I was thrilled to hear they were making such progress. It was great. Bill Harvey said, "There's nothing there. I don't want to pick up the option; it's not worth it". That was it.'

Elektra terminated The Stooges' contract, as a third album for the label was not deemed commercially viable. The *Ann Arbor Sun* broke the news about The Stooges' break-up on 6 August 1971: 'The Stooges are no more. Last Sunday (Aug. 1), Iggy finally broke it off from the rest of the band, saying that he might form a new group to take the old name sometime in the future. It's fairly well known that most of the Stooges have been plagued with the jones for several months now and that's what caused their music and general state of organization to crumble.' Thus, the band's career reached a standstill in the summer of 1971. Iggy said that he 'never planned to stop. I took the chance that if I stopped playing and tried to straighten myself out, I could start again. I took the gamble. I had too much at stake personally to go out and do a crummy show.'

Iggy embarked on a methadone and valium treatment program, paid for by his parents: 'I went home and got some help. My parents pulled-off something; I had an illegal monitored professional methadone supply. America was a smaller place at the time. There was a family pharmacist in the area that they'd known for a long time. My dad walked into the pharmacy, and he said, "Bob... my son's duh... I don't want clinics and people like that duh duh...". And the guy said, "Don't worry about it. I'll buy a large bottle". It was something called Dolophine. It was a form of methadone, Cherry-flavoured.' Meanwhile, the Ashetons laid low in Ann Arbor while James took refuge with his sister to cure a case of hepatitis. 'The drug thing was just ripping everything apart,' reflected Scott. 'I'm not saying I was an angel. I was also in the pit with it. The band had to break up to help everyone's health. I always felt bad for him (Ron) that he had to have his career end with other people's disgusting habits.'

Even after the record contract was canceled, Elektra executives had vague plans for Iggy as a solo artist, working in a more commercial pop format. According to Iggy, 'I did hear at one point a murmur from Danny that, "The guys at Elektra say they would like to do like a David Cassidy kind of thing on you." That was the word that was used.' The plans were never directly relayed to Iggy, and nothing came of them.

Iggy went to Miami in August 1971 to meet with Steve Paul, who expressed interest in managing Iggy. A friend of Fields, Paul was the manager of Johnny Winter, amongst others, and owner of the New York club, The Scene. Paul suggested that Iggy work with guitarist Rick Derringer, who had been a member of The McCoys and played with brothers Johnny and Edgar Winter. Fields had mixed emotions about Paul's involvement: 'Steve was always my best friend and then suddenly he was making a move on Iggy professionally. The three of us were really close and I "invented" Iggy and brought him to Steve's attention. They started to toy with the idea of Steve working for him. Steve was very smart and very canny and had been in show business since he was 14. He thought he was explaining to me things that he understood about Jim. I thought that was very patronizing of Steve. To hear that he and Iggy had been planning Iggy's career after me. "Oh, really? I hope the two of you will be very happy together". I never wanted to talk about it again and I don't think I ever did.' Iggy met with Derringer, whom he considered to be 'a nice guy, but not my cup of tea,' but he had second thoughts about working with Paul: 'I thought, "This guy's too tough and mean. I'm not gonna survive this". And I just didn't wanna go with him.'

Iggy arrived in New York in late August 1971, initially staying with Terry Ork, who worked with Andy Warhol on his movies and would later manage Television. A few days later, Iggy moved in with Fields. 'He needed a place to stay and he just showed up. I was delighted to see him. There were probably remnants of this managerial guidance stuff: "Don't worry, I'll take care of everything" or "Go to sleep, smoke a joint and watch a movie."'

While in New York, Iggy met David Bowie one night (7 September 1971), an encounter that would prove pivotal for both, being the start of a long friendship. Bowie and his manager Tony Defries – then an employee of Laurence Myers' Gem Music Productions, a UK management and record production company – were in town to sign with RCA and hand over the master tapes of *Hunky Dory*. Following dinner at Ginger Man – where Bowie had met Lou Reed, among others – Lisa Robinson called Fields to see if he and Iggy could meet up at Max's Kansas City because Bowie was anxious to meet Iggy. According to Tony Zanetta – another Warhol associate who was part of the dinner company along with David's wife Angie Bowie, Lisa's husband Richard Robinson, and numerous RCA executives: 'Although David wasn't a major star, he had a strong following. Richard knew David was somebody to watch. I know that David wanted to meet Jim and Lou Reed. He was very taken with Andy Warhol and wanted to find out as much about Andy Warhol and the whole scene as he could.' Zanetta had met Bowie in London in August 1971, when he performed with the *Pork* ensemble along with Leee Black Childers, amongst others.

Max's Kansas City was a five-minute walk from Fields' apartment. 'Lisa and Richard Robinson were at Max's Kansas City with David Bowie,' recalled Fields. 'They said, "Do you have Iggy there?". I said, "Yeah." They said, "Well, bring him over because David's here and he wants to meet him."' Iggy would later claim that he was reluctant to leave the apartment because he was deep into a James Stewart film – *Mr. Smith Goes To Washington* – although Danny said Iggy had fallen asleep: 'I woke him up. "Wake up! David Bowie wants to meet you, come on, we're not doing anything". And the rest is history.' Bowie had picked Iggy Pop as the world's best singer in *Melody Maker* in May 1971, but Iggy had never even heard of Bowie.

'David and Iggy instantly hit it off,' said Lisa Robinson of the meeting between Iggy and Bowie at Max's. Fields concurred, 'The two of them just sat and started babbling to each other as if they'd grown up in the same eggshell, but they'd never met. The rest of us sat around babbling to each other, looking at them. Bowie liked Iggy for the right reasons. He liked his singing, the musical aspects.' There was a meeting of minds, according to Iggy: 'David and I got along, and his manager and I got along too. He (David Bowie) was an interesting person, but we were both rather aloof at first. There was a nice vibe, though, and Defries suggested we talk about management the next day.' Fields said, 'They were a house on fire. Iggy didn't have to pass any tests. He didn't have to pass the Rick Derringer scrutiny or anything like that. The musical scrutiny came from Rick Derringer; the show business scrutiny came via Steve Paul and the overview of his whole career. With David Bowie embracing him, and Tony Defries, wherever that money came from, that seemed perfect to me. So I was happy to deliver Iggy into the arms of the person who would save his career. I'll never say anything bad about Bowie because he rescued Iggy. I was out of

Above: A couple of rare photos from Iggy's white-face phase,
April 1968, at The Armory, Ann Arbor. At this stage, the band
was known as The Psychedelic Stooges and both music and
stage show were quite experimental. *(Steve Babor)*.

Left: *Michigan Daily* review of the public debut by
The Psychedelic Stooges, led by "Iggy Osterberger",
Grande Ballroom in Detroit, 20 January 1968. 'That's
where the old Psychedelic Stooges really learned how
to play,' said Ron Asheton of the Grande Ballroom.
(Michigan Daily)

Left: The Stooges' self-titled debut album, released in August 1969, was not a mainstream success. 'What's important is individual recognition,' said Iggy. 'In other words, it's not how many people recognize you; it's what the people who *do* recognize you, recognize you for.' *(Elektra)*

THE AUTHORIZED and ILLUSTRATED STORY

Left: Robert Matheu's officially sanctioned Stooges book (published 2009) with a shot from the photo session for *The Stooges*. *(Abrams Books/ Joel Brodsky)*

Right: The Stooges' second album, *Fun House*. 'Elektra had it all wrong,' Iggy said. 'They were trying to market us to college kids, and they were too educated to appreciate the Stooges' sound. I wanted them to target the dropouts, people like us.' *(Elektra)*

Left: This release shows Iggy backstage at a summer 1970 performance. 'I was getting delusions of grandeur by that time,' Iggy said as interest in The Stooges grew in 1970. 'The shows were good, and I knew I was dabbling in something that was really happening.' *(Easy Action/ Frank Pettis)*

Right: The cover of *Total Chaos*, a book by Jeff Gold (published 2016), features a shot of Iggy at Ungano's in New York, August 1970. *(Third Man Books/Dustin Pittman)*

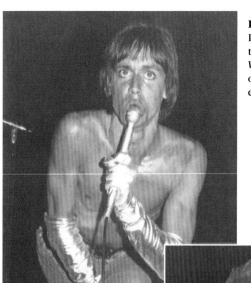

Left: Iggy at the Whisky A Go Go in Los Angeles, 7-8 May 1970. According to John Mendelsohn in *Entertainment World*, half of the audience walked out, but those who remained were entranced. *(PN collection)*

Below: St. Louis Pop Festival, Kiel Auditorium, 7 March 1970. 'We were playing all the time,' said Ron Asheton. 'We learned to play on the road. During the short time span between the first and second record, we progressed amazingly.' *(Craig Petty)*

Left: Summer Dance Concert at Rainy Daze, St. Louis, 14 July 1970. *(Craig Petty)*

Right: Iggy and Ron Asheton at Ungano's in New York during the three-night stand, 18-20 August 1970. 'That was the best I ever saw them,' said future Stooges soundman, Bob Czaykowski. 'Ungano's was the super-power one. Even for me, that was a scary show. They were intense. It was kind of scary because you didn't know what would happen.'
(PN collection

Below: Performing material from *Fun House* at Ungano's, New York, 18-20 August 1970. The audience and rock writers were intrigued. Fred Kirby of *Billboard* felt the group was 'as intense and erotic as ever' and Allen Richards of *Zygote* described Iggy as an 'impromptu performer, doing whatever makes him happy at the moment.'
(PN collection)

Below: A rare shot of the six-piece Stooges line-up, September/October 1970, with Steve Mackay, Billy Cheatham, Iggy, Zeke Zettner, Scott Asheton (and Ron Asheton, not visible in the photo). Signs of self-destruction were becoming evident despite increased interest in the band. 'Once heroin was introduced into the picture, it was the beginning of the end,' said Ron Asheton.
(courtesy of Kevin Plamondon)

Left: The Stooges played two concerts at New Old Fillmore in San Francisco, 15-16 May 1970, taking time off from recording *Fun House* in Los Angeles. They topped the bill over Flamin' Groovies and Alice Cooper. *(Kurt Ingham)*

Right: New Old Fillmore in San Francisco, 15 May 1970. *(Kurt Ingham)*

Above: New Old Fillmore in San Francisco, 15 May 1970. 'Iggy began to feel a pressure to do more outrageous things and more and more live up to his billings,' commented the band's manager Jimmy Silver. *(Kurt Ingham)*

Above: Following a four-month break, The Stooges returned to live performances in April 1971. Four-fifths of the 1971 line-up of the band are shown in the photo from Chicago Opera House, 17 April 1971: Jimmy Recca, Scott Asheton, Iggy and Ron Asheton (James Williamson is not visible in the photo). *(Bruce Dinsmor)*

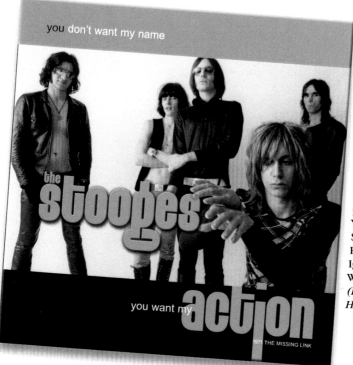

Left: This release contains four 1971 concerts, featuring a completely overhauled repertoire that did not include anything from *The Stooges* or *Fun House*. The front cover is from a photo shoot in New York, May 1971: Scott Asheton, Jimmy Recca, Ron Asheton, Iggy and James Williamson. *(Easy Action / Peter Hujar)*

Right: Iggy in October 1972 at the Beverly Hills Hotel in Los Angeles with David Bowie's entourage, having finished recording *Raw Power* in London. 'He was in a really good state of mind and he wanted to stay in California and bring his band over there,' said Tony Zanetta at MainMan, the management company headed by Bowie's manager, Tony Defries. *(PN collection)*

Left: This release, *Heavy Liquid*, features a cover shot from London's King Sound, a venue housed in the King's Cross Cinema, 15 July 1972, their only show outside North America (until the 2003 comeback). *(Easy Action / Mick Rock)*

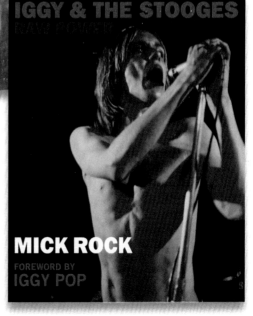

Right: Mick Rock's book features photos from The Stooges' London sojourn, summer 1972. The cover is from King Sound, 15 July 1972. 'The total effect was more frightening than all the Alice Coopers and Clockwork Oranges put together, simply because these guys weren't joking,' said Nick Kent in *New Musical Express*. *(Palazzo / Mick Rock)*

Left: *Raw Power* with a cover shot by Mick Rock from King Sound, London, 15 July 1972. *(CBS/ Columbia)*

Above: The *Extended Play* release featured a front cover from The Stooges' US homecoming gig at Detroit Ford Auditorium, 27 March 1973. Lester Bangs in *Creem* later said it was 'the greatest show many ever saw them do.' *(Easy Action / Robert Matheu of Creem)*

Left: The 2016 *Gimme Danger* documentary by Jim Jarmusch featured a cover showing the band in front of a star-studded crowd at Max's Kansas City, New York, July-August 1973. *(Amazon Studies and Magnolia Pictures)*

Above: A shot of Iggy in September 1973 during a five-night stand at the Whisky A Go Go in Los Angeles, where The Stooges performed numerous times between June and October 1973. *(Heather Harris)*

Left: James Williamson, Iggy and Scott Thurston at Whisky A Go Go, September 1973. 'It was a tremendously powerful, exciting show,' said musician and writer Don Waller. 'We just kept going back. We'd get out of there and go home, go to sleep, go to work, and then we'd get out of work and drive back up to Hollywood and sit outside the Whisky.'
(Heather Harris)

Right: St. Louis American Theatre, 18 August 1973.
(Craig Petty)

Right: Iggy on stage somewhere in the US in the autumn 1973. Some of the 1973 concerts they played were excellent, justifying many rock critics' belief that Iggy and the band were among the most exciting performers around. *(PN collection)*

Below: Backbending at Academy of Music, New York, 31 December 1973, a show which also featured Kiss, Teenage Lust and headliners Blue Oyster Cult. At one point during the concert, Iggy fell off the ramp into the photographers' pit, 15 feet downward, luckily being caught by a roadie. 'I'd just drunk a whole quart of vodka and been given some Quaaludes, I think,' Iggy said. *(unidentified photographer)*

Above: Iggy and James Williamson on tour in the US, autumn 1973. Iggy's behavior both on and off stage became increasingly unreliable over the course of touring in 1973-74. 'I realized the quality was about to taper off,' said Iggy. 'Not that the quality ever got that high, but there were some interesting, some good things about those gigs.' *(PN collection)*

Right: Iggy with James Williamson in the background, early 1974. Ron Asheton described the tour as 'never-ending torture,' as drugs increasingly impaired the performances. *(PN collection)*

Left: Iggy and Ron Asheton at Victory Burlesque, Toronto, 25 January, two weeks before The Stooges were laid to rest. *(John Catto)*

Below: James Williamson at Victory Burlesque, Toronto, 25 January 1974. 'That band could have been a real (success) and… instead, it was becoming a flop,' remarked James. *(John Catto)*

This page: Advertisements for miscellaneous 1973-74 concerts by The Stooges.

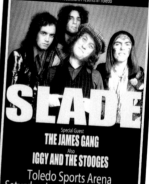

Howard Stein Presents

At The **ACADEMY OF MUSIC**
NEW YEARS EVE
December 31 at 8 and 11:30 P.M.

BLUE OYSTER CULT
TEENAGE LUST
SPECIAL GUEST STAR
IGGY POP

SCOTT PIERING PRESENTS

IGGY and the **STOOGES**
The TUBES
FRI and SAT JAN 11 & 12
8 PM – 2 AM
BIMBO
1025 COLUMBUS
ADULTS ONLY!!
No One Under 21 Ad
TICKETS · S

THE RAW POWER OF
IGGY AND THE STOOGES
MONDAY
January 21
Tickets · $3
now on sale
in the lounge

THE **BREWERY**
MSU WEST

COMING! FRI. & SAT., OCT. 5-6
IGGY AND THE STOOGES
at the
MICHIGAN PALACE
ALL SEATS $5.00
(Limited Box Seats $6.00)

Belkin Productions Presents in Toledo

SLADE
Special Guest
THE JAMES GANG
Also
IGGY AND THE STOOGES
Toledo Sports Arena
Saturday January 19th 8:00pm
$4.50 Advance $5.50 Day Of Show
All Seats Reserved

IN CONCERT AT KE_____ CENTER
MOTT THE HOOPLE
plus IGGY & THE STOOGES
Sun., Aug. 19, 8:30 p.m.
Tickets $4.00, $5.00, $6.00:
Available at Kennedy Ctr. Box Office, all Ticketron locations including Sears, Woodies, AAA and at The Bethesda Holiday Inn.
Ticket Info. 338-5992.

THE BIGGEST
7 Hours of Rock and Roll!

WNAP & SUNSHINE
PRESENTS
Second Annual Holiday Festival

RARE EARTH
REO
SPEEDWAGON
IGGY and The STOOGES
MIKE BLOOMFIELD BAND
BLUE OYSTER CULT
CAPTAIN BEYOND
and the return of Santa Claus
Surprises for One and All
Plus More
Sat., Dec. 29th—5 P.M.
Doors Open at 4 P.M.
INDIANAPOLIS
CONVENTION CENTER
Tickets $5.75 Advance

Jet Set Enterprises Presents
J. Geils Band
With Special Guest Spooky Tooth
and extra added attraction Iggy & The Stooges
FRIDAY, DEC. 7
Jacksonville Coliseum
8:00 P.M. .... $5 Per Ticket
Advance Tickets by Mail: send money

IN CONCERT FRI. OCT. 5
SAT. OCT. 6
8 PM **MICHIGAN PALACE**
THE BIZARRE
IGGY AND THE STOOGES
plus **WHITE WITCH**
& Public Foot Roman
ALL SEATS $5.00   phone 963-4624
ADVANCE TICKET SALE AT ALL J.L. HUDSONS
Also at Michigan Palace Night of Conc

any financial, emotional, and professional resources at the time. I could do nothing for him.'

The next day, Iggy met with Bowie and Defries over breakfast at the Warwick Hotel, and they drew up plans for Iggy. He would continue his methadone treatment in Ann Arbor, and when he was back in shape, Defries would try to get him a record contract. Iggy signed a management contract with Defries, who represented Laurence Myers' Gem. They decided that Iggy should go to England to record an album. 'They didn't want The Stooges on their hands,' said Iggy. 'But I figured I could sneak them in later. Their idea was basically to get this charismatic performer away from his ridiculous friends and his awful, noisy music and get him playing with some nice English boys.'

Defries was back in New York in late 1971 or early 1972. He sent for Iggy from Ann Arbor and arranged for him to stay at the Warwick Hotel. Iggy and Defries visited CBS Records' head Clive Davis. 'I met Clive Davis once and I think he just wanted to get me outta the office,' Iggy recalled of the meeting, which has taken on a life of its own in Stooges lore, as Iggy has talked about how he impressed Davis by singing a bit of 'The Shadow Of Your Smile.' Iggy attributed Davis' interest in signing him to missing out on signing David Bowie: 'That's what happened. He passed on David Bowie, realized his error, and what an exec does then ... it makes him very liable to pick up another act by the same manager, so you can say you were involved in the general movement.' Working with Defries, Zanetta was present at the meeting: 'When we walked in, it felt like it was a done deal already, that it had already been sorted out between Defries and Clive Davis.' The two-album record deal was between CBS Records and Gem Music Productions, which would 'furnish the services of' Iggy Pop, according to the contract.

While in New York, Zanetta took Iggy shopping for a pair of leather pants (including the silver ones seen on the *Raw Power* cover) and a hat: 'We went to some shops on Madison Avenue. Tony gave us $400–500 and we spent the whole $400 in the first half-hour on two pairs of pants! The way Defries acted, we thought he had millions and millions of dollars. We spent the $400–500; that was a lot of money to both of us. We didn't know each other so well, so were both pretending that it wasn't.'

Upon his return to Ann Arbor, Iggy told James about the plans, and they 'formed a handshake pact' to continue working together: 'I wanted to build a band around Williamson. The disintegration of The Stooges at that point was also, at least in my mind, a reflection of the germinal growth of what I wanted to do with James Williamson. Because we knew we could do something better.' Iggy did not believe Ron was ambitious enough and wanted to take the band in another direction with James. Ron admitted that 'James was a better songwriter and a more accomplished guitarist.' According to James, 'Ronnie had become very apathetic and lethargic and he smoked a lot of weed. He just liked to sit around and smoke weed. He wasn't gonna be the guy who was gonna make the next record for Iggy. Iggy's a very ambitious guy and he needs someone that can be the engine of the music he's gonna make, and he didn't see Ron as that guy, and I guess he saw me as that guy. I certainly wanted to make an album.'

Iggy convinced Defries of the necessity of bringing James with him to England: 'I called England to tell Defries he had to bring two of us, to which he said, "Oh. So now there are two of you?". And I was like, "Oh shit, I don't think he likes this." But I just took a deep breath, pinned him back down. I said, "Yeah, that's what we gotta do".' Iggy told Ron about his plans at a party in Ann Arbor. Ron was upset when he learned about his intention to form a new band without himself or Scott: 'I saw him (Iggy) at a party and he offhandedly said, "Oh, yeah, by the way, James and I are leaving for England in a couple of days." It was like someone just hit me over the head with a baseball bat. He didn't even tell us. If I hadn't gone to that party, I would've probably read about it in a magazine or something. I'm thinking, "Thanks a lot, pal. You shit on your two fucking buddies who started the band". I was shattered.'

Tuesday, 13 April 1971: Vanity Ballroom, Detroit, MI

Following a four-month break, the reformed Stooges returned to live work. The band now featured Iggy along with Ron Asheton and James Williamson on guitars, Jimmy Recca on bass and Scott Asheton on drums. The Vanity Ballroom concert also included MC5, Jam Band, Frut and Werks. Built in 1929, Vanity Ballroom was a beautiful art deco-style building with an Aztec theme.

The Vanity Ballroom gig featured a 43-minute set: 'I Got A Right,' 'You Don't Want My Name,' 'Fresh Rag,' 'Black Like Me,' 'Big Time Bum' and 'Do You Want My Love?' Danny Fields' cassette recording of the show was released in 2009 on Easy Action's *You Want My Action* box set.

Jimmy Recca was excited to make his debut with the band: 'It was a homecoming for me because everybody I knew in Detroit, local musicians, kids I grew up with, was there cheering me on. Now they had something to really like The Stooges for – that I was in the band! Every friend that I knew came to see me at that show, so it was a big thing for me.'

Stooges fan, Bill W. Ten Eyck, recalled the show: 'Chris Huntoon and I went to the grand opening of the Vanity Ballroom to see The Stooges on April 13 1971. Like the Grande Ballroom, the venue was on the second floor, and we waited in line to get in on the stairs. We got there a little late and had to sit on the floor center-stage halfway back. Iggy was doing his thing on the floor in front and we wanted to see better. "Iggy's afraid to come more than 20 feet from the stage", I yelled. "Who said that! Who said that!" Iggy yelled into the mic. We were both nervous that someone would point me out and then we would be in for trouble, but the younger crowd sitting around us did not snitch. The next thing we knew, Iggy grabbed the microphone stand, waded out into the crowd, and proceeded to set up right in front of Chris and I! It was a moment in Rock History! Chris even remembers sweat spraying on us as he danced three feet away. The band was playing a new song, a wicked version of "Who Do You Love?" when the rhythm section broke down and the song stopped. Iggy berated the new musicians, and the show degenerated into another practice session on stage.'

New York rock journalist, Lisa Robinson, was present to report for *RPM*: 'I realized just how much I'd missed the band, as they went into their super loud, high energy set. All new material – and it sounded great. Two songs more that stood out especially were "1971" (not clear which song she is referring to) and "Black Like Me." One of these should be a single.' She met up with Iggy after the show and he 'was talking about how this band is the most musical he's played with.'

Saturday, 17 April 1971: Opera House, Chicago, IL

The show was headlined by Alice Cooper, with Jam Band appearing first on the bill. The Stooges were billed as 'the Stooges with Iggy Pop.' Having opened many shows for The Stooges in the preceding years, Alice Cooper's popularity had now surpassed The Stooges.' Danny Fields said, 'It would come showtime and there would be the boys in Alice's band looking for a mirror to put on eye make-up, you know being real professional, and then we'd have to go look for Iggy. And I'd find him lying there, down around the toilet bowl with a spike in his arm. I'd have to pull it out, with blood spurting all over the place, and I'd be slapping his face, saying, "It's showtime!". I thought, "This band is in trouble if they can't whip themselves into shape to go on stage because they're too busy getting high."'

Despite Fields' reservations, Lisa Robinson of *RPM* was excited and believed Iggy and the band were even better than in Detroit: 'Iggy Pop jumped down into the orchestra pit and then climbed over that until he was halfway into the orchestra seats. In the midst of the Midwest, these perfectly archetypical Midwestern punks were alive and well and outrageous ... and it was fun to go to a concert for a change.' In contrast to Robinson, the Chicago press showed little enthusiasm for The Stooges, focusing mostly on Alice Cooper. The *Chicago Daily News'* Wayne Crawford complained that Iggy's 'old movements just can't feed the imagination anymore.' Al Rudis of the *Chicago Sun-Times* thought The Stooges were 'merely noisy' and 'without exciting music, Iggy's antics are doomed to frustration, no matter how loud the guitars.' Similarly, Lynn Van Matre of the *Chicago Tribune* said that 'while fascinating in a diseased sort of way for a while, Iggy soon gets terribly boring. His basic antics seem never to vary, and after a while, the self-indulgence, no matter how weird, begins to pall.'

The Stooges' performance also received a negative review in *Playboy*: 'After giving his crotch a couple of test shakes to make sure it was in proper working order, he launched the group into 50 minutes of the most earnestly awful Rolling Stones imitation we have ever heard. By the third number, we noticed that the pot smokers near us were toking down a little desperately, apparently in the vain hope of improving what they were hearing. The band, which knows at least three chords, was careful to use no more than two in any given song – and Iggy cooked along in the same spirit, rolling on stage, crawling down into the audience, flapping his legs and arms like a duck possessed. We were happy to see that his work permitted him to get so much exercise, but as the lady who was with us put it, "He's just like Mick Jagger – except he doesn't have any moves and he can't sing." We had to agree – and to be grateful that the audience didn't cheer hard enough to encourage an encore.'

Saturday, 24 April 1971: Palladium, Birmingham, MI
This concert was attended by 'probably one of the biggest crowds ever to pack into the Palladium,' according to the *Ann Arbor Sun*. The Stooges' performance was recorded by some guys who formed the Stooges-influenced band, The Punks, in the Detroit suburb of Waterford in 1973. The band learned a few of the songs from the tape, which they mixed in with their original material during shows. The band later evolved into Matt Gimmick, which recorded and released their versions of 'You Don't Want My Name' (as 'Ya Don't Want My Name') and 'Fresh Rag' (as 'Rag') on their *Detroit Renaissance '79* EP in 1979. The cassette containing The Stooges' concert has been lost to the ages. Matt Gimmick called it a day in the early 1980s.

Saturday, 1 May 1971: Dewey's, Madison, WI
Nothing is known about this show, but it was listed in the *Post-Crescent*: an Appleton, Wisconsin, newspaper.

May 1971: Grand Valley Armory, Grand Rapids, MI
The date and venue have not been verified. It could have been Kentwood Memorial Hall because it also staged rock concerts at the time.

Wednesday, 5 May 1971: Psyche-Dilly Lounge, McKees Rocks, PA
Nothing is known about this show. McKees Rocks (also known as 'The Rocks') is a small town just outside Pittsburgh. The club itself, which had hosted MC5 and the Amboy Dukes in the two months preceding the Stooges appearance, started advertising live music in mid-1967 and ceased as a venue under this name in December 1971, when it reopened as The Carnival, although still promoting rock bands.

Friday, 7 May 1971: Auditorium, Saginaw, MI
No details about this show are known. It has not been verified that the venue was the 3,000-capacity Saginaw Auditorium, but many acts played there at the time, which makes it likely that The Stooges did too.

Sunday, 9 May 1971: The Depot, Minneapolis, MN

The band was billed as 'Iggy and the Stooges.' *Minneapolis Star* reported that they replaced Little Richard, who had canceled his tour. Denny Burt, writing for the *Winona Daily News*, was captivated by Iggy: 'When Iggy's not gyrating like limbs at the end of a high wire, he flops on the floor, in people's laps, on tables, whatever's handy and might work. Iggy's probably the last of the great body singers, carried to a logical and absurd conclusion.' Calling The Stooges' two albums 'horrible,' the writer thought the live format was The Stooges' strength: 'Save your money for the real thing. They're nothing without their spectacle, and everything imaginable with it.' Michael Anthony in *Minneapolis Tribune* believed Iggy made 'Mick Jagger look like Rudy Vallee. He minces, prances, crawls on the floor, and turns his long pouting lips to the audience. He works mainly in the audience, falling, shoving, jumping on the back bar and up onto the balcony, and occasionally singing.' The only number Anthony recognized was *Fun House's* 'Dirt,' but it is questionable whether it was played.

Interestingly, Morris Day of The Time – a funk/R&B act masterminded by Prince – mentioned seeing The Stooges play at The Depot in his 2019 autobiography, *On Time – A Princely Life in Funk*. The Depot would later evolve into Uncle Sam's in 1972, and the club became First Avenue in 1982. The venue was put at the forefront of the Minneapolis music scene when Prince used it for several scenes in *Purple Rain* in 1984.

Wednesday, 12 May 1971: Arena, Richmond, VA

Nothing is known about this show. A gig planned for the next day, 13 May, at Northport High School, Long Island, New York, was canceled at the last minute by the authorities of the school, who were partially concerned about Iggy's reputation for wild antics, but mostly because a concert by the group, Shocking Blue, had lost money for the student council the previous year. Brownsville Station was planned as the opening act.

Friday and Saturday, 14 and 15 May 1971: Electric Circus, New York, NY

The Stooges returned to New York for two gigs at Electric Circus. There was no support act. Hell's Angels members surrounded the stage, acting as if they were security and making it difficult for photographers to shoot the concert. The Stooges opened the Electric Circus residency by giving an inspired 45-minute performance. The set featured 'I Got A Right' (aborted attempt), 'I Got A Right,' 'You Don't Want My Name,' 'The Shadow Of Your Smile' (briefly, Iggy a cappella), 'Fresh Rag,' 'Black Like Me,' 'Big Time Bum' and 'Do You Want My Love?' Lenny Kaye's review of *Raw Power* in 1973 referred to this gig and reported that, as the crowd applauded at the set's conclusion, Iggy recited a few lines from the 1931 film *Dracula* (directed by Tod Browning and starring Bela Lugosi as Count Dracula): 'Flies, big juicy flies, and spiders!' However, all that can heard on the recording is Iggy muttering, 'The little white face, getting closer and closer... The children of the night...' before the tape runs out.

Labeling The Stooges 'the darlings of the avant-garde this year,' the review by Lillian Roxon in the *Sydney Morning Herald* (Australia) praised Iggy and the band: 'His newly-augmented band, rather menacing in leather and dark glasses, backed him with an even stronger sound than in the past. The fans who crowded the *Circus* screamed and whistled nonstop throughout the entire performance, especially when he strutted around the stage Mick-Jagger-fashion, made faces at the audience and, some insist, spat at the front row.'

Fields threw a party after the first show, inviting Andy Warhol, Lillian Roxon, Germaine Greer (Australian author, then famous for the 1970 book, *The Female Eunuch*, dedicated to Roxon), as well as Tony Zanetta, Jamie Andrews, Cyrinda Foxe and other members of the cast of *Pork* – a play based on Andy Warhol's taped phone conversations. Zanetta recalled, 'It was a big party, and somebody was passing out these little pills, some kind of Spanish pill. Everyone was taking them. They were either Quaaludes or Mandrax, but they made everybody sick because people were throwing up. It was disgusting. That was my introduction to Jim.'

The second Electric Circus show was a different affair from the first night. The concert was delayed because Iggy did not want to perform until he had injected heroin backstage. When he finally came onstage, he was glassy-eyed, and his speech was somewhat slurry. The 41-minute set featured the same songs as the previous night, although Iggy did not sing 'The Shadow Of Your Smile,' and the band nailed 'I Got A Right' on their first attempt. After 'Fresh Rag,' Iggy went behind one of the amplifiers to throw up, although it was not much more than a retch despite wildly exaggerated reports that he threw up on the audience. Leee Black Childers remembered, 'Iggy had gotten an outrageous reputation for self-destruction and being a junkie onstage. Geri Miller was right down in the front again. She had this horrible little voice and she was right down in the front screaming, "Throw up! Throw up! When are you gonna throw up?". And he did! He threw up. Iggy always satisfied his audience.' According to future Stooges soundman Bob Czaykowski: 'I saw them playing at the "Puke Show" where he threw up. That was a pretty good show before he got sick. That's another concert where people are like ... it gets bigger from the retelling. I don't remember it being such a big deal. The guy was obviously loaded.'

The review in *Circus* of the two concerts was positive: 'The Stooges returned to New York triumphantly a short time ago and for two nights at the Electric Circus, the band excelled. Iggy seemed to have a little trouble adjusting to the Circus' unique audience the first night, but by the second, he was in top form, delivering the kind of legendary rock performance that he is famous for.' The *Circus* critic noted that nothing was played from *The Stooges* or *Fun House*, but the writer believed the new material 'was more tuneful and striking than anything he's done before. The band was impeccable as it ground out the incredible high energy wall of sound rhythm that fits so well next to Iggy's singing. Both nights he walked on the audience's hands. In fact, he spent almost half of the concert within the grasp of the audience.'

Dee Dee Ramone of the Ramones recounted in his autobiography *Poison Heart* how he and his friends would listen to their tape recordings of the Electric Circus gigs over and over in their car. The shows were also taped by Danny Fields, whose recordings emerged in 2009 on the *You Want My Action* box set. The band did a photo shoot with Peter Hujar after the second concert, as featured in Robert Matheu's biography of The Stooges. Photos by Lisa Gottlieb from the first of the two shows are also featured in Matheu's book.

Before the Electric Circus engagement, Iggy and Scott took Ron's vintage Stratocaster guitar and traded it for 50 dollars' worth of heroin. Ron recalled, 'They said it got ripped off. I was heartbroken, man. Years later, my brother, Scott, told me what really happened. Yeah, by the time of the Electric Circus gigs, I'd given up.'

Sunday, 16 May 1971: Creelman Hall, University of Guelph, Canada

This was a sparsely-attended gig. The band and crew drank tequila before the show, to the extent that one of the lighting guys actually passed out during the set, splitting his head open. The concert finished earlier than expected because at one point the band was interrupted by the head of the university, who lived nearby and could not sleep due to the loud music.

Wednesday, 19 May 1971: Painter's Mill, Ownings Mill, MD

After playing this concert in Ownings Mill, which is close to Baltimore, Scott Asheton drove the band's rented equipment truck into a bridge on the way to the next concert – at Eastown Theater in Detroit, 21 May – ruining the truck and $3,000 in band equipment. Scott ended up in hospital with two of the band's roadies. Ron Asheton explained: 'We had a rented U-haul truck for taking the equipment. My brother says he wants to go along. He wants to go with the roadies. He loves to drive, so they let him drive the truck. So right here in Ann Arbor on Washington St., there's a train trestle that goes across, though this one is real small and it's posted at a certain height. He wasn't paying attention. He was doing about 35 mph, went under the bridge and "bam," took the top off the truck.'

'Nobody told me it was a twelve-foot-six truck and a ten-foot-six bridge,' said Scott. 'I got thrown out of the truck about 15 yards. One guy hit the dashboard and knocked all his teeth out, he was unconscious, and the other guy hit the windshield, which put a big gash in his head and he was wandering around with blood all over his face. I thought the other guy was dead. I was going, "Oh no," still not knowing what the hell happened, and then I turned around and saw that the truck didn't fit under the bridge. So they made the gig that night without me. They had to put six stitches in my chin, but what I'll never forget is that stitch they put in my tongue. It was the worst pain I ever had in my whole life. I thought I was gonna snap. I thought I was just gonna lose it. You can look at the bridge even now, and you can tell. That bridge is still fucked up.'

'They destroyed the truck, destroyed the musical instruments, which were rented, and destroyed the bridge,' Danny Fields recalled. 'So they were being sued by the owners of the truck, the owners of the instruments, and the city of Ann Arbor. And they wanted to know, at four o'clock in the morning, what was I gonna do about that. What was I gonna do about it? I was gonna go back to sleep.'

The *Ann Arbor Sun* wrote about what happened: 'While on the road last week, the Stooges had a bad accident that set them back temporarily, but they'll be kicking them out this weekend at the Tumbleweed (Walled Lake). Their 16-foot equipment truck didn't make it under a 14-foot bridge, and drummer Scott Asheton was injured, but not seriously. At least not as seriously as the truck, which had the top half ripped away.'

Saturday, 22 May 1971: Eastown Theater, Detroit, MI

Due to the truck accident, The Stooges only played the second of two advertised shows at the Eastown Theater. The gig on Friday, 21 May, was canceled. With Scott in hospital, Iggy called up former Stooge, Steve Mackay, to play drums. Steve practiced with Iggy, Ron and James in the afternoon before the concert: 'I got an amplifier in front of me and a pair of drumsticks. I'm tapping out a beat and it's fine, "That's fine, OK!". So we get there, and I'm not that good a drummer to know I have to readjust all these drums so I can play; they're all set up for Scottie. No ride cymbal, just crash cymbal. He'd play ride on the crash; that's part of his style.'

Steve was a good drummer, but the concert turned out to be a shambles, with Iggy repeatedly stopping Steve to instruct him how to play the beat. According to Steve, 'I made it through three or four songs unassisted, but he was stopping the songs and restarting the songs and showed me the beat to play. Part of me was feeling bad about it, the other part was, "That ain't what we played this afternoon, motherfucker. You thought it was fine on top of the amplifier". But you can't argue at a point like that. This is the crowd, the Eastown in Detroit, they're going "Come on Iggy, let's see ya puke, come on motherfucking junkie, fuck you asshole." That was going on. I lasted the whole set; I did not leave my seat for the whole fuckin' set. There were some times where I would get it right enough that it didn't fuck them up too bad. It wasn't like I wasn't keeping the beat. Maybe I wasn't playing the right one ... I'd never heard any of the songs; it was all new material!'

Jimmy Recca remembered the concert: 'He gets up there onstage, and in our first song, he just falls apart, he's not there. I'm looking over, and I look at James, and James just gives me that silly smirk. I couldn't hear the hysterical laughter that goes underneath that smirk, and I look like a camera's lens opens up the iris, and who's standing right behind him in the wings, just having a ball with it, but Michael Bruce and Glen Buxton from Alice Cooper's band. At the Eastown, I walked off the stage, and Glen and Michael told me, "Man, you gotta go back!". I turn around and Iggy's going, "Come on!" and I'm like, "Oh, Jesus, man. Go back out there and take your licks". But I was a fan of those guys in the Alice Cooper band. Those guys were like my older brothers; I love those guys. But they gave me shit: "You're gonna have one distinction. They'll always remember you for this". Thanks, guys.'

'It was terrible because he (Steve) just stiffened up,' said Ron, who could see the humor in the situation. 'I looked around, he was beet red, spotlights on him, he's just like ... arms of lead. It was disastrous, but it was funny. I was never at first so embarrassed, mad, then laughing because Iggy's going, "Steve, one, two, just the beat, one, two, three, four...". We stopped songs; the crowd's going, "Ooooh, aaaaah...". I couldn't have felt worse than Steve. On the way back... complete silence in the car. Steve wouldn't take his pay and I just started laughing. I couldn't stop laughing.'

The band had their next concert scheduled for 23 May at the Taft Theatre, Cincinnati, Ohio, but it was canceled to allow Scott's wounds to heal. A few days later, Scott was back in action for the next concert in St. Louis.

Wednesday, 26 May 1971: Music Palace, St. Louis, MO

The Stooges were in St. Louis but did not play this concert because the band's equipment had not arrived at the venue. Road manager Eric Haddix had contracted hepatitis and asked a friend to bring the equipment to St. Louis, but he failed to make it on time.

Jimmy Recca was sent out on stage to explain to the crowd of around 700 people why they could not perform: 'The equipment never showed up, so they were stomping, going "Iggy! Iggy! Iggy! Stooges!". So, what were we gonna do? The guy comes back, the fucking fire marshal's there, cops are all out there, and he said, "Somebody's got to go out there and talk to this crowd before they tear the place apart!". And nobody was going to do it. So the new guy in the band gets to go do this "public relations" thing. "Go introduce yourself!". I'm out there, and I think I incited the riot. I saw some state trooper knocking some kid around and I said, "Y'know, that ain't cool," and then they turned the lights on, and I said, "If you keep the lights on, we'll *never* come out," and when I said that, the whole crowd went nuts. They fucking started sailing chairs, and Missouri state troopers came flying in there and started beating everybody. They were rushing the stage and they pulled me off and took me back to the room. I was like, "Did I do good?"'

Despite Recca's best efforts, the resulting fracas ended with 22 people being arrested for peace disturbance. In their report, *St. Louis Post-Dispatch* quoted one of the audience members, Betsy Harris: 'We were told that the Stooges would be half an hour late. Everybody was cool. Policemen, who were on the scene, were asked to leave by promoters of the concert. They began shoving people out of the door and blocking other exits.'

Thursday, 27 May 1971: The Factory, St. Charles, MO

This hastily-arranged concert replaced the scheduled gig for St. Louis' Music Palace the previous day. The Factory was a 'terrible little stage at a horrible place,' according to Ron Asheton. The show featured the same six songs played previously on the 1971 tour: 'I Got A Right,' 'You Don't Want My Name,' 'Fresh Rag,' 'Black Like Me,' 'Big Time Bum' and 'Do You Want My Love?' The gig was recorded by an audience member and later released on *You Want My Action*. The concert was curtailed after 40 minutes when Iggy accidentally hit Ron in the head with his microphone. Iggy told the crowd that they were unable to finish the show because Ron needed medical attention. Afterward, Iggy hung out in the lobby and talked to people because the band felt bad about cutting the show short.

As a result of the shortened set and the additional costs caused by the rescheduled show, the promoter withheld the money and did not pay the band. To make matters worse, The Stooges discovered that someone had taken their rented car, leaving them trapped in St. Louis without money and mode of transport, with a scheduled concert at the Tumbleweed in Walled Lake, Michigan (28 May). 'The guy took our rent-a-car before the show was over, split with the money and the car he rented for us,' said James Williamson. 'And that night, we had to be at another place to do a show where we were getting a lot of money. We couldn't make the show.' They called Danny Fields, asking him to wire them money so they could return, but it was too late, and they missed the next gig. Said roadie, Bill Cheatham; 'That was a mess, it was a disastrous tour. The guy who promoted the show fucked us royally, never paid us. Then we couldn't get the plane out for our next job in Michigan. So we lost tons of money.'

Saturday, 29 May 1971: Sports Arena, Toledo, OH

This was the last regular gig The Stooges played in 1971 and their last US gig for almost two years, as Iggy and James left the band later in the summer when Elektra did not pick up the option for a third album. The Stooges topped the bill over The Frut, The Sunday Funnies and Bob Seger, in an event that was billed as 'People's Concert #1.' It was the Stooges' fourth concert at the venue, as they also performed there in 1969 and twice in 1970.

Stooges fan, Chazz Avery, recollected the show: 'This was my first concert ever and, at 14 years old, I didn't know what to expect. I was the first, but my close friends soon followed suit to get *Fun House*, prompted by reports in *Creem, Circus* and *Rolling Stone* of Iggy's over-the-top stage antics. By the time of this show, we were fully entrenched in Stoogeland. I remember our reaction to seeing the advertisement in the newspaper. We 'had' to see this show. My mother took me and three friends to the show (she didn't come in). I took a recorder but had forgotten the damn batteries. Believe me, I've 'really' been kicking myself in the ass ever since. I still vividly remember my dismay when I discovered no batteries.'

Said Avery; 'The opening bands, The Frut and The Sunday Funnies were quite enjoyable but fairly generic local bands. Bob Seger was solo with an acoustic guitar and a mic under his platform, which he tapped his foot on for beat, or he played a couple of songs on piano. Seger was very good but not quite what we had expected after growing up listening to The Bob Seger System. And his solo set was quite a contrast to what was about to follow. Anyway, it seemed forever for The Stooges to take the stage. Finally, there they were. I easily recognized Ron (I think he had Nazi stuff on) and Scott. I thought Recca was Dave, but who the hell is this fifth guy? As Iggy entered the stage a few minutes after the band, 'he was silver' and looked totally alien. We thought it was pretty fuckin' cool. They seemed to take a while to get started. Meanwhile, Iggy taunted the audience with gestures and words. Finally, the music started. We didn't recognize the first song (we were expecting to hear the first two albums). We rightly assumed they had written some new songs since *Fun House*, and we'd probably hear old stuff later in the set. However, in the end, we realized we didn't recognize any of the songs. I also remember that the songs were a bit repetitive and rambling. There was also a lot of time between songs.'

Avery continued, 'I remember Iggy writhed and bounded around the stage. He was in the audience at least once. As teenage boys, we were slightly disappointed we didn't see the bloodletting we had read about, but we figured he can't be doing that shit all the time. The music churned and oozed cool. The dual guitar play was great. I don't remember specifics but do recall what we thought and talked about afterward. We were almost speechless. We all absolutely loved the show and couldn't stop talking about it afterward. I can imagine the stuff my mother had to listen to on the way back home.'

Several further 1971 gigs were canceled, including a festival performance, Soundstorm '71, East Coast First Great Lighter Than Air Fair, at Monroe Estates in Pittsburgh, Pennsylvania, 30–31 May 1971. Also canceled were advertised concerts on 26 June at Pilgrimage Theater, Hollywood, California, 16 July at the Palladium, Hollywood, California, and 7 August at the Pavilion, Wampler's Lake, Michigan.

Saturday, 24 July 1971: Pavilion, Wampler's Lake, MI

This show was played without Iggy and James. Ron and Scott Asheton, together with Jimmy Recca, played a short set, with Jimmy singing a couple of songs. A guy from the audience named Steve Richards filled in for Iggy during part of the show. Ron said, 'We went on and explained to the crowd that Iggy quit the group. They were disappointed, but ironically the thing turned into an amateur night. There was a kid about 15 years old in the audience who was really into Iggy and imitated him perfectly, even down to hitting me in the knee with the mic stand, just like Iggy used to do. So this kid filled in for Iggy the entire show.' Jimmy recalled: 'I think I started to sing a couple of songs, then we started doing this other thing that was kind of like a Stooge jam, I think it was like "No Fun" or something like that, and there was this guy down in the crowd who was just standing there singing every song, and when we stopped jamming for a second, Ron said, "Anybody who wants to come up and thinks they can be Iggy...". And this cat was already up there. He got up there, didn't sing much, just did a bunch of contortions, but for what he did, man, he should have got paid too.'

Two numbers from this gig emerged on the *You Want My Action* box set: an instrumental jam (often referred to as 'Ron's Jam') and 'What You Gonna Do?' (tentative title).

1972

With The Stooges no more, Iggy and James Williamson left for London in mid-February 1972 to recruit musicians for a new band and record an album for CBS Records. Iggy had a new name for the band in mind: The Users. 'I wanted to call it that back when we were with MainMan, but Defries vetoed it,' Iggy said. Iggy and James were put into a nice, small house in St. John's Wood, London, which belonged to Laurence Myers, the head of Gem: the company for which Tony Defries was an employee. Defries had brought David Bowie to Gem with a promise of a 20% ownership 'if everything worked out,' according to Myers. Defries had ambitions to achieve world domination with his stable of artists, which included Bowie, Iggy, Mott the Hoople and Dana Gillespie, and he aimed to surround them with the aura of major stars, regardless of their commercial status. However, Defries' plans clashed with Myers' more traditional business-like approach to management. Later in the year, Myers and Defries agreed to end their association, and Defries went alone under the name MainMan, to which Gem assigned all the rights that it had in the artists Defries had recruited. In the summer of 1972, Defries opened MainMan offices in London and New York.

Iggy and James were 'parachuted into the ground zero of glam,' recalled James. They attended a concert by Marc Bolan's T.Rex at Wembley Empire Pool, 18 March 1972 (filmed as *Born To Boogie*, directed by Ringo Starr), and were amazed by the audience adulation. 'We were extremely impressed with Marc Bolan,' said James. 'It was like "Holy Jeesuz, it's like The Beatles again." It really was like that over there. So it was like, "Let's get some of this".' Bolan was at the vanguard of a loosely-defined genre of glam or glitter rock, which attracted a new generation of teenagers who were coming of age in the early 1970s. The glam artists were image-conscious and favored showmanship over the earnest artistry of the late-'60s hippy-era rock. Suddenly, both new and established artists camped up in glitter, satin, lamé and make-up: Bowie, Roxy Music, Elton John, Sweet and T. Rex. In many ways, glam represented a retreat from the political and collective ambitions of the 1960s in favor of individualized escape through stardom. Glam artists played around with gender conventions, dressing in outlandish, androgynous costumes and make-up, which were important reasons why glam never really caught on commercially in the US.

Meanwhile, Iggy and James moved into the Portobello Hotel in Notting Hill, as Myers said that he discovered 'burn marks on our carpet where he (Iggy) had made little fires' in his house. They did not last long at the Portobello Hotel, though, as Iggy complained about the 'little tiny basement rooms.' So after only a week, they were installed at the Royal Garden Hotel: a first-class hotel off Kensington High Street by Hyde Park. 'They put us in the honeymoon suite together, this two-room suite,' recalled James. 'Ig took the outer room and I took the room with the beds in it.' At this time, Iggy had a meeting with Bowie about the planned album. They agreed that Bowie would not produce it. 'We didn't want Bowie to produce us,' said James. 'We were adamant about that; we didn't want Bowie in the studio. We didn't want Bowie messing with our songs.' At a meeting with Bowie, Iggy politely declined his offer to produce the album: 'I had my vision, and his wasn't right for what I wanted.'

The search for musicians continued in London. Bowie proposed that they should seek out drummer Russell Hunter, or his later replacement, Twink, from Pink Fairies – a band that was active on the London underground and psychedelic scene. Other potential candidates were bass player Jim Avery and drummer Paul Olsen from World War Three – a London group labeled England's first punk band. However, Iggy and James were skeptical of working with any of the proposed musicians. James, in particular, was wary: 'The kinda guys that were around in those days were more from the... I don't know ... the Yes, kind of frilly shirt, long English hair and platforms era. It just wasn't us; it didn't make any sense to us because of the style we played.' In the end, no auditions were held during the time in London.

Realizing that they were wasting their time looking for British musicians, Iggy eventually called up Ron and Scott Asheton to ask them to join them in London. James recalled, 'We were watching television one night and I said to him (Iggy), "Hey, we know a rhythm section, why don't we call the Ashetons up and get 'em over here?". Ronnie is a great bass player, which is what he was when I first met him, and he was a great bass player in that line-up. Anyway, Ig agreed and called them up.' Iggy's version of the events was that the first idea was to recruit only Scott: 'Anyway, so I said, "Well if we're gonna get Scott, might as well get Ron", and he (James) didn't argue.'

The brothers were hesitant at first, feeling that they had been asked merely as a last resort when no other options were available. Said Ron, 'Iggy calls me up and goes, "We can't find any guys that are good enough on bass and drums." At first, I thought, "Well, fuck, thanks a lot, man! You're calling me out of desperation after you have tried out every limey that was available in England".' Ron felt slighted, considering himself primarily a guitarist: '"Eventually you'll switch over to guitar, we'll get another bass player." I wasn't thrilled, but I wanted to go to England to do something.' While initially disappointed, Ron swallowed his pride and told James that he would be 'the best bass player you've ever had.' James explained why two guitars would not work: 'Because of my style of guitar, there's not a lot of air for someone else to be there and fill in. We did it for a little while with the two-guitar line-up in the beginning, but that was mostly because we were playing those earlier Stooges-type tunes, which had room for that. Once I started writing the stuff for *Raw Power*, there was no room for anybody else. So that's why he stayed on bass and he did a great job but always resented it.'

The Asheton brothers arrived in London on 6 June 1972 and took up residence with Iggy and James in a small house on Seymour Walk in Chelsea/ Fulham that David Bowie's wife Angie had found for them, along with a cook.

The reformed Stooges immediately set about rehearsing at Underhill Studios, which were used by several Gem acts. They initially worked on numbers that they had played in 1971, such as 'I Got A Right,' and new material Iggy and James had written in London, including 'Gimme Some Skin,' 'I'm Sick Of You,' 'Scene Of The Crime' and 'Tight Pants.' The songs were not released on *Raw Power*, with the exception of 'Tight Pants,' which was re-recorded for the album as 'Shake Appeal.' The five songs emerged in 1977 on a Siamese Records single and a Bomp Records EP. Ron claimed to have song ideas that he wanted the band to work on, but the rehearsals made it clear that the new center of the band was the songwriting partnership of Iggy and James. This situation caused some antagonism to well up between Ron and James, yet they worked effectively together, and Ron had a high regard for James' songwriting.

Focusing their energy on the music, the London stay was a highly creative period for the Stooges. 'Those were the times when I matured as a guitarist and songwriter,' James reckoned. 'I think the hard work and long hours that we put in initially during the spring and summer of 1972, paid off for me and the rest of the band. We went through many different sessions and songwriting exercises, but ultimately it resulted in my "writing in the zone."' Ron also appreciated the discipline. 'It was a totally work-oriented situation,' according to Ron. 'There was no fooling around; we had schedules for rehearsals – all we did was rehearse every day up until the recording of the record.' With the Ashetons back in the fold, the band reverted back to referring to itself as The Stooges. 'Since it was now all the members of The Stooges, we just called it The Stooges, by default, I suppose,' said James. 'It wasn't planned, but all of us together, we were The Stooges.'

The band members had few distractions from the music in London. No one in the band was involved with any hard drugs during this period. 'It was pretty clean over there,' James observed. 'Near the end, Ronnie found some hash and we found out you could buy Codeine at the drug store. But we weren't druggies over there. It was beer-oriented stuff.' Ron concurred: 'No one was taking any drugs – that was the deal. It was a good chance for him (Iggy); he was working with Tony Defries and he's got a record deal with CBS, so you don't want to screw up – he'd already screwed his life up and he pulled himself out of that hole.' Still, Iggy had brought a supply with him, which he continued using in London: 'During the writing of *Raw Power*, those songs were written musically-speaking without the drugs, by a couple of junkies on a break, and we were using, after I got off the Dolophine from the pharmacist, I had a doctor – I think he was in Livonia – and he prescribed Valium and an anti-depressant for me.'

Billed as just Iggy Pop, The Stooges played a concert at King Sound on 15 July 1972. It was to be their only concert during the London period and their only show outside North America. Defries had flown in a dozen American journalists to see Bowie perform at the Aylesbury Friars earlier in the evening. The journalists would spend a weekend at the Inn on the Park in London and have an opportunity to meet Bowie, Iggy and Lou Reed (who played at King Sound the night before the Stooges' performance). Buses carried the journalists to London after Bowie's concert to watch Iggy and the Stooges' comeback concert. The next day, Defries organized a press conference for Bowie at the Dorchester Hotel, with Iggy and Lou Reed in attendance.

Later in July, Bowie and Defries were able to listen to some of the material Iggy and the band had put down on tape during the time in London. According to Iggy, Bowie believed they 'could do better,' while Defries told them that he was not going to present the recordings to CBS. Said James, 'MainMan turned up the nose at them (the songs) and said, "Keep trying boys."' However, the band also believed that they could improve on the initial material. 'All the *Raw Power* material was very fresh,' commented James. 'We went through the demo sessions and just didn't feel they were quite what we wanted, so we continued to write new material, and *Raw Power* gradually fell into place.'

Following months of songwriting and studio work in London, The Stooges were finally able to record the album at CBS Studios in London, between 10 September and 6 October 1972. 'The only reason *Raw Power* got made the way it did, was that David got quite popular and he got busy, and they quit paying attention to us and just let us go in and do our own thing in the studio,' James observed. Bowie and Defries left England for Bowie's first American tour. Iggy insisted on producing the album himself, a decision they would come to regret, as his lack of experience would ultimately compromise the sound. 'It was my first record, so I was deferring to Ig in the studio, and that's a bad thing to do,' James said. 'He thinks he knows this stuff and he's a very bossy guy, but he doesn't know squat. He's telling the engineer to do all this stuff that they did on *Fun House*, live things, and the poor guy is doing his best, but what can he do? He's gotta do what his customer wants him to do so.' Iggy would later take some of the blame for the problems: 'The *Raw Power* sessions didn't work because I was a poor communicator and I didn't understand tracking, and sometimes I only used eight tracks when there were like 16 or 24 available. My behavior was just insane and there is no excuse for it.'

Upon completion of *Raw Power* in October, Iggy returned to the US, initially staying with MainMan's entourage at the Beverly Hills Hotel when Bowie played concerts in Los Angeles and San Francisco. James, Ron and Scott left London shortly afterward, first going to Ann Arbor, before James joined Iggy in Los Angeles. 'We all had bungalows,' said Tony Zanetta, who was now employed by MainMan to head up their New York offices. 'There were 30 of us! Everyone was at the Beverly Hills Hotel. Iggy was really healthy. He was eating only vegetables; he was a vegetarian. No drugs. He was in a really good state of mind and he wanted to stay in California and bring his band over there.'

During a gap in Bowie's tour schedule, he went into Hollywood's Western Sound Studios to mix the *Raw Power* tapes – 24-25 October 1972 – with Iggy and James present in the studio. In early November, the Asheton brothers joined Iggy and James in Los Angeles. Tanned, with newly bleached hair and in better health than he had been in years, Iggy was planning Los Angeles as the center of the Stooges' next career phase. 'Iggy wanted to be there,' said Leee Black Childers. 'That was his pick. It was sunny; he could swim all the time.' As Bowie's entourage left to continue his American tour, The Stooges remained at the Beverly Hills Hotel, running up a huge bill. Defries instructed Childers – also now employed by MainMan and tasked with managing The Stooges' day-to-day affairs – to rent the band a house which would also function as MainMan's Los Angeles headquarters, enhancing the illusion of MainMan as an international entertainment conglomerate since they already had offices in New York and London.

Childers found the band several potential houses: 'But Iggy wouldn't settle on any of them. By his choice, he was going out in Beverly Hills Hotel limousines to look at the houses. It all went on the hotel bill.' Childers' friend, Cyrinda Foxe, eventually helped them locate a large, comfortable house on Torreyson Drive off Mulholland Drive in the fashionable Hollywood Hills area. Rented at $900 a month, the house was equipped with five bedrooms and floor-to-ceiling windows overlooking a large swimming pool. 'It was an incredible, beautiful, magic house,' said Childers. 'Right on top of the Hollywood Hills. From one window, you could see all of Burbank, and from another you could see all of L.A. It had a huge, huge swimming pool and absolute privacy. The house had to have a pool, that was a prerogative. It was a gorgeous place.' Childers arrived on Christmas Eve 1972 to live with The Stooges in the Hollywood Hills mansion. Using one of the rooms as his MainMan office, Childers' responsibility was to take care of rehearsals and report back to Defries in New York.

With management support, a record deal, and an album awaiting release, the future prospects for Iggy and the band seemed bright. They had gone 'from absolute poverty to the lap of luxury,' according to James. 'First time in L.A., I get picked up by a limo with Ig in the back, palm trees everywhere, beautiful summer day, what's not to like.' Ron also thrived and enjoyed being associated with MainMan, which he considered 'the hippest organization' at the time, as Defries kept them ensconced in the Hollywood Hills house: 'Happy and dumb, just stupid, in that luxury.'

Saturday, 15 July 1972: King Sound, London, UK

Billed as Iggy Pop ('ex Iggy and the Stooges'), King Sound played host to the only concert The Stooges performed during their stay in England. It was to be their only show outside America until the band reformed three decades later. Tickets cost just £1.00. The show was not attended by more than 200 people. The band now featured James Williamson on guitar, with Ron Asheton playing bass and Scott Asheton, drums.

King Sound was a new rock concert venue opened in 1972, housed in the King's Cross Cinema (later the Scala), near King's Cross railway station. The balcony of the venue was closed, and a special platform had been constructed for The Stooges, which extended out from the stage into the audience. Mick Rock was at hand to photograph the performance, as later featured on the *Raw Power* album sleeve, including the famous cover shot.

Iggy was dressed in silver leather trousers and had sprayed his hair a matching silver. He wore black lipstick and made-up eyes. James also put on make-up: 'We see all these people – Bolan and Bowie and everybody – and they're all wearing makeup. So there we are and we got to do a show and we said, "Maybe we should be wearing make-up too." We literally went out and got a box of a clown's make-up. If you look at us in those pictures, we both have this whiteface on. And Iggy's got black lipstick on.'

Scheduled to start at midnight, Iggy and the Stooges came on at 2 am. There was no dramatic entrance, as Iggy just walked onto the stage and stood looking at the audience while the band tuned up. After prowling over the stage in the first two numbers, Iggy decided to wander into the audience, followed where possible by the spotlight. He occasionally stopped to stare deep into people's eyes, talking about wanting to find something 'interesting' and calling the crowd hippies that did not inspire him. The concert was attended by a group of noisy skinhead types, who voiced their impatience during one of several breaks due to technical problems, which caused Iggy to respond, 'What did you say, you piece of shit,' as he advanced threateningly across the stage. During another break, Iggy sang an a cappella version of 'The Shadow Of Your Smile.' The Stooges then commenced another song, but halfway through, one of the amplifiers broke down, causing another long delay. Later in the show, the leader of the skinhead gang went down to the front of the stage to shout obscenities. This time, Iggy leaped across the stage to aim a boot in the guy's face. Roadies pounced on the guy and bundled him out of a side exit.

The Stooges' brief 40-minute set at King's Cross Cinema was comprised entirely of songs they had rehearsed and recorded in London during June and July 1972. Based on recollections from both band members and press reports, they most likely played 'I Got A Right,' 'Gimme Some Skin,' 'I'm Sick Of You,' and 'I'm Hungry,' which was a prototype for 'Penetration.' Nothing from *The Stooges* or *Fun House* was played. No audio or video recording from the gig is known to exist, so speculation about the precise setlist continues to this day.

The Stooges drew predominantly positive reviews, although it was obvious that Iggy's performance made many critics and audience members somewhat uneasy. Rosalind Russell described Iggy's actions in *Disc*: 'He slimed offstage and wound his way among a somewhat nervous audience, still screaming into his mike, and berated the people for being so apathetic. He wrapped himself around the barrier poles and hung there, "waiting for inspiration" before he would start singing again. Then he found a young lady in the audience. He held her by the hair and sang close to her face. His next victim was an embarrassed gentleman who was a little upset by Iggy sitting in his lap and playing with his hair. He utterly destroyed a rash soul who began to shout out suggestions by screaming back at him from the stage, then finally coming over to find the culprit. Everyone else laughed nervously, glad it wasn't them.'

Glenn O'Brien – who was among a group of journalists flown over from the US – reported for *Interview*, 'Iggy does several things London has never seen. He swings his microphone around his head in a big circle just like Roger Daltrey, but when Iggy wants it back, he lets it wrap around his neck. Iggy likes to visit with the audience. He likes to sing a song to a particular girl in the audience. He likes to grab her by the hair and shake her head like a handful of dice when he sings to her. But he'll settle for a boy. The show goes on.' Nick Kent concluded in *New Musical Express*: 'The total effect was more frightening than all the Alice Coopers and Clockwork Oranges put together, simply because these guys weren't joking.' Michael Oldfield of *Melody Maker* believed Iggy and the band were on the verge of the dangerous, which made him uncomfortable: 'It's like a flashback 200 years, to the times when the rich paid to go into insane asylums and see madmen go into convulsions.' Mick Rock admitted to being 'distinctly intimidated' as he photographed the show.

Kent later reflected on the concert: 'No one had ever witnessed anything like this in England before. The Who had been loud, anarchic-sounding and genuinely shocking as a live attraction once upon a time, but they'd never physically confronted their audiences in such an alarming fashion. Four years hence, UK crowds would become totally entranced by just this sort of spectacle, but in 1972 it was way too much, way too soon. The audience at the Stooges show looked genuinely traumatized by the end. As soon as Iggy had leaped off the stage and into the crowd, people generally scattered backward and stood close to the exit doors, peering nervously at the action and praying that the singer wouldn't come over and start tormenting them. At the same time, they couldn't keep their eyes off him, so it made for an interesting dynamic in the room, to say the least.'

In attendance at the King's Cross Cinema were several aspiring rock musicians, who would go on to become highly influential in the British punk rock movement that exploded a few years later, including Joe Strummer (The Clash), Johnny Rotten (The Sex Pistols) and Siouxsie Sioux (Siouxsie and the Banshees). The concert has been called the birth of British punk rock. Nick Kent opinioned, 'Iggy and the Stooges invented punk rock just like James Brown and the Famous Flames created funk. They were the first and they were the best. Many self-styled punk experts have since come forward to chronicle the genre in lofty tomes, but unless you were one of those 200 jittery punters watching the Stooges' only European show in the summer of '72, you weren't there at the real beginning and don't really know what you're talking about.' Iggy stated, 'That show changed the history of English music because of who was there. People checked us out and realized we had changed the playing field for what was possible.'

1973–1974

Raw Power was released in late March 1973 in the US, to glowing reviews by the band's many followers in the music press, including Lenny Kaye (*Rolling Stone*), Dave Marsh (*Creem*), Ben Edmonds (*Phonograph Record Magazine*) and Lester Bangs (*Stereo Review*). Although David Bowie's magic touch had worked wonders for Lou Reed and Mott The Hoople, *Raw Power* was too uncompromising for a wider, mainstream audience and did not repeat their commercial success. It reached number 183 in the US and failed to chart in the UK. 'Now, of course, some people say that they like that album, but at the time they said that that was one more step downhill in a tragic story,' Iggy later commented.

While the band members were pleased that *Raw Power* finally was out, they were disappointed in the thin, brittle sound of the album. Ron Asheton was particularly upset and disowned 'Bowie's and Iggy's cocaine "artsy-fartsy" mix,' complaining that the mix they had done when recording the album was 'much, much better.' Iggy lambasted Bowie at the time as 'that fucking carrot top' who 'sabotaged' the album, but he would later defend Bowie's mix as the best job under the circumstances. Similarly, James Williamson's critique was harsh at the time, but he later revised his appraisal as he recognized that Iggy's recording of the tracks had left few options for the mixing: 'For all the grousing I've done about this mix, which is a strange, arty kind of thing that certainly has David's fingerprints on it, you know what? He pulled it out; he pulled out an almost unusable session.' Iggy remixed the album in 1998. Although Iggy's remix was deemed by most to be an improvement, Bowie maintained his preference for the 1972 mix because 'it has more wound-up ferocity and chaos' and features 'a hallmark roots sound for what was later to become punk.'

Having played only one concert under MainMan's auspices, The Stooges were anxious to tour behind the new album. However, Bowie occupied all the attention of Tony Defries and the MainMan organization as Bowie was touring the US and Japan from February to April 1973. 'There was an enormous frustration on our part because we felt pretty jealous of the attention that Bowie, his people, and his whole project were getting,' said Iggy. 'We were seeing them go out and play for nobody, but still getting a big push, and we weren't.' The Stooges speculated that Defries did not want them on the road to avoid competition with Bowie and to build the expectation for their return. 'He (Tony Defries) had theories about that kind of stuff,' Tony Zanetta observed. 'He didn't want Iggy to do small clubs, or as an opening act or any small gigs. He wanted everything to be right, but none of us MainMan had the time to make that happen.' James said, 'We still don't know why we didn't play; why didn't Defries play us more over in London? We'll never know. I think he wanted David to be in the limelight, and The Stooges were just for association.' Leee Black Childers said The Stooges 'were put out to pasture and forgotten.'

The Stooges kept themselves busy with writing new material for a potential second CBS album and rehearsals at Studio Instrument Rentals (SIR) – a large studio complex on Santa Monica Boulevard, a 15-minute drive from the Hollywood Hills house. They worked up several new numbers, including 'Cock In My Pocket,' 'Head On,' 'She-Creatures Of The Hollywood Hills,' 'Heavy Liquid,' 'Johanna,' 'Open Up And Bleed,' 'Rubber Legs' and 'Wild Love,' as well as numerous song drafts. Some of the new material was played live in 1973-74, but nothing was released at the time. The material has since emerged on various semi-official and more-official sanctioned albums. James would later record new versions of many of the songs for inclusion on his 2014 album *Re-Licked*. 'It was kind of the pinnacle of The Stooges, in between *Raw Power* and *Kill City*,' James reckoned. 'We had every reason to believe they were gonna pick up our option to do another album on our CBS contract. In typical fashion, we started writing new material like crazy and we were pretty prolific back then, and we would play it live because we were pretty ADD and we didn't want to just play our album; we wanted to play the new stuff.'

The band's schedule also left time for hanging out at Hollywood clubs like Rodney Bingenheimer's English Disco, The Rainbow Bar & Grill and Whisky A Go Go, and socializing with groupies and local celebrities such as Bingenheimer, Kim Fowley and Danny Sugerman. Ron embraced the lifestyle: 'In the beginning, living in the house on Torreyson Drive was great. We'd come back from practice and there'd be naked girls in the pool. It was classic rock and roll: naked girls in the pool, Cadillac in the driveway, getting paid, maids, plenty of pot....' Heavier drugs slowly crept into the picture. 'Once we got back and got the groupies and the drug connections, then everything started coming back in,' noted James. 'In Hollywood, you got guys who don't have much to do except rehearse for a couple of hours a day and get stoned.' Childers remembered that there were 'a lot of unauthorized parties,' as he witnessed the debauchery first-hand. 'A lot of broken glass in the pool. A lot of fights with me. They brought in a bunch of junkie groupies and they were shooting up around the pool! All I ever said to Iggy was, "Be discreet, just be discreet." Therefore, the one thing he couldn't do was to be discreet. It's the old "I must break the rules" syndrome. He did! But it's understandable. He was driven so crazy because he was totally ignored until he went completely bananas.'

The Stooges became increasingly despondent about the lack of work and exposure. MainMan's concentration on Bowie's career bred resentment towards both Bowie and Defries within the Stooges' camp. They protested loudly to Childers: 'They weren't working, and Iggy was feeling second-banana to Bowie. He was feeling left out, and he was most insecure and upset. I guess I wasn't very good at receiving all the complaints. We were all so in awe of Tony Defries. He was like a God. I just didn't want to disturb him. Iggy's complaints disappeared into me. Very few of them were communicated to Defries in New York.' Zanetta said, 'He (Iggy) began calling all the time. He was looking for attention and there wasn't anybody to give him that. He felt left out. Everybody

117

at MainMan was really too busy to deal with that kind of behavior. There were robberies; there were abortions. It was a new problem every day. No one had the energy to deal with Iggy any longer.'

Defries eventually scheduled a show for The Stooges: a Detroit homecoming on 27 March 1973. Prior to the concert, former Prime Movers member, Bob Sheff, joined the band on piano to thicken the sound. Said James, 'I started telling Iggy that I thought we needed keyboards. I remembered Bob (Sheff) from the Prime Movers, and we got in touch with him because Iggy knew him.'

Shortly after the Detroit concert, Defries issued an ultimatum: either fire James Williamson or Iggy would receive no more support from MainMan. James was deemed to be a bad influence on Iggy and was accused of taking drugs. The decision was influenced by James' strained relationship with Childers and his friend Cyrinda Foxe, whom James had been living with for a while. Said James: 'I was the first to get axed from the band. While I was no angel, I was certainly not the worst either. In hindsight, I think that Leee Black Childers didn't like me much. Feeling's mutual. I had been living with one of his girl pals from the New York/Warhol scene: Cyrinda Fox. Our relationship became complicated and resulted in her returning to New York. I then took up with Evita Ardura, who was a very young girl from Hollywood High School. She became my steady girlfriend, and this also seemed disturbing to Leee. This left some hard feelings, both from Cyrinda and Leee. We were informed that something had to give, and where it ended up was, I had to leave the band, so I left the band because I was supposedly a bad influence.'

The situation was exacerbated by the overall alienation of the band from Defries. Said Iggy; 'Defries' leverage that he tried to use for that one was that he said if we didn't accede to his wishes, he would use every trick in the book to see to it that I would never step out on a stage again at all. He promised court injunctions that would tie me up for the rest of my life.' The band took a vote and reached the conclusion that they wanted to continue with MainMan, even if it meant losing James. Subsequently, James left the group and moved into a motel in Hollywood, as Iggy and the Asheton brothers began looking for a replacement.

Defries approved of another show in Chicago on 15 June 1973. The band recruited Warren Klein – a Los Angeles session guitarist who had been recommended to them by Kim Fowley. Klein was a founding member of Lowell George's band, The Factory, and played with *Easy Rider* film soundtrack stars, Fraternity of Man. He auditioned for Iggy and the Stooges at the Hollywood Hills mansion. Encouraged by Iggy, he came up with the stage name Tornado Turner: 'It was Pop's idea. He said, "I don't call myself James Osterberg," and wanted me to have a nickname.' During rehearsals with the band, he co-wrote a tune with Iggy called 'Wicked Dick from Detroit.' Iggy recollected: 'We tried one gig in Chicago with this sort of guy who had, as Kim Fowley said, "the personality of a shoe salesman." Tornado Turner: a guy who could play anything you showed him to play on a guitar. I didn't really feel that, and my instinct was, "Keep moving forward."'

Shortly before the Chicago gig with Turner, Defries terminated Iggy's management contract with MainMan. Having been informed about the band's drug use – with Childers filing reports about discovering burned spoons and broken needles in the mansion – Defries decided that he had enough evidence of the band's drug use to cancel the contract. 'They had a blackened spoon from my room,' said Iggy. 'They sent Leee Childers on orders, MainMan sent him into my bedroom to gather evidence.' According to Zanetta, 'There were arguments; "Here is this problem and that problem and none of us have the time, and you (David Bowie) don't have the time, and we just feel..." – David was very frustrated. There was a helplessness about it, but he realized that he wasn't going to go in there and sort it out by himself. It would be best for Iggy to go his own way.' Childers recalled, 'Tony (Zanetta) just called me and said, "Get them out of the house!". Lo and behold, they all did. No fuss. They didn't destroy things. They didn't pour cement down the toilet or sugar in the gas tank. They just packed up and left.' Ron remarked, 'We're by the pool, I'd just called my mom: "Is it snowing in Michigan?". I'm sipping my rye and ginger, and Leee comes, almost in tears, "You've just been dumped by MainMan." And we all start laughing because we were glad. MainMan was doing nothing for us.'

Iggy and the band expressed discontent and frustration with the lack of support from MainMan, accusing Defries of stalling their career. 'The entire saga has reached such mythic proportions, and Defries is always blamed for sabotaging poor Iggy and the Stooges,' said Zanetta. 'But there are always two sides to every story. Defries took a recovering drug addict, got him a record deal, brought him to the UK to record and rehearse, and supported him in comfortable if not quite grand style. He eventually imported his entire band to the UK and supported them as well. During this time, the 27-year-old Defries was breaking away from his employer, Gem, to form his own company, MainMan, and trying to break two other acts – Dana Gillespie and David Bowie. He moved the entire operation to the US in order to tour Bowie and establish him in the US. While touring Bowie, he set up Iggy and the Stooges in a very nice house in the Hollywood Hills. All of their expenses were paid for, including unlimited rehearsal time. Within three months, they had repaid his largesse by reverting to their drugs of choice, causing constant mayhem, and stealing from their own house in order to buy drugs. If there was a leash that they were on, it was largely of their own making, because of their irresponsibility and passivity and inability to be trusted.'

Breaking away from MainMan, the band moved into a Hollywood motel where James was already staying. 'We got kicked out of the house, and luckily for Iggy and Scotty, I'm a saver of money, and I had squirreled away about five grand,' said Ron. 'I literally had it hid in my mattress, there was a hole in the box springs, and I'd stick my arm way in there and stash it. James Williamson had moved down to the Riviera Hotel, so he said, "Hey, you guys, you gotta come down to the Riviera, it's only 70 bucks a week". So I got Iggy, Scotty, and myself a room. I paid the whole week upfront; that way you got the discount, and I put those guys on a per diem, ten bucks a day. Then it was five bucks a day...'

With Defries and MainMan no longer dictating their moves, there was nothing to stop James from rejoining The Stooges. Turner said, 'Since MainMan was no longer in the picture, and I was a hired hand to fill in, I assumed Iggy would get James back in the band, best for everyone, and he did.' James said, 'Iggy called me up and said that the entire band had left Defries, and would I come back and play guitar with them again? I did and the period that followed was only equaled by the London period in terms of creativity. We practiced very hard at SIR and other practice studios. I wrote a lot of new music.' The reformed Stooges set about rehearsing, again recruiting Bob Sheff to play piano. They were able to secure a five-night engagement at the Whisky A Go Go in Los Angeles in June 1973. 'After MainMan dropped me, it was a losing game, but I thought I would (still be) doing good work, and I was determined to let people see it,' said Iggy. 'Booked myself, took whatever I could get. Crazy. Five nights at the Whisky, four at Max's, five in Atlanta, two in Vancouver. Made no sense. Just do the shows, stumble back to L.A. with a few hundred, and flop until I could go back out. What I didn't spend on motels, I'd spend on drugs.'

While Iggy, James and Scott were healthier than in the heroin days of 1970-1971, The Stooges were not drug-free. 'Iggy told me he had been having trouble with drugs and he was getting off them,' said Bob. 'He was trying to do that. But as the gigs went on, I saw that he continued taking them. It was obviously a conflict for him. I know for sure Quaaludes were around. He seemed to be acting very ... I think it maybe was heroin. This is a supposition, but he would be very up and then sometimes be like shockingly insulting.' Bob's stint with the band was short-lived, as he left during the June 1973 Whisky A Go Go engagement. 'The Stooges were ultimately too weird for Bob,' remarked James. Another reason was the lack of payment. 'The money situation was weird, and I wasn't getting paid,' said Bob. 'Iggy was getting paid because they had to keep him happy, but no, the rest of us weren't getting paid. I told Iggy, "Look, Iggy, I'm running out of money, I don't have any money, I have to catch a plane back to Berkeley," and he said, "Well," and I just packed up and left.'

As a replacement, James brought in Scott Thurston, who made his debut with the band at a concert in St. Clair Shores on 6 July 1973. Said James, 'One day, I was over at Capitol Records (studio), and as I was going out, I was watching a guy recording, and it was Scott Thurston with this other band. He was cool. I could hear that he was a great piano player, so I got his contact info. When we put the band back together, I asked him if he wanted to play with us, and he said, "Sure," and the rest is history.'

Realizing that they needed management to be able to play with any regularity, The Stooges enlisted the services of Jeff Wald, who was introduced to them through journalist Lillian Roxon, one of the band's many well-connected followers in the rock media. Wald set up a US tour that began in Vancouver,

Canada, on 10 August 1973. Some of the concerts were excellent, justifying many rock critics' belief that Iggy and the band were among the most exciting and promising performers around. They often did better shows in smaller cities than in Detroit, Los Angeles, and New York, where the expectations of both critics and audiences were usually higher. Iggy managed to cut down on his onstage excesses, and he and the band concentrated on delivering a professional, high-energy rock 'n' roll show. 'We did some of our best shows with that management team,' James reckoned. 'We did a lot of shows. Unfortunately, you couldn't book The Stooges on any organized tour – we couldn't play everywhere – there were places where they didn't want to know about us.'

Wald did not last long with the band, as he severed ties with them during another round of Whisky A Go Go concerts in October 1973. He was disturbed by Iggy's unreliable behavior and worried that his own career would be negatively affected by the band's reputation. The band hooked up with the New York-based American Talent International (ATI) booking agency to set up more concerts. A string of gigs was scheduled, from late November 1973 to February 1974, making this the most intense period of live work for the *Raw Power*-era Stooges. The band retained a few *Raw Power* numbers but introduced new material in the winter of 1973-1974, augmenting their set with 'Rich Bitch,' 'Wet My Bed' and 'I Got Nothin',' as well as an occasional cover of 'Louie Louie.' Iggy also revamped his stage attire, alternating between an outfit consisting of ballet-style leotard and what seemed like a fringe from a lamp around the waist and another outfit with a bow tie and white trousers.

Despite drawing good crowds, life on the road was a bare existence without the MainMan support. CBS also took the decision not to pick up the option for a second album, leaving The Stooges without management and record company backing. Iggy relied on downers and alcohol, referring to the tour as his 'Vodka tour.' Ron described the Stooges' tour as 'never-ending torture,' as drugs impaired Iggy's and the band's performances: 'The drugs really started fucking him (Iggy) up and he just got burned out. He was physically and mentally wrecked. He had driven himself too hard, and he was doing lots of downers. He'd become so nervous and tense that he had to take downers just to relax.'

Iggy's behavior both on and off stage became increasingly unreliable over the course of touring across the US. 'I realized the quality was about to taper off,' said Iggy. 'Not that the quality ever got that high, but there were some interesting, some good things about those gigs.' The decline was witnessed by followers of the band, including Bob Czaykowski, who had worked as The Stooges' soundman at Max's Kansas City in July and August 1973: 'During the summer, as it progressed over the next couple of months, when I saw them in Michigan (5-6 October 1973), you could see it was starting to crack. Then when it came to around New Year's Eve, that's when it started to get really bad. You could see the signpost up ahead: "The End is Near."' Bob Mulrooney – a musician who had seen The Stooges in July 1973 – observed, 'They just got progressively worse 'cause of the dope and traveling and shit. Everything was going wrong for them.'

The band members became discouraged and lost confidence in Iggy as he delivered too many lackluster performances. The atmosphere in the band quickly deteriorated. 'Iggy had lost the plot a little bit and the rest of them hadn't,' noted Czaykowski. 'But it was getting tough. It's tough to be in a band with an erratic personality.' James admitted that he 'never really trusted Iggy' after being kicked out of the band in the spring of 1973. 'I had to be taught many times about how unreliable Iggy really is,' remarked James. 'That band could have been a real (success) and... instead, it was becoming a flop. Iggy was very screwed up at that point, and I had pretty much lost all respect for him and confidence in him as a person. I wasn't really sure I wanted to continue on with all my chips in that basket.'

The band returned to Michigan in early February 1974 for concerts. The Stooges' polarising effect on their audience was evident when they played a concert at Detroit's Michigan Palace on 9 February 1974. Iggy and the band came under fire from rowdy audience members who threw bottles, eggs, ice cubes and coins on the stage. While Iggy confronted the hail with insults, he and the band members were genuinely scared for their own safety. 'That night was probably the most violent and paranoid,' Iggy later commented. 'Probably the height of paranoia and violence of that edition of the Stooges. In fact, too paranoid for my taste – and a little too violent.' The Stooges' followers believed that Iggy anticipated the end of the band. 'You got the feeling that it was his farewell concert, although you didn't know for sure,' said Bob Baker, who had seen the band numerous times. 'It was such a hostile environment; people were obviously trying to mess with his head. I thought, "This guy's not going to live to be very old."' Mulrooney said, 'I thought, Iggy's just – he's like my hero – he's just embarrassing himself. He was just really belligerent, and it just wasn't a good show.'

The band had some time off after the Detroit concert before leaving to play further gigs, including going to the UK for a tour in the spring of 1974. Iggy, James, and Scott Thurston flew back to Los Angeles, while Ron and Scott remained in Ann Arbor. However, a few days before they were about to go on the road again, Iggy called Ron and told him he was quitting. 'We had a few days off. I was at home with my mother, and Iggy suddenly calls me one day and he goes, "Look, I'm sorry, Ron, but I have to quit. I can't go on any longer. I can't handle it any longer".' According to Iggy, 'nobody was surprised' by his decision.

The touring and drugs had taken their toll on Iggy's mental and physical health. He recognized that he needed a break: 'We had another tour to go on and I just said stop! Time out! Because I can't stand to go out on stage and not feel proper about what I'm doing. I thought I should quit. I didn't want to look back on all those shows and think that they had been bad. I thought it was better to take a break, even if it meant that I might never be able to get started again.' James said, 'We'd been on the road for months and months and months, hand to mouth, and it wasn't working. We were living like dogs – hardly ever eating, never sleeping, drugs like you wouldn't believe, burning ourselves out like maniacs. You can't live like that for very long.'

Tuesday, 27 March 1973: Ford Auditorium, Detroit, MI
This was The Stooges' first US concert while under the auspices of MainMan, and just the second gig they had played in the 16 months that Iggy had been contracted to MainMan. Keyboard player, Bob Sheff, augmented the band, i.e., Iggy, James Williamson, Ron Asheton and Scott Asheton. Photos from The Stooges' concert at the venue, by Lisa Gottlieb and Bob Matheu, were featured in Matheu's Stooges biography.

With a new management and record label, there was a great deal at stake for The Stooges. Defries invited many media people, including most of the *Creem* staff and several music journalists, who were flown in from New York. Iggy's parents were also in the audience. Iggy admitted that he was 'really nervous' about the concert. 'I wanted it to be really good. That was something that was bigger than we had ever done on our own, and also a nicer joint and with a new repertoire.' According to Ron Asheton, 'That was still pre-everyone getting a little weird. Everybody was excited about the prospect of carrying on and getting back onto the scene. It was pretty upbeat.'

Bob Sheff preceded The Stooges' act with a brief solo piano performance, 'Just before the show in Detroit and Iggy sent me onstage by myself. He said, "Just go on out there and play." I started playing off some of the simple rock licks of primitive, rock licks and a couple of little gospel things before they came out, and then they gradually came onstage, and people were getting more and more excited and screaming and hollering.'

Wearing a skirt and tights, Iggy looked to be in good health. James showed the most glam influence, wearing thigh-high silver platform boots. Iggy was fully in control, diving from the drum risers and spending some time in the audience. The Stooges delivered a professional 40-minute set focused on *Raw Power* material. At least one new number was played: 'Cock In My Pocket,' which Iggy told the audience was a song 'co-written by my mother,' after introducing his mother in the audience. The band did not finish their set with a long cacophony as they had done in the past but simply left the stage after the final number. Defries did not allow the band back for an encore, so there was some booing when they returned to take a bow instead of playing more.

'It wasn't just a gig – it was an event: the return of The Stooges to their hometown,' said Skip Gildersleeve, who attended several Stooges concerts in 1973–1974. 'There was a big hype because MainMan was behind it. I remember being very excited about it because I had the record. I remember staring at Iggy's mic stand before they came out, and it was like a dream come true. He introduced his mother, she stood up and he said, "Now I want to introduce my mother," and he said, "Now I'd like to do a song I co-wrote with my mother, it's called 'I've Got A Cock In My Pocket.'" As a 15-year-old, it was pretty outrageous. He did one thing where he went out in the front row, grabbed a girl, made out with her, then grabbed her by her hair and threw her back in her seat. I thought it was totally crazy.'

Ben Edmonds – then a *Creem* editor – thought The Stooges 'played really well' and believed Bob Sheff was an excellent addition to the band line-up. 'I loved Bob Sheff; he was a revelation,' said Edmonds. 'My memory was that the concert was a little on the short side. It was more professional than their earlier shows but without the energy. They were obviously doing their best to be The New Stooges, more professional and polished. They didn't have the oddball careening, unhinged quality that they used to have. This one had that kind of MainMan atmosphere. The show was very tight.'

The concert drew mostly enthusiastic reviews from the press. Writing for *Interview*, Glenn O'Brien believed it was 'one of the greatest rock and roll shows ever' and was full of praise for The Stooges' return to the stage: 'The highlight of the show is when he enters the audience. It's the theatre of cruelty come alive. Iggy jumps off the stage. He grabs a girl in the first row and kisses her hard. He holds her and grinds into her while he sings. When he's finished, he pushes her down to the floor. Then he goes chasing after a boy. Some kids run, afraid that they're next. Others watch in awe. Nobody's going to rush the stage. The stage has rushed the audience.' Lester Bangs later in *Creem* described the concert as 'the greatest show many ever saw them do.' John Weisman of *Detroit Free Press* was positive but indicated that The Stooges faced more competition than ever before: 'His performance these days is mild compared to the complicated theatrics of Bowie or Alice Cooper.' He described Iggy as a 'monochromatic performer whose shock value has long worn off.'

Some concerts in May and June 1973 were canceled, including gigs planned for 15 May at Carnegie Hall, New York, New York, and 8 June at Civic Auditorium, Santa Monica, California.

Friday, 15 June 1973: Aragon Ballroom, Chicago, IL

The Stooges played this concert at the 4,500-seat Aragon Ballroom with Tornado Turner on guitar instead of James Williamson, but still with Bob Sheff on keyboards. Ben Edmonds attended the show but felt it lacked the excitement of earlier Stooges performances: 'It was bland. There was nothing Stooge-like about them. Suddenly it was just like any other band; it was like watching a bad covers band. Warren Klein was faceless and had no musical personality. He is an excellent player. Whatever you want to say about James' desire to make The Stooges more professional, he was completely incapable of doing that. It still made them The Stooges. When they got a "professional" guitarist, it turned it into nothing. Iggy wasn't feeling it. There was nothing happening, no theatre, no performance.' In contrast, Turner said in a 2020 interview that 'the show went really well and Ron ran up to me and gave me a big hug when the show ended, happy it went so well, unlike their previous comeback show in Detroit.'

Thursday, Friday, Saturday, Sunday and Monday, 20, 21, 22, 23 and 24 June 1973: Whisky A Go Go, Hollywood, CA

With James Williamson back in the band, The Stooges performed two sets each night at the 500-capacity Whisky A Go Go, playing in front of an adoring throng that included most of Los Angeles' scene-makers and friends of the band. They drew a total of 3,500 people, and the Whisky management reported its best business in years. Rufus featuring Chaka Khan opened for The Stooges on some of the dates. Prior to The Stooges' first concert, a small party was thrown for the band at the Continental Hyatt House, hosted by Les Petites Bon-Bons and Columbia Records. The party was attended by various celebrities and wannabes, including Rodney Bingenheimer, Divine, Gilda Glitter and members of the then-current television show, *An American Family*.

The Whisky A Go Go setlist mixed *Raw Power* tracks ('Raw Power,' 'Gimme Danger,' 'Search And Destroy,' I Need Somebody') with more recent material, including 'Head On,' 'Cock In My Pocket,' and 'Heavy Liquid.' Iggy performed in a small pair of underpants that said 'Soho' on the front, having purchased them at a tourist kiosk in Piccadilly Circus in London the previous summer.

Bob Sheff played with The Stooges but left the band after the two first nights; they played on without a pianist the last nights. 'Everybody at the Whisky were hipper than shit,' recalled Bob. 'The concerts were very crowded. Just in the dressing room, it seemed like there was an open door. The playing was probably the best. The audience was totally into the theatre of the thing; nobody was sitting … they were waiting for Iggy to throw himself out into the audience. There was an old upright piano they had miked and the thing literally fell apart through the gig. The manager (of the club) was mad, but the thing was a wreck. I couldn't see the band very well cause of where they put the thing. A lot of people said the band sounded 1,000 times better with me playing piano.'

Many of the Stooges' Los Angeles followers were in attendance. Musician and writer Don Waller – who founded the Los Angeles music journal *Back Door Man* in 1975 – attended several of The Stooges' Whisky concerts during 1973: 'I saw nine shows. It was back in the day when you did two shows a night at the Whisky. There was an opening act and a headliner, and each act did two shows a night. The Whisky's policy was to clear the house after the first show if there was a huge amount of people that wanted to get in. You could see two shows if not that many people wanted to get in. Since The Stooges, at that point in time and unbeknownst to us, Iggy was just completely fucked up out of his mind on heroin, so there were many nights during these runs where they didn't play the second show.'

Phast Phreddie Patterson – writer, manager, DJ, and co-founder of *Back Door Man* with Waller – was there with friends: 'It was amazing. We had never seen

125

The Stooges before, but we were all big fans of the albums. We were knocked out by Iggy's commitment to entertain, his dancing, excellent stage presence, etc. I remember opening night; the place was pretty well packed, a lot of glitter folks from Rodney's English Disco and other Hollywood types. At the time, the dance floor was raised and fenced-off; I suppose to keep people from losing their balance and falling off the dance floor. We got on the dance floor so we could be up close. It was packed with people. During the set, several girls, and a guy or two, groped Iggy's legs and private parts whenever he came close to the edge of the stage. Every once in a while, he would fall into the audience, and the folks there would pass him around the dance floor. I remember thinking that he had movements like a lizard, especially the way he would stare out at the rest of the audience from his position above the folks on the dance floor.'

Another fan of The Stooges, Raul Pineda, attended two sets on Friday, 21 June: 'The Whisky is a small club and it wasn't fully sold out for the first set. We arrived and quickly made our way to the front table and ordered drinks (I was not of age, but they served me anyway). As the place started to fill up, we noticed a distinctive black couple at the table next to us. Figured they were CBS Record execs. As the lights went down, we noticed they were gone. Next thing we saw was them and other musicians being introduced as Rufus. They did a danceable set, which we used as an excuse to move to the front of the dance floor. We drank and danced (very badly). They finished, exit stage-right and the lights come up. We didn't budge. We were front and center, waiting for The Stooges. Okay, anticipation building, The Stooges were about to come out. Lights out, Stooges on stage, starting the familiar 'Raw Power' chords. Iggy came out. The band sounded much more powerful than on record. Every member came off loud and clear. Iggy did his now standard dances and acrobatics. We were teenagers and felt his presence to be somewhat dangerous. In short time, Ig stripped down to some black pantie briefs. He flung himself recklessly, oblivious to anything or anyone around him. He jumped into the crowd, got back on stage with the agility of wrestler/ballet dancer/acrobat. Amazing show, but it was relatively brief (well under an hour), but better than anyone I've ever seen live. We watched the band go back to their dressing room and decided to follow.'

Pineda and friends backstage after The Stooges' first set on 21 June: 'We knocked on the dressing room door. A scraggly looking guy opened and said, "What you want?". We asked very politely if we could meet The Stooges. He asked if we had a dollar to buy Iggy some beer. He put it in his pocket and let us in. My date was very beautiful, with long blonde hair and very short shorts – I think that was more a factor than the dollar. Inside the small, smoke-filled room were many hangers-on, and all Stooges in various parts of the room. First, we approached James Williamson. He had that rock star look and attitude. Still, he was kind enough to talk to us and give me his autograph. Next was Scott "Rock Action" Asheton. He was all laughs and good cheer (he also signed my paper). Third was Ron. He was so warm and friendly. He smiled and put up with our stupid teenage questions, like "Wow, how much money are you guys making?". We talked to him longest and he was an absolute gentleman. All this time, Rufus were doing their second set. Fourth, Iggy himself. He was sprawled out on the couch, very different from the strange animal he was onstage. Someone in the room yelled, "Hey, it's Jethro!". This brought Iggy to life. "Jethro who?" asked Iggy. "Jethro Bodine (Max Bear Jr. from television show, *The Beverly Hillbillies*). "Go get him," said Iggy. A couple of Iggy's guys flung open the door and complied. A few minutes later, they brought back the actor. As he walked in, all cameras, press, and hangers-on flock to the door. He looked like a cool version of the character he played on television. All the commotion spooked him, and he quickly left. This gave us an opportunity to approach Iggy. He was slouched on the sofa. Before this, a guy in a nice suit was sticking a business card down Iggy's briefs. We asked him a few stupid, teenage questions. He answered with a simple "yes" or "no" reply. He wasn't so much rude as just tired and out of it. Rufus was finishing their second set downstairs, and we were all instructed to leave.'

'We fought our way to the dance floor,' Pineda continued. 'The place was fully packed, and we couldn't get to the front. Lights out, Stooges hit the stage. We thought, "No way will they be as energetic as the first show." Wrong! "Raw Power" riffs playing, Iggy runs to the front. "I Need Somebody" was so much more powerful live. As we looked around, we saw Jethro standing a few yards behind us. He remained cool and composed but seemed to be enjoying the music. 45 minutes later, the show ended. We talked excitedly about how incredible the performance was. The Stooges stood like stoic gangster accomplices, while Iggy performed with superhuman energy and agility both shows. I remember Iggy once mentioning how if he could get away with a half-hour show, he could put on an even more incredible show. I believe him. The brevity of the Whisky shows showed a level of intensity I haven't seen since.'

The Stooges were in good form during the Whisky engagement, but playing two sets each night took its toll on Iggy. Ron Asheton observed, 'Once again, people want Iggy to get fucked up. Lots of people offering him things; he got pretty stoned. And being it's L.A., it's pretty hard to try to top yourself every night for six nights, and he was really working it. But by the end, he was pretty ragged. It's really hard being Iggy, and it's even harder if you're expected to top yourself every night and you've got two shows every night.'

Three nights into the Whisky stand, Iggy injured his back on a miscalculated dive into the audience. Attempting to finish the set when he barely could stand up, Iggy delivered 'Search And Destroy' from a stationary position until a guitar break inspired him into a vain attempt at motion. In a few seconds, he fell to the floor. Able to walk only with great pain, he was helped backstage. The Stooges completed their engagement, doing one show a night.

Press reception to the Whisky shows was excellent. Richard Cromelin raved in his *Los Angeles Times* review: 'Iggy is very real and very scary. There's no pretending in his challenges, no escape from the pain in his singing and in

The Stooges' primitive rock 'n' roll. If you're willing, you'll get everything you're looking for; if not, you'll be instantly repulsed.' Mike Saunders of *Phonograph Record Magazine* was no less optimistic: 'The Stooges have come back from the dead to become one of the most powerful groups in the world today. Williamson's addition has made them a potential supergroup, and Ron Asheton has proven to be an equal dynamo on bass, playing it almost as if it were rhythm guitar. If they can ever develop a feel for dynamics, and if their material keeps improving until it matches their indisputable capacity for mania, The Stooges might etch their name into the annals of rock history in a big way.' Richard Cuskelly of *Los Angeles Herald Examiner* felt that 'Iggy didn't let anybody down as he leaped across the stage bare-chested singing about "Raw Power" and a lot of other unprintable subjects.' There were also reviewers who were unimpressed. Writing for *Los Angeles Free Press*, Stann Findelle reckoned that Iggy 'explored heretofore unknown galactic extremities of non-talent during his stay' and that Rufus 'was vastly superior to the lowlife that proceeded (after) it.'

Friday, 6 July 1973: Civic Arena, St. Clair Shores, MI

Bob Seger was billed as 'special guest star' at this show with The Stooges in St. Clair Shores. Catfish Hodge, and Mutants, also appeared. This was pianist Scott Thurston's debut with the band. He had rehearsed some of the material with James Williamson and was flown to Detroit, where he first met Iggy and the other band members right before the concert.

It was a balmy, hot day, and the band ate watermelons backstage. As he entered the stage, Iggy hurled a watermelon into the crowd, accidentally hitting a girl in the audience. At another point, Iggy took a cup of ice and emptied it down his briefs, then fished it out piece by piece, sucking it or throwing it at the audience. Art Lyzak of opening act Mutants was not impressed by Iggy and the Stooges: 'The band came out and started playing "Raw Power," and it was about ten or fifteen minutes before Iggy even came out. And right before he came out to the front of the stage, he took a dump behind the Marshall amp. I guess that's a junk thing or something. Then he kind of came out with a little skimpy thing on; it was just like fucking horrible. I mean I stood there for like ten or fifteen minutes after he started and thinking, like, just how bad they'd gotten.' Contrary to Lyzak's view, Stooges fan, Skip Gildersleeve, believed it was one of the band's best performances of the 1973-1974 gigs he attended: 'That was one of the best times I saw them. I don't think the abusive part of the audience was there in full forces that early. We were all so happy that Bob Seger opened for The Stooges.'

In late July, the band went to New York to set up rehearsals at Columbia's studios. They worked on their repertoire, trying out new material and honing their set in preparation for a prestigious engagement at Max's Kansas City. Former band member, Dave Alexander, came to visit during rehearsals. Bob Czaykowski – who worked at a rehearsal studio in New York – was hired to oversee the sound at the Max's concerts: 'I'd seen them play and I was familiar with the music; everybody else I was working with didn't want to have anything to do with them. I'd seen them at Ungano's during *Fun House*, and I saw two different shows at the Electric Circus (1970 and 1971). They sent me down to CBS studio, where they were rehearsing. I remember being struck by how normal they were, how "average guys" they were. They were like, "Oh you must be the backline guy! Come have a seat". We just hung out and then they went through their set. In those days, whenever the studio was operational, they had to have a union studio guy there. So this guy who is normally watching Tony Bennett has got Iggy Pop dancing on the piano, pulling his pants down. I was like, "Wow, this stuff rocks! These guys are crazy!"'

Monday and Tuesday, 30 and 31 July 1973: Max's Kansas City, New York, NY

Billed as just Iggy Pop, The Stooges were booked for a four-night engagement at Max's. The concerts were set up by Columbia Records Vice President Steve Harris. J. F. Murphy and Salt opened for The Stooges. Their 40-minute set of the opening night featured a blend of *Raw Power* and more recent tunes: 'Raw Power,' 'Head On,' 'Gimme Danger,' 'Cock In My Pocket,' 'Search And Destroy,' 'I Need Somebody,' and 'Heavy Liquid.' The set was released on the *Heavy Liquid* box set in 2005.

The Max's gigs saw the premiere for the band's new stage clothing, which had been crafted by Bill Whitten, a Los Angeles designer. Iggy performed in what he termed 'a strange human fly outfit,' and James wore a *Star Trek*-inspired costume. Iggy did not feel completely comfortable, though: 'I remember that I was pretty unhappy when we got to the gig to find that the entire room was organized with folding chairs. It was like going to a Pentecostal church or something, and I didn't think it was right for the group.'

The Stooges' return to New York was eagerly anticipated, with followers lining up for several hours before the opening show. Max's upper floor – with a small stage and the audience seated at tables – was packed. The star-studded crowd included Lou Reed, Alice Cooper and his manager Shep Gordon, Wayne County, Todd Rundgren and his fiancé Bebe Buell, Johnny Thunders and David Johansen of the New York Dolls, present and future members of Blue Oyster Cult, Ramones, Blondie and Teenage Lust, as well as many friends of the band, including Danny Fields, Lisa Robinson, Tony Zanetta and Leee Black Childers. Ivan Kral – then in a New York rock band called Luger, and later with Patti Smith and Iggy – saw The Stooges for the first time: 'I was sitting right up in front of him. I was stunned! My God, what a performer! There was so much power and energy. It was just pure energy.' Press was also in attendance, causing Iggy to remark later, 'I don't think I have ever seen so many rock critics in one room in my life, nor will I ever. If they weren't rock critics, they looked like rock critics. It was just wall-to-wall.'

The press response was enthusiastic. Fred Kirby of *Variety* felt The Stooges had become 'one of the tightest of rock combos,' adding, 'If Iggy can reach beyond his devoted cult following, he could prove more jarring than Alice Cooper.' Lenny Kaye, writing for *Rock Scene*, was full of praise: 'Through the course of four energetic outings, they honed their act with a steadily-controlling hand, tight and triumphant each step of the way.' *Billboard*'s Phil Gelormine, meanwhile, concluded simply that 'Iggy Pop will be a star.' The writer from *Daily News* thought Iggy 'was in good form, aggressive, pugnacious, throwing the songs from his new album at his audience as if he were throwing punches.' He commented, 'He did not spit at the audience, as is his custom, but he did throw a very heavy microphone stand into it, and he also threatened to kill a fuzzy-haired person from an out-of-town fanzine.'

Halfway through the second Max's show, Iggy cut himself badly after accidentally falling on a table in the audience with glasses. Many in the crowd did not see it happen, but there was a large amount of blood gushing from his chest when he got up. The Fast member, Paul Zone, was a witness to the accident: 'At Iggy and the Stooges' set in the summer of 1973, it was fantastic to see him dancing and jumping around, collapsing onto a table covered with drinks, then emerging on stage, dripping with blood from the broken glass on his chest.' Bob Czaykowski was also close at hand: 'I saw him walk out. We used to call it "doing a Sinatra," where he'd walk out into the audience rather than dive. He started walking out on these tables and the tables were like any table in a rock club, not really that stable. He slipped and went down, and when he came back, I said, "You're cut pretty bad here." I was on the side of the stage. I've seen him get scraped up even in rehearsal, but he had a pretty good puncture going in his ribs. He walked to the side of the stage and crashed into me, and I noticed that my shirt was all covered in blood, so I said, "Let's pull it. Let's stop it, man. You can't do this."'

Iggy played on, but by the end of the set, he was bleeding so much that he had to be taken to hospital. 'He wanted to finish that show,' said Czaykowski. 'That's why when people said he cut himself, I was like, "I didn't see that." I saw him fall and I saw him get up with cuts, and if you fall on a table full of glass, you're going to get cut up. They wouldn't stop until they'd played their seven songs or whatever. Then he went upstairs. We used to have this thing that a piece of tape will fix everything, but he was bleeding so bad the tape wouldn't even stick. That's when Alice Cooper came up and said, "No you're coming with me. I've got a car waiting to go and get that looked at".' According to Michael Tipton, a friend of the band, 'Alice Cooper put him in the car. He literally picked him up and carried him to the car.'

Under doctor's warning, the remaining two concerts were postponed four nights, until Iggy's stitches would have time to set. Later the same week, Iggy attended a show by the New York Dolls and Mott the Hoople at the Felt Forum in Madison Square Garden. Once again, Iggy had to undergo treatment after colliding with a glass door, and he spent the Dolls' set in the Garden's emergency room.

Monday and Tuesday, 6 and 7 August 1973: Max's Kansas City, New York, NY

These two shows replaced the canceled shows on 1 and 2 August. An improved PA system had been assembled, making Iggy's vocals more audible than during the opening gigs. 'After he got cut, we had a couple of days off and we decided we were going to go to bring more PA,' noted Bob Czaykowski. 'The funny thing about it is that the PA at Max's was no way up to dealing with the kind of firepower The Stooges were capable of putting out. They played loud. We brought in more Sun amps into that place than any band would have used. We used to call it the "clang"; it was this really bright, loud sound. The bass was loud, and the drums were loud; it was all loud.'

Iggy was stitched up but as irrepressible as ever for the last two Max's shows, which were deemed to be amongst the best The Stooges ever performed by some of the band's followers. The setlist on 6 August was the same as the opening gig, but with 'Open Up And Bleed' added as a final number.

Friday and Saturday, 10 and 11 August 1973: Pender Auditorium, Vancouver, Canada

The Vancouver concerts were the start of a brief tour. Pender Auditorium started life in 1906 as the Myers Hall. It burned down in 2003. The Vancouver gigs were described as packed, in the press. Support act was the blues-based group Mojo Hand (described as 'Seattle's hottest!')

Flying to the concert, Ron Asheton wore one of his Nazi uniforms, which almost got him kicked off the plane from Los Angeles: 'I was wearing my SS uniform. It didn't have any swastikas or SS bolts or anything like that, but it did have the cuff band that said "Adolf Hitler" on it! The next thing I knew, the pilot was standing there glaring at me. I was surprised because usually, they wouldn't let Iggy on the plane because he was filthy or he had torn pants, or he still had silver make-up from his hair and glitter all over. Then the stewardess comes back and goes, "I'm responsible for you. The pilot wanted to kick you off the plane because he thought you were some Nazi guy. But I said that you seem like a nice guy, so I vouched for you". That was starting the tour off, so I decided not to wear the jacket anymore.'

A Vancouver fanzine review of the concert by Marsac, described the audience as a mixture of 'curious rock and roll devotees, Iggy Pop fans and a fair number of couples out for a night's clubbing.' He believed Iggy 'appeared to be very tired, perhaps a little bored even,' but was impressed with the band: 'Their collective musical ability is far greater than that of some of the bands backing various Iggy contemporaries/imitators, and their driving, metallic rock has an energy and near fury like that of Beefheart's Magic Band.' The audience response was 'respectable,' but applause seemed to dwindle considerably as the show went on. 'Half of the audience would appear to be more than a mite confused, if not suffering from a mild traumatic experience. By the time the show ended, it took the audience some ten minutes to muster the kind of applause that Iggy and the Stooges considered worthy of an encore. But after one last song, it was over.'

Don Stanley, reporting for *Vancouver Sun*, thought the music lived up to the album title *Raw Power*: 'Without Bowie's magical production touch, Saturday night's live sound was particularly crude and crunching, similar to the sound at the Pacific Garden appearance of another Bowie protégé, Lou Reed.' Stanley concluded that 'many people might not like Iggy Pop, might think his music is too simplistic, too repetitive, too crude, but no one could forget seeing him.'

Tuesday, 14 August 1973: Celebrity Theatre, Phoenix, AZ
The Stooges performed with Dr. John at the Celebrity Theatre, which is a 2,650-seater theatre-in-the-round. While in Phoenix, Iggy gave an interview to a St. Louis radio station from the hotel. He said that they had been well received on the tour and were 'playing real well.'

Saturday, 18 August 1973: American Theatre, St. Louis, MO
The Stooges played two sets at this 1,400-seat theater. Both sets were recorded and have since been issued on various releases. The first set (50 minutes) included: 'Raw Power,' 'Head On,' 'Gimme Danger,' 'Cock In My Pocket,' 'Search And Destroy,' 'I Need Somebody,' and 'Open Up And Bleed.' The second set (55 minutes) featured the same songs, but ended with 'Heavy Liquid,' which was played after 'I Need Somebody' ('Open Up And Bleed' is not included on the tape recordings, but it might still have been played as it usually closed The Stooges' set at this time). Some seconds of live footage from one of the sets was included on the DVD, *Search And Destroy – Iggy & The Stooges' Raw Power*, which was part of the officially released *Raw Power* box set in 2010.

Sunday, 19 August 1973: J. F. Kennedy Center for the Performing Arts, Washington DC
The Stooges opened for Mott the Hoople at the plush, modern J. F. Kennedy Center, adjacent to the Watergate complex in Washington, DC. They played in the 2,400-seat concert hall, which opened in 1971.

Bebe Buell – who had befriended Iggy during the New York stay for the Max's concerts – was visiting from New York with Cindy Lang (Alice Cooper's girlfriend) and another friend who brought the drug, THC. Before the concert, Iggy snorted a couple of lines of the powerful drug, thinking it was cocaine, which had an adverse effect on him. After 'Raw Power,' he laid down on stage and muttered, 'My doctor told me not to play tonight.' Iggy had trouble standing up during the show, stumbling to the floor a few times. After a visit to the audience, he appeared to be caked with blood, but it turned out to be a pie.

Stooges fan, Tommy Keene, experienced Iggy's visit to the crowd at close hand: 'He started staring at little ol' me on the aisle in the fifth row. He got down off the stage with the follow spot following him and started walking like a zombie straight for me. I looked up to my brother and friends in the second row and saw them pointing and laughing at me. What the fuck was he doing? All eyes were upon me as he walked up to me. He stuck out his hand and motioned, "Come on, shake it, baby!". This was too surreal; I went to shake his hand, and he did the limp thing and pulled away. A guy behind me then smashed a Hostess cherry pie on Iggy's bare chest, while another squirted wine on Iggy from a wineskin. Iggy just rubbed it all onto himself, grunted, and turned back to the stage.'

The Kennedy Center officials did not seem too pleased with the pie incident and sent the message to the band to get Iggy off the stage. They ignored the request, and the set proceeded through two or three more numbers before Iggy was led offstage by a stagehand.

Iggy returned to make a comment but found the microphones dead. He mouthed the words 'they turned off the mics' to moans from the audience. He walked off, looking resigned.

Tom Zito from the *Washington Post* was unenthusiastic about The Stooges: 'After 10 minutes of ear-blowing noise, one stagehand asked the concert promoter if he could pull the plugs. His request was denied. Fortunately, Iggy ended his performance moments later, after leaping down into the audience and finding himself unable to return. He was hoisted up by several stagehands, sang one encore and walked off.' Quite differently, Mark Jenkins writing for *Hype*, believed 'both Iggy and the band were in fine form that night, with Iggy looking like a spastic that even the occasional spurts of agility couldn't completely offset the feeling that he was going to die onstage.' He felt Iggy and the Stooges 'mesmerized the two-thirds full hall' and 'scared the shit out of the Kennedy Center officials.'

Following the Washington, DC, concert, The Stooges were scheduled to appear at the Southern Michigan Pop Festival, held in Simons Park, Dundee, Michigan, 25–26 August 1973, along with Brownsville Station, Luther Allison Blues Band, Wiz Kids, Frijid Pink (listed as 'Frigid Pink'), Heavyn & Strange Tongue, 'plus three surprise guest stars' according to the advertisement. However, the event was canceled on 23 August as a result of an injunction obtained by the Munroe Country Prosecutor, citing the need to 'protect the welfare of the public.' The Munroe Sheriff's Department instigated roadblocks to prevent festival-goers from entering the grounds, and a number of arrests were made.

Further, The Stooges were scheduled to play on 2 September 1973 at a rock festival at Donnybrooke Speedway, Minnesota. Other acts scheduled to appear at this 12-hour festival included REO Speedwagon, Black Oak Arkansas, and Quicksilver Messenger Service. More than 6,000 advance tickets had been sold for the event, which the promoters hoped would attract 20,000 to 30,000 people. However, on 28 August, a judge issued an order that prohibited the festival because 'many serious problems often develop from the bringing together of such large groups of people without adequate planning.'

Saturday, Sunday and Monday, 15, 16 and 17 September 1973: Whisky A Go Go, Hollywood, CA

The Stooges returned to the Whisky A Go Go for further concerts in September. The opening act was Chris Jagger – brother of Mick – who played a set of country music. A 60-minute recording of the 16 September gig exists, featuring a seven-song setlist: 'Raw Power,' 'Head On,' 'Gimme Danger,' 'Search And Destroy,' 'I Need Somebody,' 'Heavy Liquid' and 'Open Up And Bleed.' This set has been issued numerous times, notably on Revenge's *Live At The Whisky A Go-Go*. The band also introduced 'She-Creatures Of The Hollywood Hills' and 'Johanna' during this engagement at the Whisky A Go Go. According to Don Waller, who saw some of the concerts: 'The shows didn't vary that much from one show to the next. It was more a question of how fucked-up Iggy was on any given night.'

'The Stooges played so fucking loud, they were blowing the PA out constantly,' Waller recalled. 'The PA would cut out and there'd be howls of feedback throughout the shows. Iggy would come out and do his thing. He jumped into the audience; stage diving was there. There was this chick continually grabbing at his crotch, and he's slapping her hand away and she just keeps grabbing at him. So finally, he just pulled his foot back and kicked her square in the face. He hit her right on the chin, and her head snaps back and she staggers back through the crowd and turns to us and says, "He's fucked!". It was a tremendously powerful, exciting show. We just kept going back. We'd get out of there and go home, go to sleep, go to work, and then we'd get out of work and drive back up to Hollywood and sit outside the Whisky, waiting for a couple of hours for the doors to open because we're paying for these shows. We would make a bunch of brownies because you couldn't smoke in the place – or reefer anywhere at that time – and eat them and take generous handfuls of white crosses, amphetamine. Then we'd go in there, and you'd get hassled on the two-drink minimum. There was a two-drink minimum per show, so if you're not 21, you can't buy alcohol, of course, and if you are, you'd get hosed for whatever the price of a beer was. We were sleep-deprived because we're all working blue-collar gigs back then, and it was just such an incredibly powerful thing.'

Raul Pineda – who attended The Stooges' Whisky concerts in June – was back for the opening Saturday concert: 'We were Stones fans and were curious about Mick's bro Chris, but it was a big disappointment. He played a standard country-rock set that didn't really impress anyone. Audience was polite, but impatient for The Stooges. Lights out, Stooges hit the stage, everyone energized. They played their usual set with a few new songs. "She-Creatures..." was a standout. Iggy was in the audience even more, this time around. He would just jump in with reckless abandon. You had to make sure you didn't get kicked in the face during his assent. Now, sometime during the performance, Iggy got hurt. It wasn't apparent at the time. He just got back on stage and continued. Great set, as usual, and we planned to go backstage.

Security wouldn't allow it, and there seemed to be some commotion at the scene. I noticed one guy coming downstairs with Iggy's iconic leather jacket. My assumption was that he gave Iggy a good deal of money, drugs, or both. Then, the announcer came out to explain that Iggy would not be able to do the second show. For some reason, I was under the impression that he had broken a rib jumping into the crowd. I was later informed that he had hurt his back. Either way, Chris Jagger came out for an extended set, and the night was over. The most impressive thing about this set is that no one realized that Pop was hurt at the time. He continued singing and flailing about as if nothing had happened.'

Waller and friends met with band members after one show: 'We hardly ever went backstage because we thought there was some kind of sacrosanct quality and we weren't cool enough. But we got so frustrated waiting for the second set to start, that we actually went backstage, and we walked in there to see Iggy with his head in Sable's lap; Ron, Scotty and Williamson all in different corners, and all these glitterati-type people hanging around, and we're scratching our heads.'

Friday, 21 September 1973: Ellis Auditorium, Memphis, TN

The Stooges opened for the New York Dolls at the 12,000-seat Ellis Auditorium in downtown Memphis, performing in the smaller South Hall of the auditorium. Memphis police stopped the show towards the end of the Dolls' set due to the crowd rushing the stage, encouraged by Dolls singer David Johansen. The policemen ripped the microphone from Johansen and arrested him onstage. He was dragged off stage, blowing kisses to the audience. He spent a night in jail for 'disorderly conduct' before being let out on bail.

Saturday, 22 September 1973: State Theater, Toledo, OH

With the cancellation of the Southern Michigan Pop Festival, 25–26 August 1973, came information and advertisements that The Stooges – supported by Wiz Kids – would instead perform at Toledo State Theater on 25 August. However, this concert also was never played. A subsequent listing appeared in *Billboard* for the band to play Toledo on 10 September, which in turn was rescheduled for later in the month, as a news article in *The Toledo Blade* stated that The Stooges were due to play Toledo soon, but no date was given. However, a flyer for the concert confirms the date as 22 September 1973.

The concert was witnessed by Stooges follower Chazz Avery: 'I recall they played a few common songs, "Search And Destroy", "Raw Power" and "Gimme Danger." I remember they also played several songs I didn't know at the time, which were surely the likes of "Head On" and "Cock In My Pocket." One specific memory I have is, my friends and I were sitting in the aisle seats a couple rows back from the stage. At one point, Iggy was in the audience. My friend, who had never seen The Stooges but had heard of Iggy's antics, was in the actual aisle seat. Iggy came up and was blabbering some lyrics right in my

135

friend's face. My friend, not knowing what to expect, kind of pulled back with a concerned look on his face. We all had a good laugh over it.'

Friday and Saturday, 5 and 6 October 1973: Michigan Palace, Detroit, MI

The Stooges returned to their home turf for two shows at the Michigan Palace: a venue housed in the elegant Michigan Theater, built in 1926 (converted into a three-level parking garage later in the 1970s), which had only started staging rock concerts after being closed for several months, following a failed attempt to turn it into an exclusive nightclub in the spring of 1973. The second of the two gigs was released on the classic *Metallic KO* (and later configurations of the album) and on *Michigan Palace 10/6/73* (Bomp Records). The Stooges' set lasted 45 minutes and featured six songs: 'Raw Power,' 'Head On,' 'Gimme Danger,' 'Search And Destroy,' 'Heavy Liquid' and 'Open Up And Bleed.'

Bob Czaykowski – who was recruited as a soundman for the two concerts – witnessed the band's escalating drug use: 'It was the first time I'd ever seen copious amounts of cocaine. I mean, like, on the table, just stick your hand in and have a good time.' Still, Iggy and the band put on fantastic concerts, according to Czaykowski: 'The band was killing, and you don't really get that from those tapes, because you're not seeing and feeling the dynamic between the band and the audience. Those shows in Michigan were some of the greatest live shows I've ever seen.'

'The band had this guy who they called Don Cool from Liverpool, and I was glad to see him there because when Jim went into the audience, he was usually right there to look for him,' said Czaykowski. 'The Michigan Palace had an orchestra pit that could go up and down, and they left the pit up, so as the show progressed, the stage was flooded with people. It turned up into this "rock 'n' roll open up and bleed melee." And the second day, we called them up and said, "You should probably leave that down." So they left the pit down, and I think Iggy went out and forgot that it was down, because he very gracelessly went down, and Don went, "Oh shit!" and went out after him. I went to go get him and he was buried in some girl's dress, and I was like, "Are you OK?". Iggy said, "You got to carry me." I had to carry him back. I remember Don was beating the hell out of somebody, and that's why I had to go out and do it.'

Monday, Tuesday, Wednesday, Thursday, Friday and Saturday, 8, 9, 10, 11, 12 and 13 October 1973: Richards, Atlanta, GA

The Stooges played six consecutive nights, doing two sets each night in Atlanta. A band called Hydra opened for The Stooges. Billing itself as 'Atlanta's finest rock club,' the 800-capacity Richards was short-lived, opening in February 1973, only to close in December the same year. Some of the Richards shows are considered amongst the best The Stooges ever did.

Stooges admirer Elton John had been to see one of the shows and came back the next night dressed in a gorilla suit to give Iggy a surprise. 'I love practical jokes,' said John. 'No one recognized me, of course, and no one could hear me shouting from within the costume. I couldn't see properly and was fainting with the heat. I suddenly realized that there were all these great big men looking down on me, and any minute they were going to pick me up and hurl me off the stage. Eventually, just as they were about to push me over a ten-foot drop at the front of the stage, I managed to wrench the head of the costume off. I hate to think what might have happened if I hadn't managed it in time.' Iggy revealed later that he was genuinely scared at seeing a gorilla raid the stage because he was 'unusually stoned, to the point of being barely ambulatory, so it scared the hell out of me.'

Wayne Bruce of opening act Hydra reminisced about the Atlanta engagement with The Stooges. 'That was pretty wild. We did a week with them and it was getting kind of strange. All these drugged-out people were watching us play, and when we got sort of a half-assed response, Iggy came out on stage yelling, "Come on, let's hear some goddamn noise and bring these guys back." So we came back out and jammed Chuck Berry's "Nadine," only it kept coming out from him as "Maybelline." I never saw anybody control an audience the way he did, not having them do the usual clap-hands kinds of thing. He'd just totally try to be as outrageous as possible while knocking himself out in the process. Not saying that they're good musicians, they're terrible, but every night the crowd was getting larger, and people kept coming back because they never saw anyone do a show like that before.'

One of the Richards shows was recorded for an Atlanta radio station broadcast, featuring a 60-minute set comprised of eight numbers: 'Raw Power,' 'Head On,' 'Gimme Danger,' 'Search And Destroy,' 'I Need Somebody,' 'Heavy Liquid,' 'Cock In My Pocket' and 'Open Up And Bleed.' The recording was never broadcast at the time but emerged in 2010 as *Georgia Peaches:* part of the officially released *Raw Power* box set (the tape recording was attributed to Joe Neil).

Wednesday, Thursday, Friday, Saturday and Sunday, 17, 18, 19, 20 and 21 October 1973: Whisky A Go Go, Hollywood, CA

Following the Atlanta stand, The Stooges were back in Los Angeles for five more nights at the Whisky. Attendance was sparser than it had been for the June and September gigs at the club. The opening act was called The Hayden Project: a band from San Francisco area. The first concert on 17 October was taped and released on the *Heavy Liquid* box in 2005, featuring a 55-minute set containing the same eight numbers as at the Atlanta gig: 'Raw Power,' 'Head On,' 'Gimme Danger,' 'Search And Destroy,' 'I Need Somebody,' 'Heavy Liquid,' 'Cock In My Pocket' and 'Open Up And Bleed.'

The Saturday concert – 20 October – was attended by Harry Young of *Billboard*, who wrote, 'Crowd-surfing Iggy: "Keep your hands off my cock, s'il vous plaît." Responding to a heckler: "That sounds pretty funny coming from a girl with a nose like yours." I'm sitting in the front row of the bleachers. As Iggy exits stage left, he pauses in front of me. I blurt out, "That was great!" He looks me in the eye and calmly replies, "Thanks." The headline in the next morning's *Los Angeles Times*: "Nixon Fires Cox, Abolishes His Office; Richardson Quits." Saturday Night Massacre, indeed.'

Wednesday, Thursday, Friday, Saturday and Sunday, 24, 25, 26, 27 and 28 October 1973: Whisky A Go Go, Hollywood, CA

The Stooges returned for a fourth engagement at the Whisky A Go Go, replacing Bachman-Turner Overdrive, who had been booked for 24-28 October. The British band, Babe Ruth, opened for The Stooges.

The reviewer for the *LA Free Press* was positive, although he had gotten miffed at The Stooges during the previous week, because of the long wait after the opening set by the Hayden Project (or Hansen Project as the reviewer incorrectly insisted on calling them), and left before The Stooges started. 'Surprisingly... Iggy and the boys are quite good at what they do. Which is to make a lot of noise, with Iggy dancing about, flailing his arms and insulting his audience in the time-honored tradition of such marginal acts as Kim Fowley and Screaming Lord Sutch and the Savages. Like Fowley and Sutch, Iggy surrounds himself with high-grade musicians and concentrates on the showmanship aspects of the performance, letting the music take second or third priority. Most of the "better" (a relative term in this context) songs owe more than a little to what Van Morrison was doing with Them, not that it matters. Iggy, who from time to time throws himself into the audience, performs semi-obscene acts with the microphone, and screeches inanities, obviously realizes exactly what's going on; at one point he refers, presumably, to his set as "a tale told by an idiot – full of sound and fury, and signifying less than nothing" and asking one particular trendy-looking fan "how many months have you been wearing that glitter on your cheek?".'

Two shows planned for 31 October and 1 November 1973 at The Matrix in San Francisco – with support from local band, The Tubes – were canceled and rescheduled to Bimbo's in January 1974.

Friday, 30 November 1973: Prince George's Community College, Largo, MD

Following a month-long break, The Stooges were back in action. They performed in the gym at the college, with headliners Blue Oyster Cult and the opening band The Dictators, for which this was their debut gig. Prince George's Community College is a college just east of Washington, DC. Photographs of Iggy backstage with members of Blue Oyster Cult and the Dictators – as well as a couple of The Stooges on stage – were taken by photographer David Ramage and posted on the Internet.

Bill Bouchard – brother of Joe and Albert Bouchard of Blue Oyster Cult – was impressed with Iggy: 'I was totally blown away by Iggy Pop, not for his music, but by his performance. He seemed like he was from another planet. It was my first and only time I saw Iggy, and he was quite a sight, walking through the gym with the audience just sitting on the floor staring up at him.'

Friday, 7 December 1973: Memorial Coliseum, Jacksonville, FL

The show was headlined by J. Geils Band, followed by Spooky Tooth, with The Stooges as third on the bill. Ron Asheton remembered: 'Afterwards we wound up meeting with Peter Wolf, who said, "What do you want to get high on?". So he sends the roadie out, and he comes back with a doctor's attaché case full of drugs. So I just had a couple of puffs of something and headed back to my room, and there's a blood smear from the top of the wall, and there's Iggy – he'd cracked his head on the side of the wall going back to his room, and just sort of passed out. I took him to his room, and there's this inch-wide split, open to the skull. So I kind of squeezed it back together with a bunch of bandages and told him he should see a doctor, but he said, "No way."'

A concert scheduled for 14 December 1973 at Chicago Auditorium Theatre – with Blue Oyster Cult headlining – was canceled for unknown reasons. Raspberries filled in for The Stooges.

Saturday and Sunday, 22 and 23 December 1973: Muther's Music Emporium, Nashville, TN

No details are known about these concerts, which were held at the recently opened 300-capacity Muther's Music Emporium club. The advertisement billed the band as 'Iggy & the Stooges.' No opening act was listed.

Wednesday, 26 December 1973: The Latin Casino, Baltimore, MD

On Boxing Day, The Stooges (billed as 'Iggy & the Stooges') performed with a group called Max, at The Latin Casino nightclub (not to be confused with the Latin Casino in Cherry Hill, New Jersey). They played an unusually long eleven-song set lasting 75 minutes that added three new songs worked-up in rehearsals: 'Raw Power,' 'Head On,' 'Gimme Danger,' 'Rich Bitch,' 'Wet My Bed,' 'I Got Nothin',' 'Search And Destroy,' 'Cock In My Pocket,' 'I Need Somebody,' 'Heavy Liquid' and 'Open Up And Bleed.' A recording of the show was released as *Double Danger* by Bomp Records.

Friday, 28 December 1973: Joint In The Woods, Parsippany, NJ

The Stooges played two sets, with a band called Daylight as the support act. The club was located in the woodland in Parsippany (on a site now occupied by a Sheraton hotel). The audience was quite small, as Bob Czaykowski noticed: 'We picked up dates and we'd go to this place out in the woods; it had only just opened and almost nobody was there. When they did "Search And Destroy," Iggy jumped into the audience, and they just moved out of the way.'

Ron Asheton introduced the band in German, over the opening chords of 'Raw Power,' having been convinced by Iggy to dress up in a full Nazi uniform. Iggy said, 'I told him people would love it, in full SS gear, right? So he comes out in his authentic, full dress, mint condition, superb detail, black SS colonel's outfit, with jodhpur riding boots and full accessories, and a good fit, too. There was a little kid in front saying, "How could you do this?" pointing at the SS gear. It must have been an Italian kid. But it didn't faze me. I was very relaxed. It's all part of the show.'

Czaykowski noted the audience response: 'People were horrified. Ron had got his typical Nazi outfit on, and Iggy had found a baseball bat, so he came out swinging this baseball bat. And this is out in rural New Jersey. I was very popular at that show because I had a car. "Get us out of here right now!". I guess they had one vehicle to move what little gear they had brought. I think it was Ron and his brother going, "You have a car? Let's leave right now". So we got in the car and drove back.'

Ron's introduction resulted in complaints from representatives for the Jewish Defense League. 'Afterwards, I get a call from Danny Sugerman because news of this had spread all over the place,' recalled Ron. 'We were scheduled to play the Academy of Music with Kiss and Blue Oyster Cult, and Danny said, "I just saved your ass! The Jewish Defense League was gonna beat the shit out of you at the show tonight, so I donated a hundred dollars to them in your name". But of course, Iggy still wanted me to wear the SS jacket that night.'

Saturday, 29 December 1973: Convention Center, Indianapolis, IN – Second Annual Holiday Festival

The seven-hour concert saw The Stooges play on a bill that featured five other acts: Rare Earth (headliners), Blue Oyster Cult, REO Speedwagon, Mike Bloomfield Band, and Captain Beyond.

Monday, 31 December 1973: Academy of Music, New York, NY

Presented by Howard Stein, The Stooges closed-out 1973 with a gig at the 3,000-seat Academy of Music, built as a deluxe movie palace (it became the Palladium in 1976). Kiss opened the proceedings, followed by Teenage Lust, The Stooges (billed as just Iggy Pop) and headliners Blue Oyster Cult. Although two shows were advertised (at 8 and 11:30 pm), the bands played only one set each. The show was attended by Patti Smith, Todd Rundgren, Bebe Buell, Danny Sugerman, and many of the band's friends and followers.

Kiss was added to the bill on the day of the show; their addition was not known by the other bands until right before the start of the show. Their 30-minute opening act was memorable because it was their music industry debut, and bass player Gene Simmons accidentally set his hair on fire during his fire-blowing act. Kiss guitarist, Paul Stanley, said in his autobiography *Face The Music* that 'despite all the hype and legend, I thought The Stooges were awful.'

The audience was polarised, with half being there for The Stooges and the other half for Blue Oyster Cult. Stooges follower, Chaz Miller, observed: 'BOC fans were pretty hostile towards The Stooges beforehand. It was a very partisan audience!' Still, the writer from *Friday Morning Quarterback* believed The Stooges got 'the strongest crowd reaction of the evening.' An audience recording of 42 minutes of The Stooges' concert was later issued on Bomp's *Double Danger*: 'Raw Power,' 'Rich Bitch,' 'Wet My Bed,''I Got Nothin',' 'Cock In My Pocket,' 'Search And Destroy,' 'Gimme Danger' and 'Heavy Liquid.'

The Stooges' concert opened with Ron Asheton doing his German speech introduction, in full Nazi regalia. The band started playing 'Raw Power,' as crew members carried Iggy from the dressing room and almost threw him onstage. Iggy's performance was erratic throughout the concert, due to alcohol and drugs. His backbends collapsed, and he kept introducing songs they already had played. At one point, he fell off the ramp into the photographers' pit, 15 feet downward, luckily being caught by a roadie. 'I'd just drunk a whole quart of vodka and been given some Quaaludes, I think,' Iggy said. 'Anyway, the only thing I remember is laying there on stage and saying "Thank you! Thank you! The next song we're going to do for ya is called 'I Got Nothin'," and James coming up behind me and saying, "Pop! Pop, you've said that four times already". After that, I just blacked out.'

Bob Czaykowski attended the concert: 'Iggy could hardly stand up. He kept falling into the pit. That was my job, to go get him, but at one point, the photographers would catch him and throw him back on. He just couldn't properly stand up. I was like, "How can you do this?" when two months before, he would do the show without getting messed up. That was the big difference that I saw. It was not good. He would break mic stands like nobody's business. He'd snap them in half, and I'd have to pay the PA guy to give him another mic stand. We decided at that New Year's Eve show that I didn't want to be paying for mic stands anymore, so I hammered a drumstick into the bottom because the weakest part of a mic stand is where the threads are at the base. We hammered this drumstick in there, and he couldn't break it. I started saying, "You've lost it, man. You're weak". And then he'd fall down, and we'd have to go pick him up.'

Ivan Kral was in attendance, having become a fan after seeing Iggy and the Stooges at Max's Kansas City earlier in the year: 'It was the second time I saw Iggy and the Stooges. My God, what a performer! I brought a film camera; I still have the films. I was in the seventh row, totally into shooting this guy. The footage was incredible. I didn't know people were into Quaaludes and drank heavily; I was so naïve.' Danny Sugerman later revealed that it was he who gave the Quaaludes to Iggy. After The Stooges' set, many Stooges followers left the concert to go to Times Square in Manhattan for the customary New Year's Eve celebrations, instead of watching Blue Oyster Cult.

Andy Warhol had heard rumors that Iggy was to have committed suicide on stage that night. In conversation with a journalist after the show, Iggy seemed apologetic of his performance: 'It was the worst show we ever did, alcohol was responsible, and we've been so good lately.' Journalist Anne Wehrer – whom Iggy knew from Ann Arbor – met up with Iggy afterward to discuss writing a book about Iggy's life (which eventually became *I Need More*, published in 1982). 'Backstage, he was flat-out on the red concrete floor, rolling in spilled beer, dead cigarettes and broken dreams,' recalled Wehrer.

Despite Iggy's lackluster performance, The Stooges' followers in the press were sufficiently impressed. Jon Tiven, writing for *Zoo World*, felt the show was 'thoroughly titillating' and said that 'Iggy was incredible, mixing with the audience and getting sprayed with silly string while members of the crowd poured tequila over his head.' Fred Kirby of *Variety* simply said that Iggy 'gyrated, insinuated and sang up a storm.' Gordon Fletcher of *Rolling Stone* devoted most of his review to Kiss and Blue Oyster Cult, but described The Stooges' music as 'sonic blitz,' which had James Williamson 'churning out power chords with Kamikaze abandon.'

Speculation that CBS recorded the concert with a mobile recording unit for a live album by Iggy and the Stooges has been refuted by band members and associates of the band. It is highly unlikely that such a recording took place since the concert happened around the time of the label's decision not to pick up the option for a second album.

Friday and Saturday, 11 and 12 January 1974: Bimbo's 365 Club, San Francisco, CA

These shows at the 700-capacity club replaced two canceled shows at The Matrix, 31 October and 1 November 1973. The Tubes opened for Iggy and the Stooges. Two sets each night were advertised, but reports have described the Friday gig as lasting 90 minutes, which suggests that only one set was played. Richard McCaffrey's photos from the gigs are featured in the Stooges biography by Bob Matheu. Four tracks (35 minutes) from one of the gigs were later issued, on the *Heavy Liquid* box set in 2005: 'Head On,' 'Wet My Bed,' 'I Got Nothin'' and 'Open Up And Bleed.'

The relatively small audience at Bimbo's 365 Club was clustered in front of the stage. At one point during the Friday performance, Iggy jumped into the crowd, where someone got hold of him and 'dispensed with the briefs and administered a deviant sexual act,' according to the report by Joel Selvin in the *San Francisco Chronicle*. The audience pushed and shoved their way to the front for verification, as Iggy told the crowd, 'I'm getting my cock sucked. You don't believe it, but I'm getting a blowjob.' Finally, bored with the attention, he screamed, 'Give me my cock back, you bitch!' Selvin later reported that he received a phone call from a guy after his review was published: 'That was no girl that did Iggy – that was me and my cousin Frankie!'

Selvin described the audience as a 'surprisingly straight rock crowd' and praised the band in his review for *San Francisco Chronicle*: 'The Stooges band actually plays the three-chord progressions with a certain deftness – enviably tight, reasonably original and with strong piano work from Scott Thurston and the Keith Richards-like presence of guitarist James Williamson. Stooge casts himself as the paranoid loner – "keep your hands off me, girl," he sings – alternately rudely insulting and grinning crazily. His "acting," however, is less convincing than the physical limits to which he drives himself.' Not everyone was as fascinated, though. While he believed The Stooges were a 'rather good band,' Philip Elwood of the *San Francisco Examiner* was disgusted, and felt Iggy was 'unpleasant, a verbal bore, and would have been yanked off stage in vaudeville days, after two lines of his lyrics,' and he hoped 'they'll be gone for a long time – and take The Tubes with them.'

Friday, 18 January 1974: Allen Theatre, Cleveland, OH

Slade was the headliner, with Iggy and the Stogges (sic) being billed as a 'special guest.' Allen Theatre is a 2,500-seater in downtown Cleveland. The Stooges were late on stage and played a short set consisting of four or five songs, according to reports. Audience response was mixed, as many were there to see Slade.

Two fans – Chris Yarmock and Harvey Gold – attended the show and later recounted the event on an internet website. 'It took a long time before Iggy was able to make it out onto the stage,' said Gold. 'He was real slow and real unsteady. After the first song ended, he was really holding himself up by his mic, and he just kind of looks out and goes, "I'm the world's greatest dancer."' According to Yarmock, 'It was just a mess. Iggy couldn't do anything; he was totally out of it. The band sounded tight when they got it together. It wasn't the band so much; Iggy was just totally out of it. On "Open Up and Bleed" and "Gimme Danger," he didn't know which song it was, so he was kind of like singing both of them, just in and out of consciousness. It was a pretty wild show.'

After the show, Yarmock and Gold went to the Holiday Inn where The Stooges were staying. 'There were a bunch of groupies,' recalled Yarmock. 'The hotel detectives warned us, "We smell anything weird or anything; you guys are outta here." So eventually, we got up to the room, and I'm sitting on the bed. The Stooges are roaming around; James Williamson and all those guys are there, and all these big, scary Detroit guys. So these two people come in the room, literally dragging Iggy. And I'm sitting on this bed, and they plop him down on the bed right next to me. He's totally out of it; he's totally passed out. This chick comes up to him and she goes, "Oh, Jimmy, Jimmy, are you OK?" And he just opened his eyes for like a split second and then just closed them, and they just picked him back up. His legs weren't even touching the ground; they literally dragged him out of the fuckin' room. James Williamson came in the room and we talked for a little bit. He was a really, really nice guy. I got his autograph, which I still have, and it's actually hanging on my wall in the music room.'

Natalie Schlossman remembered the aftermath of the concert: 'Iggy was so out of it, he was running around the halls of the hotel naked. Of course, everybody else was partying and they could not be bothered with him. I found him wandering, so I took him back to his room. I helped him get dressed and tried to get him to go to sleep. I thought he was drifting to sleep. I went back to my room to do whatever I was going to do in the first place. When I finished, I found him wandering the hall again, and he was naked again. This time I got him back to the room, and locked him in and took the key. I put a chair on the outside of the door so he could not get out. I guess he eventually passed out. The next day he did not remember any of it.'

Saturday, 19 January 1974: Sports Arena, Toledo, OH

Slade was again the headliner. The bill also featured James Gang (as 'special guest'), who performed first on the bill. A Stooges fan later reported his impressions of the concert on a website called *Kicksville 66*: 'Every band I'd ever seen up until that night, seemed to be at least somewhat interested in entertaining, dare I say *pleasing* we, the people. But here, Iggy and the Stooges gave the instant impression that they were not there for our measly amusement. Iggy came out shirtless, in tight white flares and a bow tie, with the band looking broody and intolerant and mean, in the shadows. We were staring at Williamson blaring away at some solo or another, unable to register clear thought or form words, when suddenly, Iggy seemed to have lost his white flared jeans, revealing nothing more than a well-honed hiney encased in what certainly appeared to be women's nylon undies. Nowadays, you may not bat an eyelash at the thought of gents opting for ladies wear, but speaking for myself – fresh from the boondocks and totally uninformed, my pea brain positively exploding with the unbelievably fantastic, super-loud mess of class favorites blasting at us, combined with this guy Iggy, who was the most macho personage I'd ever set eyeballs on, despite the no-fly zone unmentionables – heck, I was ready to burst in flames right then and there and be toted home in an ashcan. Right here! Right now! There was general mayhem when the curtain came down; we are all looking at each other with new eyes. There was an intermission; some of the older kids went out to the lobby to drink, smoke, and rehash. I sat in the aisle, feeling like I'd just finally grown up. Slade came on and entertained the people. They were wonderful, yes, but I was seeing things now, 10 minutes later, through grown-up eyeballs. I'd seen the future, and it didn't conduct sing-alongs.'

The next day, The Stooges were scheduled to play at Stone Hearth, Madison, Wisconsin, but the concert was canceled due to a snowstorm.

Monday, 21 January 1974: The Brewery, Michigan State University, Lansing, MI

The Brewery was party central for Michigan State University in Lansing, in the middle of Michigan. When Aerosmith, Rush, and BTO were just breaking out and starting to fill arenas, they were playing one and two nights to rabid crowds at The Brewery for $3 admission. At the time, The Brewery was the 'biggest nite club' in Michigan and it rocked hard every day of the week. Your dollar went far at The Brewery. It had the best pizza in the Midwest, was THE place to meet anyone and everyone, served an unbelievable amount of beer and tequila, and best of all, featured national and up and coming bands three to four nights a week. The place was full, and Iggy and the band had no difficulty in maintaining audience interest throughout the show. At one point, Iggy accepted a glass of beer onstage from a girl in the audience and walked back onto her table to return it. On another occasion, a girl ran to the front of the stage to give Iggy a long kiss. Not content with a mere kiss, he tried to force her head down between his legs. His microphone stand would occasionally fall into the audience. Iggy also slipped off stage while twirling the microphone stand. Unfortunately, the show was plagued by a faulty sound system that eventually caused an abrupt end to the show. Iggy cursed the soundman at the board several times and threatened, 'Make the sound system right or I'll take off my pants!' The show finished somewhat anticlimactically when James Williamson's amplifier blew up. Most people expected a second set and were disappointed to learn that they would not return.

Writing for *Michigan State News*, Dave DiMartino had high praise for the show: 'Controversial shows have always been a part of The Stooges' image. Even though Iggy didn't get a chance to roll in his own vomit or cut his belly on broken glass, he was sufficiently "sick" to please almost everyone in the audience. There were few people in the crowd who were not open-mouthed and laughing when Iggy stuck his hands in his pants or when he called the audience "fools." Everyone enjoyed seeing the sweating, bruised form of Iggy, staggering about onstage while mumbling about 'tales told by idiots.' This probably means a lot more than we think it does.' DiMartino also lauded the band in his review: 'Musically speaking, the band was tremendous, with James Williamson deserving much of the credit for his truly fine guitar playing. The group performed material from *Raw Power*, the last album, but there was much new material. Particularly of interest was "Wet My Bed," for obvious reasons. The group does not seem to be standing still, which is encouraging when one considers where it is standing.'

Friday, 25 January 1974: Victory Burlesque, Toronto, Canada

Two sets were played at this theater, which was originally called The Standard Theatre. The venue became the Victory Burlesque in 1961, featuring striptease artists, comedians and musical acts. Rock concerts were held during a brief period in 1974-1975, before the venue closed in 1975. The Stooges were introduced by a stripper dressed as a nun. Photos from the concert were featured in *Beetle*.

Unimpressed with the performance, Jeffrey Morgan later remembered the concert in an article for Detroit's *Metro Times*: 'The main problem was that although the Stooges were still hitting the road, the road was beginning to hit back with an ever-increasing impatient fury at five guys who simply would not stay down. Absorbing life's punches on swaying rubber legs, they continued to take standing eight-count after standing eight-count while steadfastly refusing to kiss the canvas.' Morgan had seen and been enthusiastic about The Stooges before, but felt this concert was 'bereft of any real passion and much worse than that: it was *boring*.' According to Morgan, Iggy left the stage numerous times, and 'once he was safely hidden from view by the side curtain, he'd calmly smoke a cigarette and wait until it was time for him to get back into character again. At which point he'd pick himself up and start all over again by lurching back into the spotlight to play the brain-damaged geek anew.'

A concert at The Playhouse in Winnipeg, Canada – originally planned for 7 January 1974 and later rescheduled for 25 January – had to be canceled just two days prior to the gig, as it conflicted with the Toronto engagement. *Winnipeg Free Press'* Andy Mellen blamed the double booking on the band's management.

Wednesday, Thursday and Friday, 30 and 31 January and 1 February 1974: My Father's Place, Roslyn, NY

The Stooges were scheduled to play two sets nightly, over three nights at the 400-capacity My Father's Place in Roslyn, Long Island. However, the engagement was poorly promoted, so they ended up playing just one concert each night. The concert was announced on local radio only a couple of days before the show. According to eyewitness reports, the audience was very small. Iggy seemed to be irate about the poor attendance and spent much of the show insulting Long Island. The local band, Good Rats, provided support, but they were uninteresting for the Stooges fans in attendance.

'There were 'literally' only ten people in the audience,' reckoned Stooges fan, Chaz Miller. 'Five at my table and five at the other. I attended with my current girlfriend, her girlfriend and significant others, and my sixteen-year-old sister, who used phony ID to gain access into the club. So that was five at my table. There was another table with five people as well, but we did not socialize. Ron was sharp in his Nazi gear, but I recall the rest of The Stooges looked road-weary. Their clothes seemed very tattered. Being very young at the time, I thought it strange that these "rich" rock stars couldn't afford to replace them. As hostile as Iggy was towards Long Island, in general, that night: due to the terrible attendance, I do believe he saw true fans sitting at our table. After all, my sister shot an entire roll of 36 exposures – in black and white with flash – of the performance. At one point, Iggy jumped into my girlfriend's lap, where he made out with her while the band played on. I mean, he 'really' kissed her, which she confirmed afterwards, stating, "He's got a very long tongue!". After the make-out session, he turned to me and asked, "Are you Jesus? I love your eyes!" and gave me a quick peck on the forehead before going back to the stage. He ad-libbed spoken lyrics, basically bashing Long Island for the poor attendance: e.g., "What are you doing here? This place is for assholes. Only an asshole would live here". I recall feeling bad about that.'

Miller continued: 'Obviously put off by the lack of numbers in the audience, they still put on a tight show, but with no one to catch him, his leaping into what was an empty venue had him coming up limp when he missed the table he was aiming for. Subsequently, he sat on the edge of the stage and changed the lyrics to "Open Up And Bleed" to reflect his rage at the "stupidity" and "ugliness" of Long Islanders. He delivered the lines in a spoken word manner. Iggy later fractured (or broke?) a bone when he jumped to, and missed, a table. He sat at the stage's end, still singing until flashing ambulance lights appeared outside. When the flashing of ambulance lights became visible through the glass windows of the venue, Iggy left, but the band continued for about 10 minutes. It was only after the concert that we learned that Iggy hurt himself, and hence the bizarre ending to the performance.'

Saturday, 2 February 1974: Capitol Theatre, Port Chester, NY

Blue Oyster Cult headlined over The Stooges and the opening act The Dictators, at the 1,800-seat Capitol Theatre in Port Chester, in Westchester County, north of New York (called 'The Gateway to New England'). Two shows were advertised: 8 pm and 11 pm. Built in 1926, the Capitol Theatre has a long history, with tenures as a movie theater and catering hall, in addition to hosting concerts (still active to this day). The Stooges biography by Bob Matheu, features photos from the gig by Seth Tiven.

Monday, 4 February 1974: Rock 'n' Roll Farm, Wayne, MI

Back in the Detroit area, The Stooges played a 'pick-up' gig, with local rock band Marcus, as the opening act. Rock 'n' Roll Farm was a small club in the western Detroit suburb of Wayne (it does not exist today). The venue was often used for warm-up gigs for bigger concerts in Detroit. Not more than 200-300 people were in attendance for The Stooges' performance at the club, which was a hang-out for a motorcycle club from Detroit called the Scorpions. Road manager, Chris Ehring, said, 'It was a sleazy club, a biker beer bar. Sure to be a riot! It was a very small club, and we rolled in there with all these amps. Eric (Haddix), our equipment man, said, "We'll blow this place out! This is impossible". I called our agent and said, "We're not playing here. This is crazy". They just said, "It's a day off and you need the money!". So we played it. Of course, a riot ensues. Bikers are pushing each other, slamming their heads on the floor. It was horrible.'

The Stooges faced a partially hostile audience, as a group of bikers threw eggs at Iggy to provoke a fight with him. Stooges follower, Skip Gildersleeve, was in attendance: 'I've been doing professional shows for 31 years, I've done 5,000 shows, but nothing was more dangerous or strange than a Detroit Stooges audience. There were people that would come out of the woodwork – that I don't think would ever go to shows – to see them. And there were also people who would pay money for a ticket, just to go and abuse them, which I never understood. It used to depress me. At the Rock 'n' Roll Farm I was underage, and I had to sneak in. There was this abusive factor of the audience, that people who were just idiots, who came there just to abuse them. The Stooges audience was the strangest and most dangerous. To this day, I haven't experienced anything close to that.'

Iggy responded by calling one of the egg-throwers out to a fight. Gildersleeve witnessed what happened: 'There was one guy, I didn't see a whole gang, but I was standing five feet from this guy because I worked my way up to the front. I remember Iggy said, "Who the fuck threw that?". A big biker came up, and I remember Iggy jumping off the stage and this guy punching him, and Iggy flying back and hitting the stage about the middle of his back, and he went down. I do remember he was shook up, and he came to his sense and they all ran off after that. He was twice the size, a big fucking biker. I was standing there, and as a kid, that left an impression on me. I remember that was the closest I ever was to The Stooges, and I was totally excited about it and I was rocking out, and then that incident, and that was the end of it. I was pissed off with that guy, who robbed everybody else of the rest of the show. It was a big biker. I read somewhere that he had brass knuckles, and I don't believe that to be the case. He didn't need brass knuckles. The guy was double the size of Iggy. It's just a law of physics, if you weigh 250 or 300 pounds and you punch somebody, that punch carries a lot more wallop than a 100-pound guy punching you because of the weight of the person throwing the punch. So when he hit Iggy, he just flew the room. You see this in the movies when someone gets hit with a fist and they fly through the air. Normally you don't see this in real life, but this was one of those occasions.'

Bob Baker – another Stooges follower from Detroit – was also present: 'I was not far from where he got punched-out at the end. They had brought in cartons of eggs, and they were throwing them at the stage. It was a little bar, a stage, and a dance floor in front of the stage, and tables around. I had got there early enough to get a pretty good seat: I was sitting at a table right on the edge of the dance floor, but when Iggy started playing, the whole dance floor just filled up with people. They hadn't started those mosh pits yet. They were crowded together watching him. But the bikers were at the back of the room, and they had cartons of eggs and they were throwing eggs. It was really upsetting, because I was there to see my favorite performer, and people are throwing eggs at him. These were big rough bikers, so there was no way I could do anything about it. It was scary because these guys were trying to provoke a fight with Iggy. He came out in the audience. He went right up to one of the bikers, and the guy just nailed him right in the face, and he went flying backwards through the crowd, and then they just laughed, and The Stooges left the stage and gave it up. I was depressed. This was my favorite performer, and here he is getting harassed by these big bikers. Iggy had unbelievable courage to fight anybody who would mess with him.'

Ralph Franklin reported about the incident in *Fifth Estate:* 'At the end of their fourth successful attempt at the production of utter noise, an egg was awarded to Iggy by an anonymous appreciator in the crowd. With this, the Stooge lost all control (he didn't have much, to begin with) and leaped into the audience, only to come face to face with a beer bottle and a handsome steel-studded glove, complete with a hand inside. Naturally enough, this brought an abrupt end to the Stooges' performance (Iggy was bleeding) – a performance which lasted perhaps twenty minutes.'

'The Stooges were always confrontational from day one,' James Williamson reflected. 'Iggy was always an in-your-face kind of guy. That's his style; it's part of his act. But I would never call it violent, necessarily. When I think of violent, I think of something that has consequences, and up until that one day at the Rock 'n' Roll Farm, where he got punched out by a biker, I would never call it violent. It was aggressive, is how I characterize it. That was a big defining moment for The Stooges. When somebody actually stepped up and cold-cocked Iggy, that sort of said, "Hey, you're not playing for teenagers anymore. There's these other guys out there too, and they're not nice like that". I think the band was pretty much ready to give it up at that point, and that was just the last straw.'

Down but not completely out, the next day, Iggy issued a challenge over a Detroit radio station, daring the bikers to attend the Stooges' show at the Michigan Palace later in the week. Radio DJs promoted the show by saying that Iggy was going to commit suicide during the concert. 'I think it was just the disc jockeys joking around,' said Baker. 'They said, "You've got to come up to this concert because Iggy's going to shoot himself on stage." I didn't think he'd do it.'

Saturday, 9 February 1974: Michigan Palace, Detroit, MI

The Stooges were accompanied on the bill by Elephants Memory (opening act) and Blue Ash (middle spot). *Fifth Estate* said that 'Detroit's own degenerates are back in town for what should be the most lurid show this year.' The Stooges had played two concerts at the Michigan Palace only four months earlier, but now they did not attract more than a half-full venue. Additional security was organized for the concert, and the Stooges themselves brought in some guys from a biker gang based in Ypsilanti. The concert was recorded by the band's friend, Michael Tipton, and 39 minutes of their set were released on the second side of the *Metallic KO* LP (and later configurations of the album): 'Heavy Liquid,' 'I Got Nothin',' 'Rich Bitch,' 'Gimme Danger,' 'Cock In My Pocket' and 'Louie Louie' (this was most likely not the actual sequence of songs, although 'Louie Louie' was the final number).

During the concert, Iggy and the band were again heckled by bikers. They came under fire from a deluge of garbage, bottles, cans, and other missiles, while Iggy gamely goaded his tormentors. The band members were frightened. 'They threw a Kessler's whisky bottle; it glanced off Thurston's piano,' recalled

Ron Asheton. 'I saw it coming in the light. We both turned away, and glass just sprayed us. It was a good thing we knew the songs as well as we did. It got to where I'm not even concentrating on the music, I'm scanning the area, man, looking for incoming objects. It was like a combat zone as we did it. I got hit by a coin on my head and I still have the scar.' According to James Williamson, 'There are just no words to describe that gig. There was no fear at all at the time, but listening back to it, it's frightening how out-there we'd gotten.'

Stooges follower, Bob Baker, was in the audience: 'It was the same thing (as in Wayne): bikers throwing bottles and anything they could throw to start a fight. It was getting to the point where these guys were following him around and trying to start fights. It made the concerts unpleasant, because these are the kind of guys that like fighting anybody that will fight them. They were not just throwing stuff at the band, but if anybody were to try to stop them throwing things, even the bouncers would have a problem, because these guys were tough. I think there were five or six from where I was sitting. They were heavy-set and they had beards, and they were big, and they had blue jean jackets, but on the back of it, they had their bike club logo. They weren't that old. They were probably in their early thirties. They looked tough. I wouldn't want to mess with them.'

Photographer, Robert Matheu, recalled the concert: 'I was tucked away under one of the small balconies that hung low, closest the stage of the old theater, away from the barrage, and it was one of the scariest damn shows I have ever been at. Not knowing where the breaking point would be, or if Iggy would live through it, but the previous year of his onstage self-abuse had only prepared him. It was his defense, fearless, he asked for more. "I've done it to myself – what are you going to do to me that I haven't already done?".'

'I never thought it would come to this,' Iggy shouted as the band launched into the final song, 'Louie Louie.' Baker believed this choice was intended as an insult to the audience: 'For them to do "Louie Louie" was like telling the audience, "You know what, you don't deserve to hear our good stuff, so you're going to hear the crappiest song we can think of." Three chords, repetitive.' As it happened, 'Louie Louie' turned out to be the last song The Stooges would play until their resurrection, three decades later. The band members were able to leave the stage, scared but relatively intact. The rowdy and partially hostile Detroit audience is very much evident on *Metallic KO*; the bottles and debris thrown onto the stage and at Iggy during the riot-torn concert, can be clearly heard. Ron Asheton viewed it as 'the perfect ending, but I never had an inkling that it was 'the' ending.'

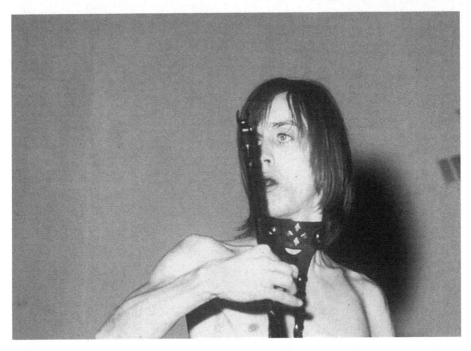

Above and below: Farmington High School, 5 December 1970. (*Gary Fletcher*)

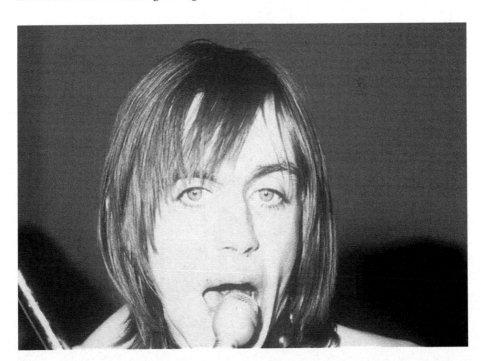

Above: Visiting the audience at Farmington High School, 5 December 1970. (*Gary Fletcher*)

Right: New Old Fillmore, San Francisco, 15 May 1970. (*Kurt Ingham*)

Above: St. Louis Pop Festival, Kiel Auditorium, 7 March 1970. (*Craig Petty*)
Below: Whisky A Go Go, September 1973. (*Heather Harris*)

Above: Iggy with James Williamson and Scott Thurston at Whisky A Go Go, September 1973. (*Heather Harris*)

Epilogue

When The Stooges disbanded in February 1974 after seven years of playing together, they had built a small, devoted following, but they were largely ignored by the wider rock audience. 'At that time, there really wasn't any market for what they were playing,' reflected Danny Fields. 'People weren't aware of the trendy European market at the time. When you look at it through the eyes of the late '70s and '80s, where things like that are custom-made. Lou Reed, Patti Smith, etc., are tailor-made for Europe, but The Stooges broke the ground, and no one was aware of it as a marketing effort to do it that way. Their music sounds so new that it still hasn't been absorbed and assimilated.' Jim Jarmusch – who directed the Stooges documentary *Gimme Danger* in 2016 – believed people were not ready for The Stooges at the time: 'They were intimidated by something that wild and uncontrolled. They were not mainstream and not predictable, and I think people didn't know how to take them. The appreciators were the young stoners and the kind of intelligentsia, but everything in between just wanted to throw bottles at them.'

Ron Asheton had ambitions for The Stooges to become 'like the American Rolling Stones,' but they never achieved anything near the mainstream popularity of The Rolling Stones. Of course, there are many reasons why broader recognition and commercial success eluded them. The Stooges never made any compromises to reach beyond their hardcore following, instead being fiercely committed to pursuing their own path. Unlike most bands, which focus on performing their most well-known material, The Stooges never gave-in to expectations and were usually eager to present new material, even to the extent that they did entire concerts and tours that did not feature any recognizable material for the audiences. The Stooges' artistic integrity created many problems for those involved with the band from the business side of things, such as managers, promoters, and record company executives. 'They were too arrogant, in a nice way, a way that I admired,' said Jimmy Silver. 'They were just too loose, really. They didn't have anything focused on success, the way you have to do it. There was no one whipping them into shape. No one could really control them and hold all the pieces together. In their own way, they had an uncompromising kind of integrity.'

Few rock bands have been more influential than The Stooges, as they laid foundations that would be built upon by multiple generations of artists. They are widely acknowledged as the forefathers of 1970s punk rock, including New York acts like Suicide, New York Dolls, Patti Smith, Ramones, The Dictators, Jonathan Richman and Blondie, as well as British acts such as Sex Pistols, The Clash, The Stranglers, Penetration and The Damned – to name but a few. The Stooges also inspired many acts that came after this initial wave of late-'70s acts, including Jane's Addiction, Green Day, Nirvana, Sonic Youth, Guns N' Roses, Slayer, Red Hot Chili Peppers, The White Stripes, Black Flag, Mudhoney, Marilyn Manson and Stone Temple Pilots. When Billie Joe Armstrong of Green Day inducted the band into the Rock 'n' Roll Hall of Fame in 2010, he read a list of 100 bands that counted The Stooges as an influence. Jack White – formerly of The White Stripes – summarised the band's influence: 'The Stooges were pioneers in sound, look and live presentation, and along the way invented a genre – punk rock – and influenced countless others that followed. There was no precedent in rock music for what they did.'

While The Stooges were powered by raw, primal music, it was the compelling stage presence of Iggy that made them legendary. 'He, as a performer, is so unique that it's difficult to compare him to others,' said Danny Fields. 'No one has been so powerful and terrifyingly extraordinary onstage.' The Stooges' performances were theatrical in an unpredictable way, with Iggy spontaneously responding to audience reactions. Iggy was passionate, fearless, inventing acts like stage-diving, crowd-surfing, and going out into crowds to confront hecklers or spontaneously interact with individual audience members who struck his fancy. It was impossible for the audience to be complacent as Iggy dissolved the fourth wall that traditionally exists between audience and performer, forcing the audience to become part of the overall performance. Not everyone appreciated having their privacy invaded, and The Stooges' performances typically generated disparate reactions, from trepidation or fear, to excitement and enthusiasm.

At times, Iggy expressed himself in a genuinely frightening way; he lived his art in a way few artists do and survive. By 1974, he was locked into an orbit of self-annihilation and drug abuse, which he needed to escape from if he was going to continue making music and performing. 'The very big problem is simply quantity and incidence of use,' Iggy said of his and the band's drug use. 'Excess, absolutely, excess and over-dependence. If the same things had been used and it had only been half, you would've found more vitality, more work ethic, more stamina, more money to spend on a roof over your head.' He reached the conclusion that he had to quit The Stooges and re-emerge with a new toned-down approach to his art, which is precisely what he did when he embarked on a solo career with David Bowie's support, three years later.

Twenty-nine years after the demise of the band, The Stooges returned in 2003 to play and perform together again. No longer ahead of the time, it was a triumphant return, as they faced large audiences and new generations of fans worldwide, who showed them nothing but appreciation and respect. 'I crawled out of my dark cave into the limelight of love and acceptance,' said Iggy of his 2000s. Interest in the band had multiplied manifold since the 1970s, with live recordings, studio outtakes, restored albums, photos and video clips on the internet, keeping the legend alive. 'Our road manager, Bill Cheatham: his children are fans,' noted Ron Asheton in the 1990s. 'When they find The Stooges, it seems new and fresh for them. It's so timeless; people can enjoy it. When we were actually doing it, it was not a big deal. We never made it, didn't get critical acclaim. And after it lays there awhile, it keeps getting bigger and bigger.'

The reformed Stooges toured for several years, with different configurations of the band: one line-up featuring Ron Asheton on guitar, and another,

James Williamson. The Stooges also released two further studio albums – *The Weirdness* in 2007 and *Ready To Die* in 2013 – neither of which could live up to the phenomenally high expectations created by *The Stooges*, *Fun House* and *Raw Power*. 'There's been a lot of worldly success after the fact for that band,' Iggy noted. 'The (original) albums are in the black now. It's satisfying, damn satisfying.' However, after a seven-year victory lap, The Stooges disbanded for good in 2016, following the deaths of Ron Asheton in 2009, Scott Asheton in 2014, and Steve Mackay in 2015. James Williamson and Iggy both believed these deaths should be the end of The Stooges. The band's career is over, yet the unique music, performances and attitude, remain relevant and influential as new generations of music fans discover The Stooges. As Iggy put it, 'Somehow there was something about this group, something that we did that no one else did, that you could never hear anywhere else.'

Decades Series
Pink Floyd In The 1970s – Georg Purvis 978-1-78952-072-9
Marillion in the 1980s – Nathaniel Webb 978-1-78952-065-1

On Screen series
Carry On... – Stephen Lambe 978-1-78952-004-0
David Cronenberg – Patrick Chapman 978-1-78952-071-2
Doctor Who: The David Tennant Years – Jamie Hailstone 978-1-78952-066-8
Monty Python – Steve Pilkington 978-1-78952-047-7
Seinfeld Seasons 1 to 5 – Stephen Lambe 978-1-78952-012-5

Other Books
Derek Taylor: For Your Radioactive Children – Andrew Darlington
978-1-78952-
Jon Anderson and the Warriors - the road to Yes – David Watkinson
978-1-78952-059-0
Tommy Bolin: In and Out of Deep Purple – Laura Shenton
978-1-78952-070-5
Maximum Darkness – Deke Leonard 978-1-78952-048-4
Maybe I Should've Stayed In Bed – Deke Leonard 978-1-78952-053-8
The Twang Dynasty – Deke Leonard 978-1-78952-049-1

and many more to come!

Would you like to write for Sonicbond Publishing?

We are mainly a music publisher, but we also occasionally publish in other genres including film and television. At Sonicbond Publishing we are always on the look-out for authors, particularly for our two main series, On Track and Decades.

Mixing fact with in depth analysis, the On Track series examines the entire recorded work of a particular musical artist or group. All genres are considered from easy listening and jazz to 60s soul to 90s pop, via rock and metal.

The Decades series singles out a particular decade in an artist or group's history and focuses on that decade in more detail than may be allowed in the On Track series.

While professional writing experience would, of course, be an advantage, the most important qualification is to have real enthusiasm and knowledge of your subject. First-time authors are welcomed, but the ability to write well in English is essential.

Sonicbond Publishing has distribution throughout Europe and North America, and all our books are also published in E-book form. Authors will be paid a royalty based on sales of their book. Further details about our books are available from www.sonicbondpublishing.com. To contact us, complete the contact form there or email info@sonicbondpublishing.co.uk